Software Engineering Handbook

From Theory to Practice

Kaushik Sinha

Copyright © 2025 Kaushik Sinha

All Rights Reserved.

This book has been self-published with all reasonable efforts taken to make the material error-free by the author. No part of this book shall be used, reproduced in any manner whatsoever without written permission from the author, except in the case of brief quotations embodied in critical articles and reviews.

The Author of this book is solely responsible and liable for its content including but not limited to the views, representations, descriptions, statements, information, opinions and references ["Content"]. The Content of this book shall not constitute or be construed or deemed to reflect the opinion or expression of the Publisher or Editor. Neither the Publisher nor Editor endorse or approve the Content of this book or guarantee the reliability, accuracy or completeness of the Content published herein and do not make any representations or warranties of any kind, express or implied, including but not limited to the implied warranties of merchantability, fitness for a particular purpose. The Publisher and Editor shall not be liable whatsoever for any errors, omissions, whether such errors or omissions result from negligence, accident, or any other cause or claims for loss or damages of any kind, including without limitation, indirect or consequential loss or damage arising out of use, inability to use, or about the reliability, accuracy or sufficiency of the information contained in this book.

Made with ❤ on the Notion Press Platform

www.notionpress.com

Dedicated To my wife and my loving sons Alip & Alapon

and

To all the educators and learners of software engineering – may this handbook serve as a bridge between knowledge and application

Contents

Preface

Software engineering is a foundational discipline within computer science and a critical skill for every aspiring engineer. As technology continues to shape the modern world, the ability to design, develop, and maintain robust software systems is more essential than ever. This Software Engineering Handbook has been carefully crafted to meet the academic and practical needs of Computer Science Engineering students. It introduces key concepts and frameworks in a clear, structured manner, ensuring students build a strong understanding of the principles and processes that drive successful software development.

Throughout this book, we follow the software development lifecycle, covering crucial topics such as requirements analysis, system modeling, architectural design, coding standards, testing strategies, project management, and maintenance. Special emphasis is placed on practical tools and methodologies, such as creation of SRS document, designing the database, design of software system using Data Flow Diagram (DFD), Data Dictionary, Unified Modeling Language (UML) and Software Project Management techniques. Each concept is reinforced with real-world examples, case studies, and diagrams to help students apply theory to practice and prepare them for both academic assessments and professional challenges.

This handbook is not just a textbook, it is a companion to your journey in becoming a competent and confident software engineer. Whether you're studying for exams, working on a capstone project, or preparing for internships, this book aims to provide the guidance and clarity you need. We hope it inspires curiosity, encourages critical thinking, and lays the groundwork for a successful career in the ever-evolving field of software engineering.

Kaushik Sinha

30 April, 2025

Introduction of the Book

About the Handbook

Software Engineering Handbook – From Theory to Practice is designed to provide a comprehensive, structured, and application-driven introduction to the discipline of software engineering. As software systems become increasingly complex and critical to every domain of modern life – from healthcare to finance, from education to transportation – the demand for well-engineered, reliable, and maintainable software has never been higher.

This handbook serves as a bridge between the foundational principles of software engineering and the practical skills required to implement them in real-world software development projects. It is intended for computer science students, budding software engineers, and professionals seeking a structured approach to software system design and management.

Why Software Engineering Matters

Software engineering is more than just programming. It is a disciplined approach to the development, operation, and maintenance of software, governed by well-defined processes, tools, and methodologies. It encompasses technical skills, problem-solving abilities, and project management techniques, all aimed at producing high-quality, cost-effective software solutions within time and resource constraints.

The goal of this handbook is to guide readers through the lifecycle of software development by exploring key phases such as requirement analysis, design, modeling, implementation, testing, and management.

How to Use This Handbook

Readers are encouraged to approach the chapters sequentially, as the content builds cumulatively—from defining problems to designing, implementing, testing, and managing solutions. However, individual chapters can also serve as standalone references for specific topics.

Whether you are a student preparing for a university examination, a project leader managing a software team, or a developer refining your understanding of the engineering process, this handbook is crafted to serve as your go-to companion in mastering software engineering from theory to practice.

Chapter 1

Introduction to Software Engineering

1.1. Basic Concept

Software

Software is a collection of programs, data, and instructions that tell a computer how to perform specific tasks. It can be classified into system software (e.g., operating systems), application software (e.g., web browsers, word processors), and programming software (e.g., compilers, code editors). Unlike hardware, software is intangible and can be modified or updated without changing the physical components of a computer.

Types of Software

Software can be classified into several types based on its purpose and functionality:

System Software – Manages hardware and provides a platform for other software. Examples: Operating Systems (Windows, Linux, macOS), Device Drivers, Utility Software.

Application Software – Designed for end-users to perform specific tasks. Examples: Web Browsers, Word Processors, Media Players, Mobile Apps.

Embedded Software – Runs on specialized hardware devices for specific functions. Examples: Firmware in IoT devices, software in washing machines or medical devices.

An Information System (IS) is a combination of hardware, software, data, people, and processes used to collect, process, store, and distribute information. Software plays a crucial role in enabling information systems to function efficiently. This book is entirely about the development of the Information System.

Software Product

A software product is a complete, packaged software solution designed for end-users or businesses to fulfill specific needs. It includes the executable program, documentation, user interfaces, and support services.

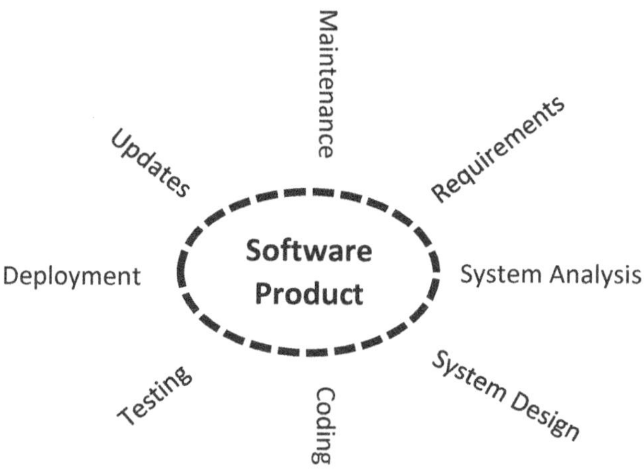

Figure 1.1: Scope of Software Product

Software products can be categorized into generic software products (developed for a broad audience, like Microsoft Office or Adobe Photoshop) and custom software products (developed for specific clients or organizations). These products go through a structured development process, including design, coding, testing, deployment, and maintenance. This is depicted in figure 1.1.

Software Engineering

Software Engineering is the systematic application of engineering principles to the design, development, testing, and maintenance of software systems. It focuses on creating reliable, scalable, and efficient software solutions using structured methodologies, programming languages, and best practices. Key aspects include software development life cycle (SDLC), coding, debugging, project management, and quality assurance. Software engineers work in various domains such as web development, mobile applications, cybersecurity, artificial intelligence, and cloud computing to build software that meets user needs and business objectives.

In other words, Software Engineering is a systematic, disciplined, and measurable approach to software development. It applies engineering principles to ensure that software is reliable, efficient, scalable, and maintainable. The primary goal is to create high-quality software that meets user requirements while adhering to budget and time constraints.

Importance of Software Engineering

- Manages Complexity – Large software projects require structured approaches to ensure they are maintainable and scalable.

- Ensures Quality – Software engineering practices help deliver reliable and high-performance software.

- Reduces Costs – Proper planning and methodologies prevent costly errors and rework.

- Improves Productivity – Well-defined processes help teams work efficiently.

Key Areas in Software Engineering

Software engineering is a broad field with multiple specialized areas, each focusing on different aspects of software development. Below is a more detailed explanation of the key areas:

1. Frontend Development (User Interface & User Experience)

Frontend development focuses on the part of the application that users interact with directly. It involves designing and coding the user interface (UI) to ensure a seamless user experience (UX). Key Technologies –

- HTML (HyperText Markup Language) – The backbone of web pages, defining their structure.

- CSS (Cascading Style Sheets) – Used to style the elements of a web page (colors, layouts, animations).

- JavaScript – Adds interactivity to websites (forms, animations, dynamic content).

- Frameworks/Libraries – React.js (by Meta), Angular (by Google), Vue.js

Key Responsibilities of a Frontend Developer

- Designing user-friendly interfaces.

- Ensuring web pages are responsive (work on different screen sizes).

- Optimizing page load speed and performance.

- Ensuring accessibility for all users, including those with disabilities.

- Collaborating with backend developers to fetch and display data.

2. Backend Development (Server-Side Logic)

Backend development handles the logic, calculations, and database interactions required to run applications. It ensures data processing and business logic work correctly. Key Technologies –

- Programming Languages – Python (Django, Flask), Java (Spring Boot), JavaScript (Node.js), PHP, Ruby on Rails

- Frameworks & Tools – Express.js (for Node.js), FastAPI (for Python)

- APIs (Application Programming Interfaces) – RESTful APIs, GraphQL

Key Responsibilities of a Backend Developer

- Writing business logic and server-side code.

- Managing authentication and authorization (e.g., login systems).

- Processing and storing data efficiently.

- Ensuring security against threats like SQL injection and cross-site scripting (XSS).

- Optimizing performance and scalability for handling large amounts of users.

3. Database Management (Data Storage & Retrieval)

A database is a structured way to store, retrieve, and manage data. Database management is crucial for handling large datasets efficiently and securely. Types of Databases –

- Relational Databases (SQL-Based) – Store data in structured tables.
    - o Examples: MySQL, PostgreSQL, Oracle DB, Microsoft SQL Server.

- NoSQL Databases – Handle unstructured or semi-structured data, often used for big data and real-time applications.
    - o Examples: MongoDB, Firebase, Cassandra, Redis.

Key Responsibilities of a Database Engineer

- Designing efficient database schemas.

- Ensuring data consistency and integrity.

- Writing optimized queries to fetch data.

- Implementing backup and recovery strategies.

- Managing database security and preventing unauthorized access.

4. Software Testing (Quality Assurance & Debugging)

Software testing ensures that applications work as expected, are free from bugs, and perform well under different conditions.

Types of Software Testing

- Manual Testing – Human testers check the software for issues.

- Automated Testing – Scripts are written to test software automatically.

- Unit Testing – Testing individual components of the software.

- Integration Testing – Checking if different modules work together.

- Performance Testing – Ensuring the software performs well under load.

- Security Testing – Identifying vulnerabilities and weaknesses.

Key Tools for Testing

- Selenium (Automated UI testing)

- JUnit (Java unit testing)

- PyTest (Python testing framework)

- Jest (JavaScript testing)

Key Responsibilities of a Software Tester

- Identifying and reporting bugs.

- Writing and executing test cases.

- Ensuring software meets the required specifications.

- Automating repetitive testing processes.

- Collaborating with developers to improve software quality.

5. Cybersecurity (Security & Threat Protection)

Cybersecurity ensures that software and systems are protected against attacks, data breaches, and vulnerabilities. Common Cybersecurity Threats are -

- SQL Injection – Attackers insert malicious SQL queries to manipulate databases.

- Cross-Site Scripting (XSS) – Injecting scripts into websites to steal user data.

- Phishing – Fraudulent emails or messages to trick users into revealing credentials.

- Denial of Service (DoS/DDoS) Attacks – Overloading servers to make applications unavailable.

Key Cybersecurity Practices

- Implementing encryption (e.g., HTTPS, TLS, AES).

- Using secure authentication methods (e.g., multi-factor authentication, OAuth).

- Regular security audits and penetration testing.

- Keeping software and dependencies up to date.

- Writing secure code to prevent vulnerabilities.

Software engineering covers multiple disciplines, and each area plays a crucial role in building and maintaining reliable software applications. Whether you're interested in designing interfaces, handling data, writing logic, testing software, or securing systems, there are plenty of opportunities within the field.

1.2. Software Development Life Cycle (SDLC)

The Software Development Life Cycle (SDLC) is a structured process used to develop high-quality software in a systematic and cost-effective manner. It defines the phases involved in software development, ensuring that software is delivered on time, within budget, and meets user requirements.

Phases of SDLC

Requirement Analysis

Understanding and documenting the client's needs and expectations.

Involves gathering requirements through surveys, interviews, and stakeholder discussions.

Output: Software Requirement Specification (SRS) document.

Planning

Defining project scope, estimating resources, timeline, and cost.

Identifying potential risks and creating a risk management plan.

Output: Project Plan, Feasibility Study.

Design

Creating a blueprint of the software system.

Two levels of design:

High-Level Design (HLD): System architecture, data flow, and module structure.

Low-Level Design (LLD): Detailed design of each module, algorithms, and data structures.

Output: System Design Document (SDD).

Development (Coding)

Writing the actual source code based on design documents.

Developers use programming languages such as Python, Java, C++, etc.

Follow coding best practices like modularity, reusability, and security.

Output: Executable Software Code.

Testing

Identifying and fixing bugs or issues to ensure the software functions correctly.

Types of testing:

- Unit Testing – Testing individual components.

- Integration Testing – Ensuring modules work together.

- System Testing – Validating the entire system's functionality.

- User Acceptance Testing (UAT) – Verifying software meets user needs.

Output: Test Reports, Bug Reports.

Deployment

Releasing the software to the production environment.

Can be done in stages (Beta release, Full deployment).

Output: Live Software Application.

Maintenance & Support

Fixing bugs, updating features, and ensuring smooth performance after deployment.

Types of maintenance:

- Corrective Maintenance – Fixing defects.

- Adaptive Maintenance – Updating software for new environments.

- Perfective Maintenance – Improving performance and features.

Output: Updated Versions, Bug Fixes.

1. Waterfall Model

The Waterfall Model is a linear and sequential approach, where each phase must be completed before moving to the next. It follows a strict step-by-step process, with no going back to previous phases. Figure 1.2 depicts this model.

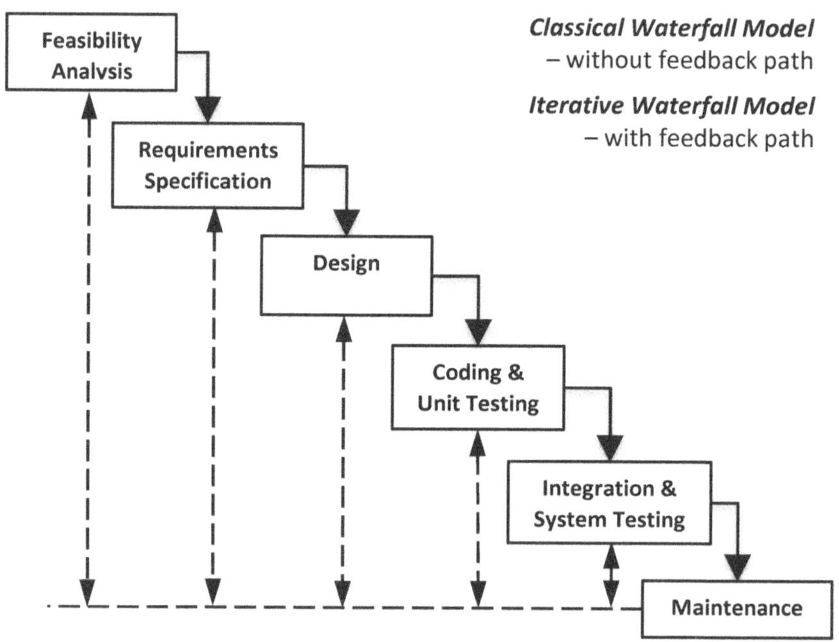

Figure 1.2: The SDLC Waterfall Model

Characteristics:

- Rigid and structured process.

- Works well for projects with well-defined requirements.

- Each phase depends on the completion of the previous one.

Advantages:

- Simple and easy to understand.

- Well-documented process.

- Works well for projects with fixed requirements.

Disadvantages:

- Inflexible—difficult to accommodate changes.

- Late detection of issues, as testing happens after development.

- Not suitable for complex, evolving projects.

Best Used For:

- Small to medium-sized projects with clear requirements.

- Projects where changes are unlikely (e.g., military and government systems).

2. Agile Model

The Agile Model is an iterative and flexible approach that breaks the development process into small increments called sprints (typically 2-4 weeks long). The product is continuously improved based on user feedback.

Characteristics:

- Development happens in small cycles (iterations).

- Frequent customer feedback and involvement.

- Focuses on delivering a working product at the end of each sprint.

Advantages:

- High flexibility—easy to adapt to changes.

- Continuous testing improves product quality.

- Faster delivery of functional software.

Disadvantages:

- Requires continuous user involvement, which may not always be feasible.

- Can be challenging to manage in large teams.

- Less predictability in project timelines and costs.

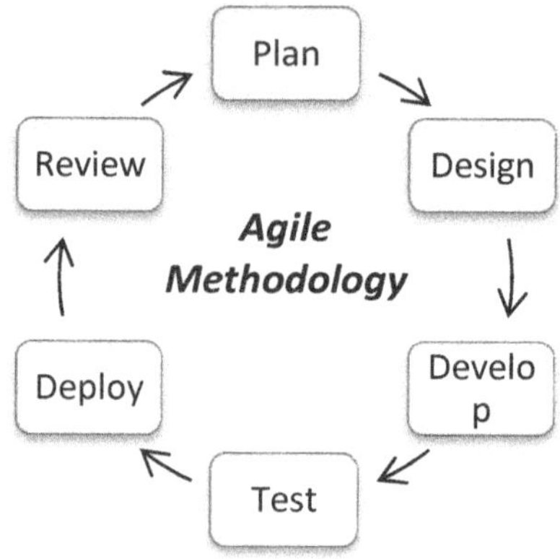

Figure 1.3: The Agile Model of SDLC

Best Used For:

- Dynamic projects where requirements change frequently (e.g., web and mobile applications).

- Startups and businesses using rapid development strategies.

3. Spiral Model

The Spiral Model is a risk-driven hybrid model, combining elements of the Waterfall and Agile models. It emphasizes risk assessment and iterative development.

Characteristics:

- Development occurs in cycles (spirals), with risk assessment at every phase.

- Each spiral includes planning, risk analysis, development, and evaluation.

- Early prototypes help detect problems early.

Advantages:

- High flexibility to change.

- Focuses on risk analysis to prevent costly errors.

- Suitable for high-risk projects.

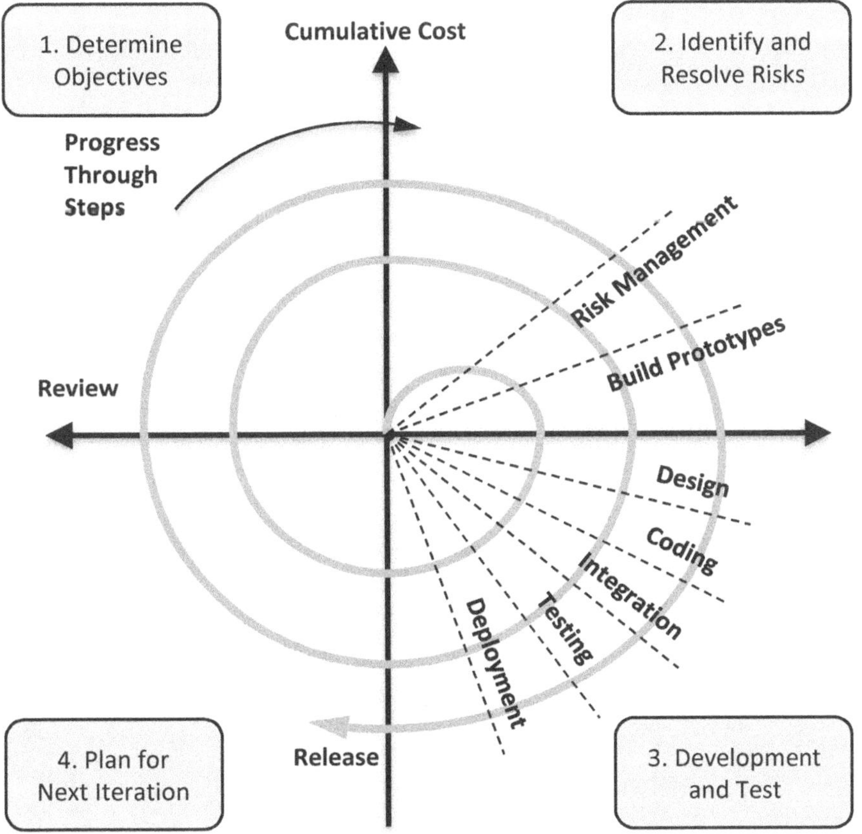

Figure 1.4: The Spiral Model of SDLC

Disadvantages:

- More complex and expensive to implement.

- Requires specialized expertise in risk assessment.

- Not ideal for small, low-budget projects.

Best Used For:

- Large, high-risk projects (e.g., financial systems, aerospace, AI development).

- Projects with uncertain or evolving requirements.

4. V-Model (Validation & Verification Model)

The V-Model is an extension of the Waterfall Model, where each development phase has a corresponding testing phase. Testing is performed simultaneously with development.

Characteristics:

- Each development phase has an associated testing phase.

- Testing is done early to detect errors faster.

- Validation and verification happen in parallel.

Advantages:

- Early defect detection, reducing cost and effort.

- Ensures high reliability and quality.

- Suitable for safety-critical applications.

Disadvantages:

- Less flexible—changes require restarting phases.

- Expensive and time-consuming due to extensive testing.

- Requires strong documentation and planning.

Best Used For:

- Mission-critical systems (e.g., medical software, aviation, automotive).

- Projects requiring extensive validation (e.g., banking applications).

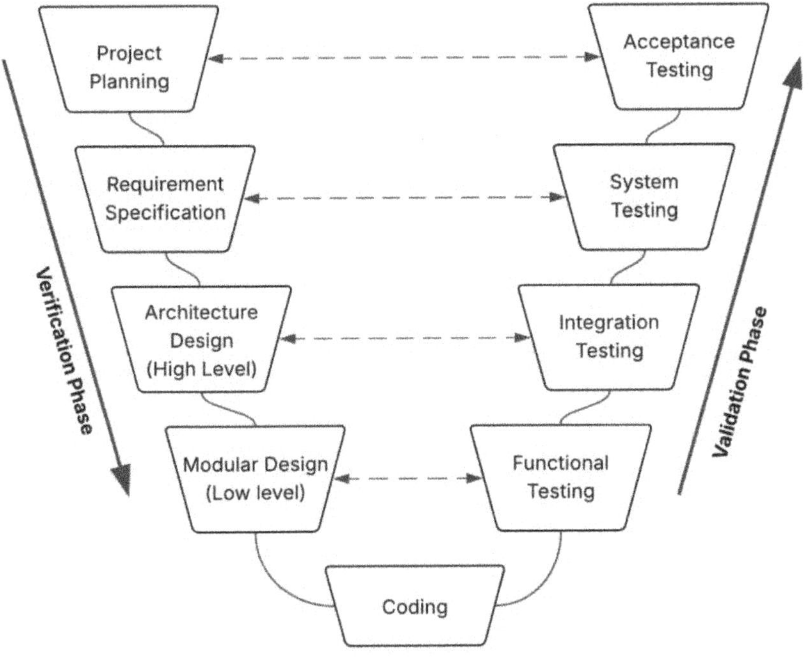

Figure 1.5: The V-Model of SDLC

5. Prototyping Model

The Prototyping Model is an iterative approach where a prototype (a working model) is built, tested, and refined before full-scale development.

Characteristics:

- Quick development of an early version for feedback.

- Focuses on UI/UX and user requirements.

- Multiple iterations refine the prototype before final development.

Advantages:

- Better understanding of requirements.

- Faster feedback loop.

- Improved user satisfaction.

Disadvantages:

- Scope creep due to continuous changes.

- Increased cost from multiple iterations.

- Not ideal for complex backend systems.

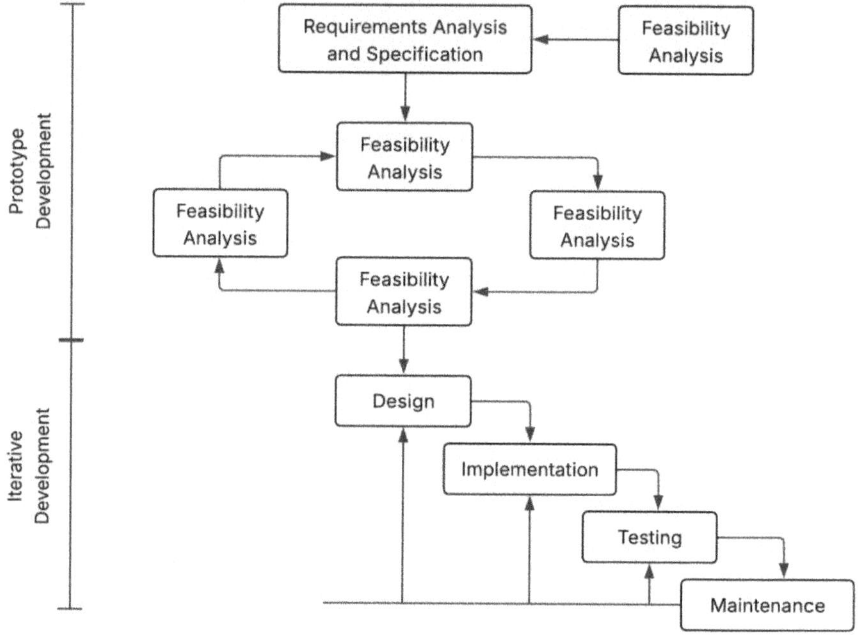

Figure 1.6: The SDLC Prototyping Model

Best Used For:

- UI/UX-focused applications (e.g., web apps).

- Projects with unclear or evolving requirements.

6. Evolutionary Model

The Evolutionary Model (Incremental & Iterative Development) builds software gradually, adding new features in each version. In figure 1.7, V1 refers to version 1, V2 is version 2 and so on. The greater number represents the later version.

Characteristics:

- Develops in small, functional increments.

- Prioritizes delivering a working product early.

- Allows continuous feedback and improvements.

Advantages:

- Faster initial delivery.

- Flexible to changes.

- Reduces risks by detecting issues early.

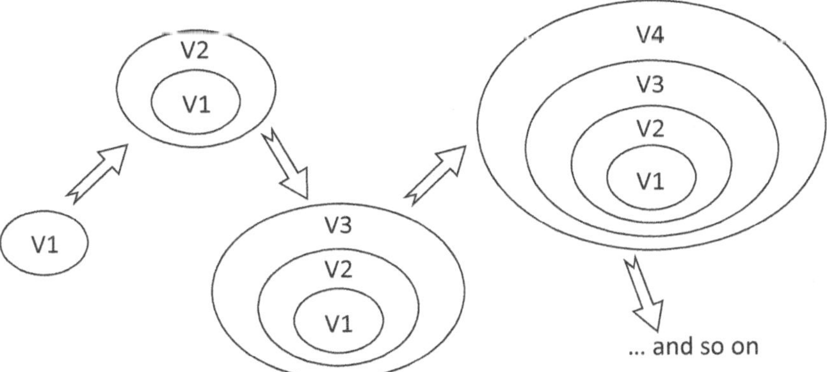

Figure 1.7: The Evolutionary Model of SDLC

Disadvantages:

- Frequent redesign may be needed.

- Increased cost due to continuous changes.

- Difficult to predict the final product.

Best Used For:

- Large-scale, evolving software (e.g., enterprise systems).

- Long-term projects requiring continuous updates.

1.3. Conclusion

Following is the comparison of all the Software Development Life Cycle models discussed in this chapter.

Model	Flexibility	Risk Management	Best For
Waterfall	Low	Low	Fixed requirements, small projects
Agile	High	Medium	Fast-changing projects
Spiral	Medium-High	High	High-risk projects
V-Model	Low	High	Safety-critical applications
Prototyping	High	Medium	UI-focused projects
Evolutionary	High	High	Long-term scalable software

Table 1.1: Comparison of SDLC Models

Choosing the right SDLC model depends on project size, requirements, risks, and customer involvement. While Waterfall is best for well-defined projects, Agile, Evolutionary, and Prototyping models suit modern, fast-changing applications. The Spiral and V-Model work well for high-risk and safety-critical software.

Chapter 2

Software Requirements Engineering

2.1. Overview of Requirements Engineering

Software Requirements Engineering (SRE) is the process of gathering, analyzing, documenting, and managing the requirements of a software system. It ensures that the final product meets user needs and business objectives.

Importance of Requirements Engineering

- Ensures that the software meets customer expectations.

- Reduces project risks and costly changes later in development.

- Improves communication between stakeholders (clients, developers, testers).

- Provides a structured foundation for system design and development.

Key Activities in Software Requirements Engineering

SRE consists of several key steps:

1. Requirements Elicitation (Gathering Requirements)

This is the process of collecting requirements from stakeholders, including customers, end-users, and business analysts. Common techniques include:

- Interviews – Direct discussions with stakeholders.

- Surveys & Questionnaires – Gathering insights from a broad audience.

- Workshops & Brainstorming – Collaborative sessions for idea generation.

- Observation & Shadowing – Understanding how users interact with current systems.

- Prototyping – Building a simple version to get feedback on features.

2. Requirements Analysis & Negotiation

After gathering requirements, they are analyzed for feasibility, conflicts, and clarity.

- Identifying missing, conflicting, or ambiguous requirements.

- Prioritizing requirements based on importance and feasibility.

- Resolving differences between stakeholders through discussion.

3. Requirements Specification (Documenting Requirements)

Once analyzed, requirements are formally documented in a Software Requirements Specification (SRS). This document includes:

- Functional Requirements (What the system should do).

- Non-functional Requirements (Performance, security, usability).

- Constraints & Assumptions (Limitations, hardware/software dependencies).

4. Requirements Validation

Before development starts, requirements must be verified to ensure correctness and completeness. Common validation techniques include:

- Reviews & Inspections – Team discussions to check for inconsistencies.

- Prototyping – Testing a working model with users.

- Requirement Testing – Ensuring each requirement can be validated later.

5. Requirements Management

Since requirements can change during development, they must be tracked and updated using:

- Version Control – Keeping records of requirement changes.

- Impact Analysis – Assessing how changes affect the project.

- Traceability Matrix – Linking requirements to design, development, and testing.

Types of Software Requirements

Software requirements are categorized into functional and non-functional requirements:

1. Functional Requirements

Functional requirements define the specific behavior, actions, or features a system must provide to meet user needs. These requirements describe what the system should do and are essential for defining the scope of the software. Below are detailed explanations with real-world examples.

These define what the system should do (features and behaviors). Examples:

- o User authentication and login.

- o Processing online transactions.

- o Generating reports and analytics.

2. *Non-Functional Requirements*

These define how the system should perform and include:

- o Performance – System should handle a certain amount of transactions per second.

- o Security – User data must be encrypted.

- o Usability – Interface must be user-friendly.

- o Reliability – System must have 99.9% uptime.

Challenges in Requirements Engineering

Changing Requirements – Stakeholders frequently modify their requirements during the development process. This may happen due to evolving business goals, market conditions, or new insights gained from early prototypes. While change is often necessary, frequent or poorly managed changes can lead to scope creep, delays, and increased development costs. It is essential to have a flexible yet controlled process for handling changes in requirements, such as change request procedures or version control in documentation.

Ambiguity – Ambiguous or unclear requirements are a major cause of confusion and errors in software development. When requirements are not stated in precise, measurable terms, different team members may interpret them differently, leading to inconsistent implementations. To minimize ambiguity, requirements should be written using clear, unambiguous language and, where possible, supported by visual models (like UML diagrams), examples, and acceptance criteria.

Conflicting Stakeholder Interests – Projects often involve multiple stakeholders, such as business managers, end-users, developers, testers, and customers—each with their own perspectives and priorities. These interests can sometimes conflict. For example, a marketing team might want rapid release cycles, while a QA team insists on more testing time. Managing these conflicts requires effective stakeholder analysis, prioritization techniques (like MoSCoW or weighted scoring), and strong facilitation skills to reach consensus.

Poor Communication – Effective communication between technical and non-technical teams is crucial but often lacking. Misunderstandings can occur when business stakeholders use non-technical terms or when developers use jargon that stakeholders don't understand. This communication gap can result in incorrect assumptions, rework, or missed expectations. Bridging this gap involves using clear documentation, collaborative tools, frequent feedback loops, and roles like business analysts or product owners who act as liaisons between both sides.

Best Practices for Effective Requirements Engineering

Requirements Engineering is a critical phase in software development that involves gathering, analyzing, documenting, and managing requirements to ensure the final product meets stakeholder needs. Implementing best practices helps reduce misunderstandings, project risks, and development costs.

1. Engage Stakeholders Early

Involve all key stakeholders—end users, business analysts, developers, testers, and project managers—from the very beginning of the project. Early involvement ensures:

- o   A shared understanding of goals and expectations

- o   Fewer surprises later in the project lifecycle

- o   Identification of conflicting needs upfront

Benefits: Builds trust, increases stakeholder satisfaction, and lays a solid foundation for collaborative development.

2. Use Prototyping & Visualization Techniques

Creating prototypes, wireframes, or mockups helps make abstract requirements tangible and understandable, especially for non-technical stakeholders. Visualization tools and models (e.g., UML diagrams, storyboards) allow stakeholders to:

- o Visualize how the system will behave

- o Provide more accurate feedback

- o Identify gaps or misunderstandings early

Tools to consider: Figma, Balsamiq, Adobe XD, or even simple whiteboard sketches.

3. Prioritize Requirements

Not all requirements are equally important. Use prioritization techniques to identify the most valuable and time-sensitive features first. This helps in managing scope and aligning development with business goals.

Common methods:

- o MoSCoW (Must have, Should have, Could have, Won't have)

- o Kano Model

- o 100-Dollar Test

- o Weighted Scoring

Outcome: Faster delivery of critical functionality and better resource allocation.

4. Ensure Clarity & Completeness

Requirements must be:

- o Clear – Free from ambiguity

- o Consistent – Not conflicting with other requirements

- o Complete – Covering all necessary aspects

- o Testable – Verifiable through testing

Use structured templates, glossaries, and formal review processes to ensure high-quality requirements.

Tip: Avoid subjective terms like "user-friendly" or "fast" without measurable benchmarks.

5. Adopt Requirement Management Tools

Utilize specialized tools to document, organize, trace, and manage requirements throughout the project lifecycle. These tools improve:

- Traceability – Linking requirements to design, development, and testing artifacts

- Change management – Tracking modifications and their impact

- Collaboration – Keeping stakeholders aligned and informed

Popular tools:

- JIRA – Agile-friendly, integrates with development tools

- IBM DOORS – Enterprise-grade requirements management

- Trello – Lightweight visual task tracking

- Azure DevOps, Confluence, ClickUp, etc.

Benefit: Helps maintain consistency and control, especially in large or complex projects.

By following these best practices, teams can significantly improve communication, reduce risk, and deliver software that truly meets stakeholder needs. Effective requirements engineering sets the stage for a successful project lifecycle, from planning to deployment.

Software Requirements Engineering is a critical phase in software development, ensuring that the final product aligns with business goals and user needs. A well-defined requirements process leads to fewer errors, lower costs, and a more successful project.

2.2. Anatomy of SRS Document

Basic concept of SRS Document

A **Software Requirements Specification (SRS)** document is a comprehensive description of a software system that outlines its purpose, features, functionalities, and constraints. It serves as a blueprint for developers, designers, and testers, ensuring that all stakeholders have a clear understanding of the software requirements before development begins.

An SRS document serves as a contract between stakeholders and the development team. A well-structured SRS ensures the software meets user expectations, remains within scope, and minimizes risks.

A well-structured SRS document helps:

- Avoid misunderstandings between stakeholders.

- Act as a reference for developers and testers.

- Estimate project cost, time, and resources.

- Maintain consistency and traceability throughout the software development lifecycle.

SRS Document Checklist

The SRS document is evaluated by testers or a review team using various verification methods, such as peer reviews, walkthroughs, and inspections. Inspections are often preferred due to their efficiency and ability to yield high-quality results. Reviews may be conducted multiple times, as each iteration enhances the document's quality. However, frequent reviews can also consume additional resources and increase software development costs.

A checklist is a widely used verification tool that ensures a deliverable contains all essential information. It helps identify missing, unclear, incorrect, or redundant content, making the review process more structured and effective.

Key Elements of an SRS Document Checklist

A Software Requirement Specification (SRS) document is a crucial element of software development. It defines both functional and non-functional requirements, serving as a central reference for all stakeholders. However, crafting a precise and complete SRS document can be challenging. This is where an SRS checklist proves invaluable, ensuring that all critical aspects are covered systematically.

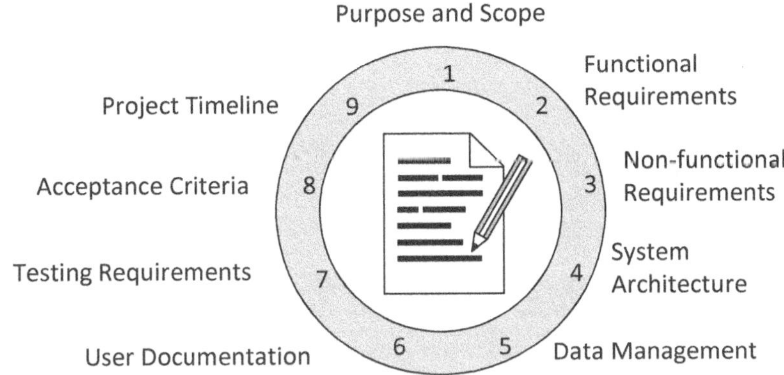

Figure 2.1: Elements of an SRS Document Checklist

1. Purpose and Scope

This section provides a high-level overview of the software, its target audience, and the specific problem it addresses. It also outlines any constraints, assumptions, and dependencies that may impact development.

2. Functional Requirements

Functional requirements define what the software must accomplish. These should be clear, measurable, and testable, covering aspects such as features, user interactions, and data processing.

3. Non-Functional Requirements

Non-functional requirements describe how the software should perform. These include metrics for performance, security, reliability, and usability, ensuring the system meets quality standards.

4. System Architecture

This section outlines the high-level design of the software, detailing its components, interfaces, and data flow to provide a clear architectural blueprint.

5. Data Management

Describes how the software will handle data, including database structures, storage methods, and backup and recovery processes to ensure data integrity and availability.

6. User Documentation

Covers how users will interact with the software. It includes information about the user interface, user manuals, and help documents to facilitate ease of use.

7. Testing Requirements

Defines how the software will be tested, detailing test cases, testing environments, and test data to ensure the system meets functional and non-functional specifications.

8. Acceptance Criteria

Specifies the conditions under which the software will be approved by stakeholders. It includes acceptance tests, validation requirements, and sign-off procedures.

9. Project Timeline

Provides a structured timeline for the software development process, highlighting key milestones, deliverables, and deadlines to track progress efficiently.

Essential Aspects of SRS Document

An SRS (Software Requirements Specification) document checklist ensures that all essential aspects of software requirements are addressed accurately. Below are the key areas to focus on during the review process:

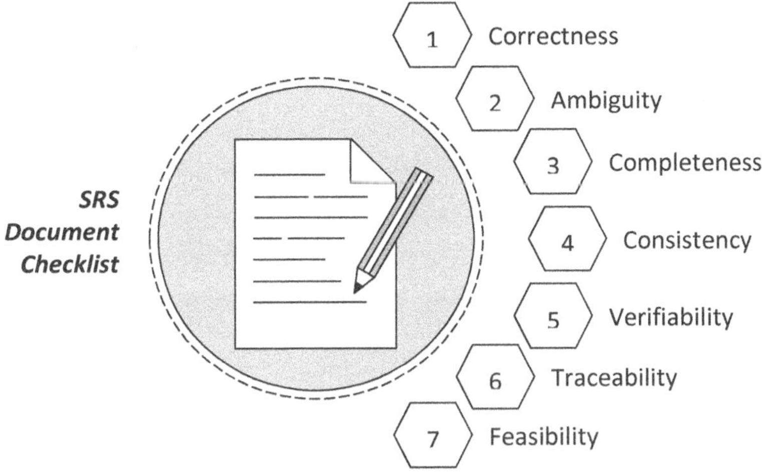

Figure 2.2: Essential Aspects of SRS Document

1. Correctness

- Every requirement stated in the SRS document must accurately reflect the expected functionality of the proposed software.

- All relevant safety and security requirements should be clearly defined.

- Each input and output must be complete and sufficient for the specified processing.

Example: If a client requires the software to respond to button presses within 2 seconds, but the SRS states 20 seconds, this discrepancy is considered an error in the documentation.

2. Ambiguity

- The SRS document must avoid any vague or unclear statements.

- Each requirement should have only one interpretation to prevent misunderstandings.

- The use of precise, well-defined language eliminates ambiguity.

- The checklist should highlight any ambiguous words or phrases to ensure clarity.

3. Completeness

- The document must include all critical functional requirements, such as handling hardware failures, input/output errors, computational issues, buffer overflows, and missing events.

- It should also cover non-functional requirements, including performance, security, and reliability aspects.

- The completeness of the document must be carefully validated using a structured checklist.

4. Consistency

- Requirements should not conflict with each other or introduce contradictions.

- Objects must be uniquely named and consistently defined throughout the document.

- Acronyms, mathematical equations, and abbreviations must be uniformly used and well-documented.

- The checklist should specifically look for inconsistencies to maintain uniformity.

5. *Verifiability*

- Every requirement must be measurable and testable.

- Vague terms such as "good interface," "excellent response time," "usually," "well," etc., should be avoided.

- The document should use precise terminology such as "shall," "will," "must," ensuring clarity and testability.

- Only measurable and well-defined terms should be included to facilitate verification.

6. *Traceability*

- Every requirement should have a clearly defined source, ensuring that it can be tracked throughout development.

- Traceability makes it easier to map requirements to design and testing phases.

- The checklist should include traceability checks to enhance document structure and maintain alignment with project goals.

7. *Feasibility*

- Some requirements may not be technically feasible or practical due to resource limitations.

- Any requirements that are unrealistic should be identified and removed.

Note: If the system depends on data from external sources, the availability of such data must be verified; otherwise, the requirement may be impractical.

A checklist helps identify other non-feasible requirements to ensure realistic expectations.

Goals of an SRS Document

An SRS document serves multiple purposes in software development:

- **Problem Breakdown** – Divides the problem into manageable parts for easier resolution.

- **Input to Design Specification** – Acts as a foundation for subsequent documents, such as the software design specification and statement of work.

- **Customer Feedback** – Ensures that the development team understands the client's requirements.

- **Product Validation** – Helps verify that the final product meets the expected standards and functionality.

Advantages of an SRS Document

- **Clarity** – Provides a precise and unambiguous description of requirements, reducing confusion and misinterpretation.

- **Consistency** – Ensures a structured and uniform approach to documenting requirements, covering all essential aspects.

- **Traceability** – Establishes a clear link between requirements and the final software product, ensuring all needs are met.

- **Validation** – Acts as a reference for validating the software against specified requirements.

Disadvantages of an SRS Document

- **Time-Consuming** – Creating a comprehensive SRS document can be lengthy, especially for complex systems involving multiple stakeholders.

- **Limited Flexibility** – Once established, modifying the document can be difficult without affecting other sections.

- Restricted User Involvement – If created before engaging users, the document may not fully reflect their actual needs and expectations.

- Potential Misinterpretation – Despite efforts to ensure clarity, some requirements may still be misunderstood, leading to errors in the final product.

2.3. Standard Structure of an SRS Document

As per the IEEE 830-1998 Format, an SRS document is typically structured into the following sections:

1. Introduction

This section provides an overview of the project, defining its purpose, scope, and key terminologies.

1.1 Purpose

The purpose defines why the software is being developed and its intended users.

Example:

- "This document specifies the requirements for an Online Banking System that allows users to manage accounts, transfer funds, pay bills, and access transaction history securely."

1.2 Scope

This section defines what the software will do and its benefits.

Example:

- The system will allow users to log in, view balances, transfer money, and pay bills online.

- It will integrate with third-party payment gateways (e.g., PayPal, Stripe).

- The system will ensure secure transactions using encryption and authentication.

- Mobile and web-based platforms will be supported.

1.3 Definitions, Acronyms, and Abbreviations

Defines important terms used in the document.

Example:

- API – Application Programming Interface

- OTP – One-Time Password

- MFA – Multi-Factor Authentication

1.4 References

Lists external documents, industry standards, or regulations followed.

Example:

- IEEE 830-1998 – Recommended Practice for Software Requirements Specifications

PCI DSS – Payment Card Industry Data Security Standard

1.5 Overview

Brief summary of the document's structure.

2. Overall Description

Provides a high-level description of the software.

2.1 Product Perspective

Describes how the system fits into the existing environment.

Example:

- "The Online Banking System will replace the current manual banking system, allowing users to manage accounts from their computers and smartphones."

2.2 Product Functions

A brief list of key functionalities.

Example:

- User Registration & Authentication
- Account Management (Checking/Savings)
- Fund Transfers & Bill Payments
- Transaction History & Statements
- Customer Support & Chatbot

2.3 User Characteristics

Describes the system's intended users.

Example:

- Customers – Individuals using the banking system.
- Bank Staff – Employees managing customer accounts.
- Administrators – IT and security teams maintaining the system.

2.4 Constraints

Lists limitations such as performance constraints, security policies, or legal regulations.

Example:

- The system must comply with GDPR and PCI DSS standards.
- The software must handle 10,000 concurrent users.
- Only English and Spanish languages will be supported initially.

2.5 Assumptions and Dependencies

Defines external dependencies and assumptions made during development.

Example:

The software assumes that users have internet access.

The system depends on a third-party payment gateway (e.g., PayPal, Stripe) for processing payments.

3. Functional Requirements

Functional requirements define what the system should do in terms of features and behavior. They are often written as "The system shall..." statements.

Example Functional Requirements for Online Banking System:

- The system shall allow users to register using their email and phone number.

- The system shall send a one-time password (OTP) for verification during login.

- The system shall allow users to view account balances and transaction history.

- The system shall process fund transfers between bank accounts.

- The system shall send a confirmation email after a successful transaction.

- The system shall allow users to reset their passwords via email verification.

4. Non-Functional Requirements

Non-functional requirements define how the system should perform rather than what it does. They cover aspects like security, performance, usability, and reliability.

Example Non-Functional Requirements:

- The system shall respond within 2 seconds for any user request. (Performance)

- The system shall encrypt all user passwords using SHA-256 encryption. (Security)

- The system shall be available 99.9% of the time. (Availability & Reliability)

- The system shall support up to 10,000 concurrent users. (Scalability)

- The system shall be accessible to visually impaired users following WCAG 2.0 guidelines. (Usability & Accessibility)

5. External Interface Requirements

Describes how the system interacts with users, hardware, and other software.

5.1 User Interface Requirements

Defines the design, layout, and interaction elements of the system.

Example:

- The system shall have a dashboard displaying account balance and recent transactions.

- The system shall have a search bar for users to find transactions by date or amount.

5.2 Hardware Requirements

Lists the hardware specifications required to run the software.

Example:

- The system shall run on servers with at least 16GB RAM and 512GB SSD storage.

- The mobile app shall support Android 8.0+ and iOS 12+.

5.3 Software Interfaces

Defines integration with other software.

Example:

- The system shall integrate with PayPal and Stripe for payment processing.

- The system shall support REST API for third-party application access.

6. System Models & Diagrams

This section contains visual representations of the system, such as:

- Use Case Diagram – Shows how users interact with the system.

- Data Flow Diagram (DFD) – Illustrates how data moves through the system.

- Entity-Relationship Diagram (ERD) – Defines the database structure.

Example: Use Case Diagram for Online Banking System

- Actors: User, Admin, Payment Gateway

- Use-cases: Login, Transfer Funds, View Transactions, Pay Bills

7. Appendices

This section includes additional information, such as FAQs, references to previous documents, or legal disclaimers.

2.4. Procedure to Create an SRS Document

Step 1: Requirement Gathering

- Interview stakeholders.

- Use surveys and prototyping.

- Analyze existing systems.

Step 2: Categorize & Prioritize Requirements

- Separate functional and non-functional requirements.

- Prioritize must-have vs. nice-to-have features.

Step 3: Write the SRS Document

- Use clear, precise language.

- Follow the IEEE 830-1998 standard.

- Use diagrams where necessary.

Step 4: Validate with Stakeholders

- Review the document with clients, developers, and testers.

- Revise based on feedback.

Step 5: Maintain & Update the SRS

- Track changes using version control.

- Keep the document updated throughout development.

2.5. Some worked-out Examples of SRS

2.5.1. Example 1 - Problem Statement: Online Magazine System

The online magazine system DigiMag is administered by different administrators managing articles belonging to several categories. The kind of articles managed by an administrator is indicated by the administrator's category. Each administrator is given an Admin ID when they register their name and date of birth. An administrator can assign articles to reviewers for approving or rejecting them for publication. However, the reviewer can also decide whether to accept or reject the review invitation sent by the administrator.

The administrators open the submission portal on particular dates and closes the portal on expiry of the deadline. A reviewer has an email and choice of review. If the reviewers decide to accept the review request, they review the assigned article and inform the concerned administrator about their decisions. The administrator then uploads the article and mails the submitter informing the reviewer's decision.

To be able to submit an article to DigiMag, one can subscribe to it by choosing a subscription type and pricing. Each subscriber will hence, have a subscription number too and will be allowed to access all articles published in DigiMag. A subscriber must pay monthly subscription fees. Only after a subscription is completed, one can become a submitter and submit an article to DigiMag. A submitter will have an article category and submission type. In DigiMag, an article should have a category and access type. An article will also have a popularity rating based on the number of views or reads.

Solution:

DIGIMAG

Online Magazine System

Software Requirements Specification

Version <1.0>

Created by: John Coder

Consultant Software Analyst, ABC Software Corporation

<u>Revision History</u>

Date	Version	Description	Author
24/12/2024	<1.0>	SRS 1.0	Andrew Ross, SSE, ABC SW Corp
19/04/2025	<2.0>	SRS 1.0	John Coder, CSA, ABC SW Corp

Table of Contents

Software Requirements Specification

1. Introduction

1.1. Purpose

The purpose of the document is to collect and analyze all assorted ideas that have come up to define the system, its requirements with respect to consumers. Also, we shall predict and sort out how we hope this product will be used in order to gain a better understanding of the project, outline concepts that may be developed later, and document ideas that are being considered, but may be discarded as the product develops.

In short, the purpose of this SRS document is to provide a detailed overview of our software product, its parameters and goals. This document describes the project's target audience and its user interface, hardware and software requirements. It defines how our client, team and audience see the product and its functionality. Nonetheless, it helps any designer and developer to assist in software delivery lifecycle (SDLC) processes.

1.2. Overview

The remaining sections of this document provide a general description, including characteristics of the users of this project, the product's hardware, and the functional and data requirements of the product. General description of the project is discussed in section 2 of this document. Section 3 gives the functional requirements, data requirements and constraints and assumptions made while designing the DigiMag system. Section 4 and 5 are for supporting information.

1.3. Environmental Characteristics

1.3.1. Hardware

Server: A computer system with at least 2.0 GHz processor, 16 GB RAM and 100 GB space in ROM,

Client: A computer or handheld system with at least 1.0 GHz processor, 2 GB RAM and 500MB space in ROM.

1.3.2. Peripheral

Strong network connectivity

1.3.3. People

The system has four types of user – administrator, reviewer, subscriber / submitter, viewer.

2. Goals of Implementation

Primarily, the scope pertains to the DigiMag features for an online magazine system which will facilitate the users to read, submit, and review etc. for the digital magazines.

This SRS is also aimed at specifying requirements of software to be developed. The standard can be used to create software requirements specifications directly or can be used as a model for defining an organization or project specific standard. It does not identify any specific method, nomenclature or tool for preparing an SRS.

3. Functional Requirements

3.1. Managing articles belonging to several categories

3.1.1. Administrator registration

3.1.2. Administrator can assign articles to reviewers for approving or rejecting them for publication

3.1.3. Open the submission portal on particular dates and closes the portal on expiry of the deadline

3.1.4. Administrator sends email to reviewer

3.1.5. Administrator uploads articles and mails the submitter informing the reviewer's decision

3.2. Review articles by reviewer

3.2.1. Reviewer can decide whether to accept or reject the review invitation

3.2.2. Reviewer review the assigned article and informs the concerned administrator about their decisions

3.3. Subscription of articles

3.3.1. Subscribers subscribe by choosing a subscription type and pricing

3.3.2. Subscriber must pay monthly subscription fees

3.3.3. Submit an article to DigiMag

3.4. View and feedback of articles

3.4.1. An article will have a category and access type. There will be a comment section also for the valuable feedback from subscribers.

3.4.2. The system will calculate the popularity rating of an article based on the number of views and reads.

3.4.3. The system will analyze the rating and feedback afterwards.

4. Non-functional Requirements

4.1. External Interface

The external interface specifies how the Online Magazine System interacts with third-party applications, services, and external users. These interfaces ensure smooth integration and compatibility with external platforms.

Key Aspects:

- Payment Gateway Integration – Supports third-party payment processors (e.g., PayPal, Stripe) for subscriptions and purchases.

- Social Media Integration – Allows sharing of articles on platforms like Facebook, Twitter, and LinkedIn.

- Search Engine Optimization (SEO) – Ensures content is indexed properly for better visibility on Google and other search engines.

- Cloud Storage & CDN Support – Uses services like AWS S3 or Cloudflare for faster content delivery and media storage.

- Analytics & Tracking – Integrates with tools like Google Analytics to monitor user behavior and engagement.

4.2. User Interface

The user interface (UI) defines the look and feel of the Online Magazine System, ensuring an intuitive and seamless experience for users.

Key Aspects:

- Responsiveness – The system must work smoothly on desktops, tablets, and mobile devices.

- Accessibility – Compliance with WCAG (Web Content Accessibility Guidelines) to support users with disabilities.

- User-Friendly Navigation – Clear menus, category filtering, and search functionality for easy content discovery.

- Customization – Allows users to personalize their reading experience (e.g., dark mode, font size adjustments).

- Fast Loading Time – Optimized design for quick page rendering to enhance user engagement.

- Interactive Features – Includes comments, likes, and bookmarks to improve user interaction with content.

4.3. Software Interface

The software interface defines how different components of the Online Magazine System interact internally and with external applications.

Key Aspects:

- Database Compatibility – Supports relational (MySQL, PostgreSQL) and NoSQL (MongoDB) databases for efficient data management.

- Content Management System (CMS) – Integrates with WordPress, Drupal, or a custom-built CMS for content publishing.

- API Support – Provides RESTful or GraphQL APIs for integrating with mobile apps or third-party services.

- Security Mechanisms – Implements authentication (OAuth, JWT) and encryption (SSL/TLS) to protect user data.

- Caching & Performance Optimization – Uses Redis or Memcached to enhance performance and reduce server load.

4.4. Communication Interface

The communication interface ensures seamless interaction between the system, users, and external services via different communication channels.

Key Aspects:

- Email Notifications – Sends automated emails for subscription confirmations, article updates, and user engagement.

- Push Notifications – Supports real-time notifications for new articles, special offers, and personalized recommendations.

- Chat Support & AI Chatbots – Integrates with chatbots or live chat services (e.g., Zendesk, Intercom) for customer support.

- Multilingual Support – Provides content translation options to cater to a global audience.

- RSS Feeds & Content Syndication – Enables integration with news aggregators and RSS feed readers.

5. Behavioral Description

The Behavioral Description outlines how the system responds to various inputs, events, and user interactions. It describes the dynamic behavior of the system, ensuring it functions smoothly under different conditions.

5.1. System States

System states represent the different modes or conditions in which the Online Magazine System operates. These states change based on user actions, system events, or external triggers.

Key System States (Based on Vision Document & Behavioral Models):

1. Idle State – The system is running but not actively in use.

2. User Authentication State – Users log in, sign up, or reset passwords.

3. Content Management State – Admins and editors create, edit, or delete articles.

4. Subscription Processing State – Handles user subscription payments and access control.

5. Content Display State – Readers browse and interact with published articles.

6. Error Handling State – The system encounters an issue (e.g., payment failure, server downtime) and displays appropriate messages.

These states ensure smooth transitions between different functions of the system. The Non-Functional Requirements Model helps define performance, security, and scalability factors for each state, while the Traceability Matrix links these states to specific system requirements.

5.2. Events and Actions

Events trigger specific actions within the system. An event can be a user action (e.g., clicking a button) or a system-generated process (e.g., scheduled article publication).

1. Key Events and Corresponding Actions (Based on Use Case Analysis & Structural Models):

2. User Logs In → The system verifies credentials and grants access.

3. New Article Submission → The article goes for editor review.

4. Subscription Payment Completed → The user gains access to premium content.

5. Reader Comments on an Article → The system stores the comment and notifies the author.

6. Scheduled Article Publication → The system automatically publishes the article at the scheduled time.

7. System Detects Unauthorized Access Attempt → Security mechanisms trigger an alert and block the user.

The Project Plan ensures these behaviors are implemented in a structured manner, aligning with system goals.

Example 2

Problem Statement: Online Examination System

Now-a-days, the online examination system has become popular for competitive examinations because of its unique features such as auto-evaluation, speed and accuracy. Moreover, it also helps environments by reducing the use of paper. In such a system, students are asked to select answers from multiple options given for a single question. Likewise, there are several questions which appear in the students' systems. The questions and multiple options are saved in a database along with desired answers. Typically, a student can edit an answer after saving it, however, editing cannot be done after submitting the answer. Another user is also there – administrator. The administrator can create, modify and delete questions and accordingly, the question is updated in the system.

The system is able to store subject Information with code, so that all subjects can be identified using unique codes. User Information for students and administrators must also be stored for login and other activities. Tests should be set by the administrator for a particular subject and for a particular group of students on a specific date and time with duration. Result should be published on a later date.

Constraints:

- All users MUST register themselves into the system.

- Same set of questions should appear to all students.

- Log-In information contains only Email Address and Password.

- After clicking on SUBMIT, selected answers cannot be changed.

- After clicking on SAVE, selected answers can be changed.

Solution:

Online Examination System

Software Requirements Specification

Version <1.0>

Created by: John Coder

Consultant Software Analyst, ABC Software Corporation

<u>Revision History</u>

Date	Version	Description	Author
27/04/2025	<1.0>	SRS 1.0	John Coder, CSA, ABC SW Corp

Table of Contents

      d.   Communication Interface

  5.   Behavioral Description ……………………………..

      a.   System States

      b.   Events and Actions

Software Requirements Specification

1. Introduction

1.1. Purpose

The purpose of the document is to collect and analyze all assorted ideas that have come up to define the system, its requirements with respect to consumers. Also, we shall predict and sort out how we hope this product will be used in order to gain a better understanding of the project, outline concepts that may be developed later, and document ideas that are being considered, but may be discarded as the product develops.

In short, the purpose of this SRS document is to provide a detailed overview of our software product, its parameters and goals. This document describes the project's target audience and its user interface, hardware and software requirements. It defines how our client, team and audience see the product and its functionality. Nonetheless, it helps any designer and developer to assist in software delivery life cycle (SDLC) processes.

1.2. Overview

The remaining sections of this document provide a general description, including characteristics of the users of this project, the product's hardware, and the functional and data requirements of the product. General description of the project is discussed in section 2 of this document. Section 3 gives the functional requirements, data requirements and constraints and assumptions made while designing the Online Examination System. Section 4 and 5 are for supporting information.

1.3. Environmental Characteristics

1.3.1. Hardware

Server: A computer system with at least 2.0 GHz processor, 16 GB RAM and 100 GB space in ROM,

Client: A computer or handheld system with at least 1.0 GHz processor, 2 GB RAM and 500MB space in ROM.

1.3.2. Peripheral

Strong network connectivity

1.3.3. People

The system has three types of user – administrator, paper setter, and student.

2. Goals of Implementation

Primarily, the scope pertains to the features for an online Examination system which will facilitate the student to appear in online based examinations. This system will have some unique features such as auto-evaluation, speed and accuracy.

This SRS is also aimed at specifying requirements of software to be developed. The standard can be used to create software requirements specifications directly or can be used as a model for defining an organization or project specific standard. It does not identify any specific method, nomenclature or tool for preparing an SRS.

3. Functional Requirements

3.1. Managing Examination System by Administrator

3.1.1. User Information for administrators must be stored for login and other activities.

3.1.2. Administrator can login with Email Address & password.

3.1.3. The system is able to store subject Information with code, so that all subjects can be identified using unique subject codes.

3.1.4. Test should be set by the administrator for a particular subject and for a particular group of students on a specific date and time with duration.

3.1.5. After the completion of examination, the administrator can choose a date for result publication.

3.2. Managing Examination System by Paper Setter

3.2.1. Paper Setter registration where user information for paper setters must be stored for login and other activities.

3.2.2. Paper setters can login with Email Address & password.

3.2.3. Paper setters can create, modify and delete questions with their answer and accordingly, the questions & answers are updated in the system.

3.3. Appearing Examination by Student

3.3.1. Student registration where user information for students must be stored for login and other activities.

3.3.2. Student can login with Email Address & password.

3.3.3. Student can appear in examination of a particular subject on a specific date and time with duration set by the administrator.

3.3.4. At the time of examination, student get several multiple choice questions in their systems and they are asked to select answers from multiple options given for a single question.

3.3.5. The answers given by students are saved in a database. Later the answers given by students will be matched with the correct answers stored and the results are generated.

3.3.6. A student can edit an answer after saving it and can submit his paper anytime, however, editing cannot be done after submitting the answer.

3.3.7. Students get their result at a particular date set by administrator.

4. Non-functional Requirements

4.1. External Interface

The external interface specifies how the Online Examination System interacts with third-party applications, services, and external users. These interfaces ensure smooth integration and compatibility with external platforms.

Key Aspects:

- Payment Gateway Integration – Supports third-party payment processors (e.g., PayPal, Stripe) for subscriptions and purchases.

- Social Media Integration – Allows sharing of articles on platforms like Face-book, Twitter, and LinkedIn.

- Search Engine Optimization (SEO) – Ensures content is indexed properly for better visibility on Google and other search engines.

- Cloud Storage & CDN Support – Uses services like AWS S3 or Cloudflare for faster content delivery and media storage.

- Analytics & Tracking – Integrates with tools like Google Analytics to monitor user behavior and engagement.

4.2. User Interface

The user interface (UI) defines the look and feel of the Online Examination System, en-suring an intuitive and seamless experience for users.

Key Aspects:

- Responsiveness – The system must work smoothly on desktops, tablets, and mobile devices.

- Accessibility – Compliance with WCAG (Web Content Accessibility Guide-lines) to support users with disabilities.

- User-Friendly Navigation – Clear menus, category filtering, and search func-tionality for easy content discovery.

- Customization – Allows users to personalize their reading experience (e.g., dark mode, font size adjustments).

- Fast Loading Time – Optimized design for quick page rendering to enhance user engagement.

- Interactive Features – Includes comments, likes, and bookmarks to improve user interaction with content.

4.3. Software Interface

The software interface defines how different components of the Online Examination System interact internally and with external applications.

Key Aspects:

- Database Compatibility – Supports relational (MySQL, PostgreSQL) and NoSQL (MongoDB) databases for efficient data management.

- Content Management System (CMS) – Integrates with WordPress, Drupal, or a custom-built CMS for content publishing.

- API Support – Provides RESTful or GraphQL APIs for integrating with mobile apps or third-party services.

- Security Mechanisms – Implements authentication (OAuth, JWT) and encryp-tion (SSL/TLS) to protect user data.

- Caching & Performance Optimization – Uses Redis or Memcached to enhance performance and reduce server load.

4.4. Communication Interface

The communication interface ensures seamless interaction between the system, users, and external services via different communication channels.

Key Aspects:

- Email Notifications – Sends automated emails for subscription confirmations, article updates, and user engagement.

- Push Notifications – Supports real-time notifications for new articles, special offers, and personalized recommendations.

- Chat Support & AI Chatbots – Integrates with chatbots or live chat services (e.g., Zendesk, Intercom) for customer support.

- Multilingual Support – Provides content translation options to cater to a global audience.

- RSS Feeds & Content Syndication – Enables integration with news aggregators and RSS feed readers.

5. Behavioral Description

The Behavioral Description outlines how the system responds to various inputs, events, and user interactions. It describes the dynamic behavior of the system, ensuring it functions smoothly under different conditions.

5.1. System States

System states represent the different modes or conditions in which the Online Exami-nation System operates. These states change based on user actions, system events, or external triggers.

Key System States (Based on Vision Document & Behavioral Models):

1. Idle State – The system is running but not actively in use.

2. User Authentication State – Users log in, sign up, or reset passwords.

3. Question Management State – Admins and paper setters create, edit, or delete questions and answers.

4. Examination Processing State – Handles student responses after displaying the questions and the corresponding answer options correctly.

5. Result Publish State – Students browse and view their results.

6. Error Handling State – The system encounters an issue (e.g., timer failure, serv-er downtime) and displays appropriate messages.

These states ensure smooth transitions between different functions of the system. The Non-Functional Requirements Model helps define performance, security, and scalabil-ity factors for each state, while the Traceability Matrix links these states to specific system requirements.

5.2. Events and Actions

Events trigger specific actions within the system. An event can be a user action (e.g., clicking a button) or a system-generated process (e.g., scheduled article publication).

Key Events and Corresponding Actions (Based on Use Case Analysis & Structural Models):

1. User Logs In → The system verifies credentials and grants access.

2. New Questions and Answers Submission → The Q and A go for review.

3. Selection of Test Completed → The student gains access to Test Schedule.

4. Students completes the Exam → The system stores the answers and notifies the student about successful completion of exam.

5. Scheduled Result Publication → The system automatically publishes the result at the scheduled time set by Administrator.

6. System Detects Unauthorized Access Attempt → Security mechanisms trigger an alert and block the user.

The Project Plan ensures these behaviors are implemented in a structured manner, aligning with system goals.

2.6. Conclusion

Tools Used in Software Requirements Engineering

Several tools assist in different activities of Software Requirements Engineering to ensure accuracy, clarity, and traceability. Commonly used tools include:

- Requirement Management Tools:

- o IBM Rational DOORS – For capturing, tracing, analyzing, and managing requirements.

- o Jama Connect – For collaborative requirements management and traceability.

- o Helix RM (by Perforce) – For managing requirements across the project lifecycle.

- Requirements Gathering and Analysis Tools:

- o Google Forms / Microsoft Forms – For creating surveys and questionnaires.

- o Trello / Jira – For gathering user stories and feature requests in Agile environments.

- o Lucidchart / Microsoft Visio – For drawing requirement models like use case diagrams, flowcharts, etc.

- Prototyping and Wireframing Tools:

- o Figma / Balsamiq – For building quick UI prototypes and getting early feedback.

- o Adobe XD – For designing interactive system prototypes.

- Modeling and Documentation Tools:

- o Visual Paradigm – For UML diagrams, requirement models, and documentation.

- o Enterprise Architect (Sparx Systems) – For comprehensive modeling (BPMN, UML, SysML) and requirements linking.

- Validation and Review Tools:

- o ReqView – For reviewing, approving, and validating requirements.

- o Collaborative Platforms like Google Docs / Confluence – For team-based requirements review and feedback.

- Change and Version Control Tools:

    o Git / GitHub / GitLab – For maintaining version history of requirements documents (especially in Agile or DevOps workflows).

Software Requirements Engineering (SRE) plays a crucial role in the success of any software project. This chapter introduced the key concepts, processes, and importance of gathering, analyzing, documenting, and managing software requirements.

We discussed the types of requirements — functional, non-functional, and domain-specific — and highlighted how each contributes to building a clear and complete understanding of the software system to be developed. Techniques such as interviews, questionnaires, observation, and prototyping were explored for effective requirements elicitation.

The chapter also explained the importance of requirements specification using tools like the Software Requirements Specification (SRS) document, ensuring that all stakeholders have a common understanding of the system. Further, we looked at requirements validation to detect and correct errors early, and requirements management to handle changes systematically throughout the project lifecycle.

Overall, Software Requirements Engineering forms the foundation for developing high-quality software, minimizing risks, controlling project costs, and ensuring user satisfaction by delivering what is truly needed.

Chapter 3

Software Data Modeling

3.1. Data Modeling

A model is a presentation of reality. It represents the view of a system or its component element. Data modeling is the process of defining and structuring data for a software system. It involves creating a visual representation of how data is organized, stored, and processed within a database. A data model acts as a blueprint for database design and ensures that data is stored efficiently, relationships between data entities are clearly defined, and redundancy is minimized.

Example:

- In an e-commerce system, a data model would define entities like Customers, Orders, Products, and Payments, and their relationships.

Importance of Data Modeling

- Ensures Data Consistency: Organizes data logically, reducing errors.

- Improves Database Performance: Well-structured models optimize queries and reduce redundancy.

- Enhances Maintainability: Easy to modify as business needs evolve.

- Supports Business Rules: Defines relationships and constraints, ensuring data integrity.

3.2. Types of Data Models

There are three main types of data models:

1. Conceptual Data Model

A conceptual data model provides a high-level representation of an organization's data, focusing on business concepts rather than technical details. It defines the key entities, their attributes, and the relationships between them without specifying database structures or storage mechanisms. This model is primarily used for discussions with stakeholders, such as business analysts, managers, and domain experts, to ensure a shared understanding of the data requirements. In short, conceptual data model -

- High-level representation of the data structure.

- Focuses on business concepts rather than technical details.

- Used for stakeholder discussions.

For example, in a university system, entities like Students, Courses, Professors, and Departments would be identified, along with their relationships, such as "a Student enrolls in multiple Courses." The conceptual model acts as a blueprint for later stages of data modeling, helping to align business needs with database design.

2. Logical Data Model

A logical data model provides a more detailed representation of data compared to the conceptual model, defining specific attributes, relationships, and constraints while remaining independent of any particular database system. It translates business concepts into a structured format that includes entities, their attributes, and the relationships between them. More detailed than the conceptual model. So, a logical data model

- Defines attributes, relationships, and constraints.

- Independent of any specific database system.

For example, in a university management system, a Student entity may have attributes such as StudentID, Name, Age, and Email, while a Course entity may include CourseID, CourseName, and Credits. The model also defines relationships, such as a many-to-many relationship where a student can enroll in multiple courses, and each course can have multiple students. By refining data structure details while keeping database independence, the logical data model serves as a crucial step before transitioning into physical database design. In short,

- A Student entity may have attributes like StudentID, Name, DoB, and Email.

- A Course entity may have CourseID, CourseName, and Credits.

- The relationship could be: A Student can enroll in multiple Courses, and each Course can have multiple Students (Many-to-Many relationship).

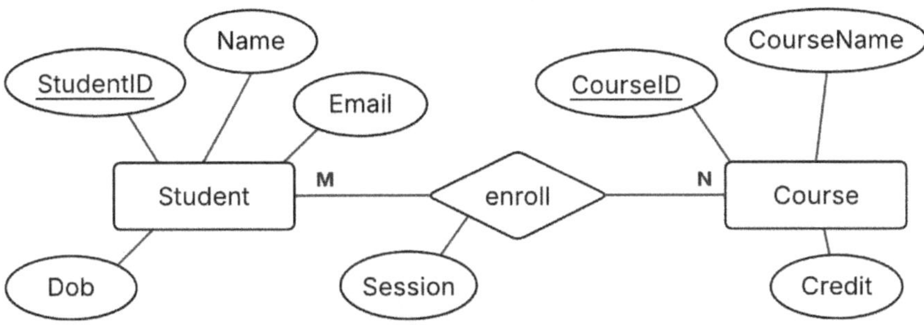

Figure 3.1: ERD for University Management System (partial)

3. Physical Data Model

A physical data model is the most detailed form of data modeling, focusing on the actual implementation of the database within a specific Database Management System (DBMS) such as MySQL, PostgreSQL, or Oracle. It defines how data will be stored, retrieved, and optimized for performance, incorporating elements like tables, columns, data types, primary keys, foreign keys, indexes, and storage mechanisms. Unlike conceptual and logical models, which remain technology-agnostic, a physical data model is closely tied to a particular database system. As a summary, we can say the followings about a physical data model -

- The most detailed model, used for actual database implementation.

- Defines tables, primary keys, foreign keys, indexes, and storage details.

- Tied to a specific DBMS (e.g., MySQL, PostgreSQL, Oracle).

Example (SQL Representation):

```
CREATE TABLE Students (

    StudentID INT PRIMARY KEY,

    Name VARCHAR(100),

    Dob DATE,

    Email VARCHAR(100) UNIQUE

);

CREATE TABLE Courses (

    CourseID INT PRIMARY KEY,

    CourseName VARCHAR(100),

    Credit INT

);

CREATE TABLE Enrollment (

    StudentID INT,

    CourseID INT,

    Session CHAR(7),

    PRIMARY KEY (StudentID, CourseID),

      FOREIGN KEY (StudentID)
```

```
REFERENCES Students(StudentID),

    FOREIGN KEY (CourseID)

REFERENCES Courses(CourseID)

);
```

This shows how Students and Courses are related through the Enrollment table in an actual database.

3.3. Key Components of Data Modeling

An Entity-Relationship (ER) Diagram is used to create a conceptual blueprint of how data is organized in a system. It helps visualize entities, their attributes, and the relationships between them. ER diagrams are commonly used during the database design phase to ensure the structure of data supports the business requirements. Followings are the key components of an Entity-Relationship (ER) Diagram depicted in figure 3.2.

1. Entities

An entity is a fundamental object or concept in a database that represents real-world objects or business elements. Entities typically store data and are translated into tables in a relational database. Each entity consists of attributes that define its properties. For example, in an e-commerce system, common entities include Customers, Products, Orders, and Payments, where each entity holds specific information related to the system's functionality. Entities play a crucial role in structuring databases and ensuring that data is categorized logically and efficiently. So, entities can be summarized as follows -

- Objects or concepts that store data.

- Represented as tables in a relational database.

Example: Customer, Product, Order.

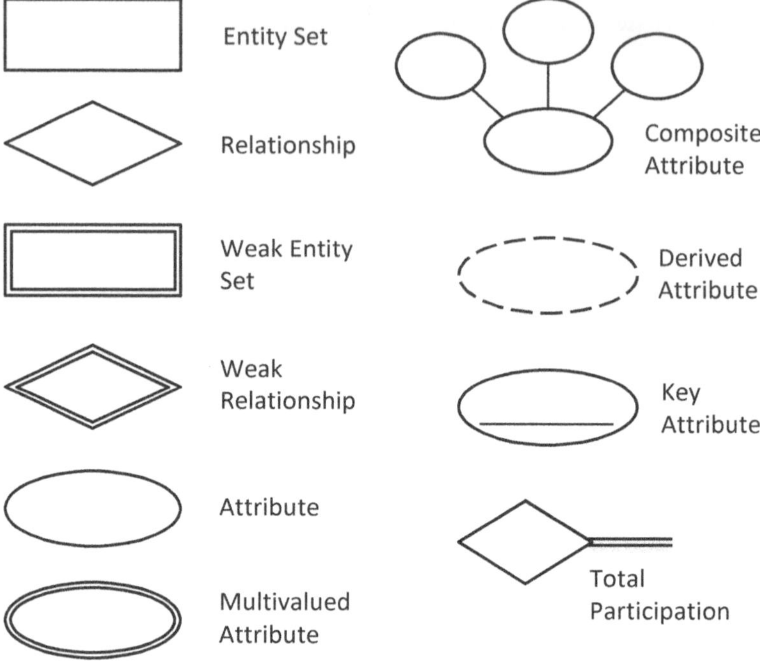

Figure 3.2: Key Components of ERD

2. Attributes

An attribute is a characteristic or property of an entity that helps describe and define it. In a relational database, attributes are represented as columns within a table. Each attribute stores specific information about an entity. For example, a Customer entity may have attributes like CustomerID, Name, Email, and Phone Number, which provide essential details about each customer. Attributes can have different data types, such as integers, text, or dates, depending on the nature of the data they store. Properly defining attributes is essential for ensuring data accuracy and integrity within a system. So, attributes can be summarized as -

- Characteristics of an entity.

- Represented as columns in a table.

Example: A Customer entity may have CustomerID, Name, and Email as attributes.

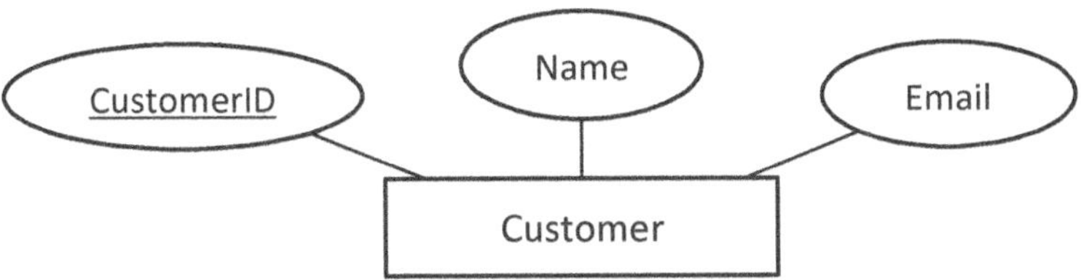

Figure 3.3: Entity with Attributes

3. Relationships

A relationship defines how entities are connected and interact with one another within a database. Relationships help establish meaningful links between data tables, allowing for efficient data retrieval and organization. There are different types of relationships, including One-to-One, One-to-Many, and Many-to-Many. For example, in a banking system, a Customer can have multiple Bank Accounts (One-to-Many), while each Account belongs to a single Customer. Defining relationships properly ensures data consistency and avoids redundancy in database structures.

In short, relationships

- Define how entities are connected.

Example: A Customer can place multiple Orders (One-to-Many relationship).

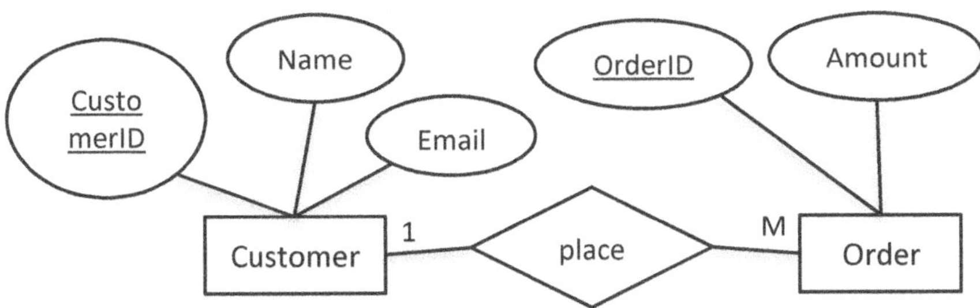

Figure 3.4: Relationships among Entities

4. Keys

A key is a unique identifier used to distinguish records within a database table and establish relationships between different tables. The Primary Key (PK) uniquely identifies each record in a table, ensuring that no two records have the same value. For example, a Student table may use StudentID as a primary key. A Foreign Key (FK) is used to reference a primary key in another table, creating a relationship between the two. For example, in an Enrollment table linking students and courses, StudentID serves as a foreign key to connect records to the Students table. Keys are critical for maintaining database integrity and enabling efficient data retrieval. Thus, keys are summarized as -

Primary Key (PK): Unique identifier for each record in a table.

Example: StudentID in the Students table.

Foreign Key (FK): Reference to a primary key in another table.

Example: CourseID in the Enrollment table.

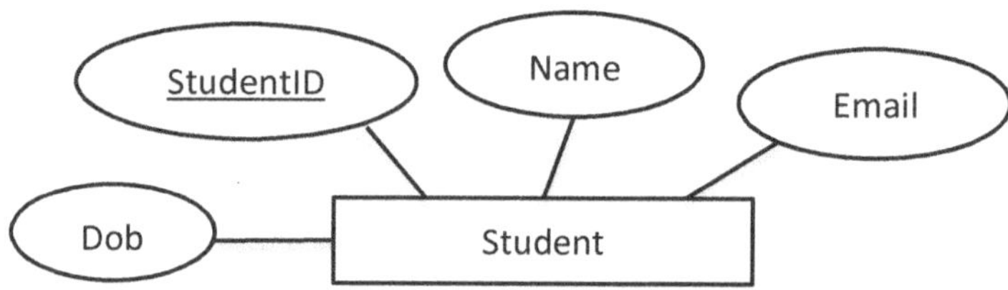

Figure 3.5: Primary Keys must be underlined (StudentID)

Types of Relationships in Data Modeling

In Entity-Relationship Diagrams (ERDs), the term cardinality specifies the numerical relationships between entities, defining how many instances of one entity can relate to instances of another. It essentially describes the "how many" aspect of relationships.

1. One-to-One (1:1) - Each record in Table A is related to only one record in Table B.

Example: Each Employee has only one Parking Slot. This example is depicted in figure 3.6(a).

2. One-to-Many (1:M) - A single record in Table A can be related to multiple records in Table B.

Example: One Customer can place multiple Orders, but one Order owned by one Customer only. This example is depicted in figure 3.6(b).

3. One-to-Many (M:1) - Multiple records in Table A can relate to only one record in Table B.

Example: Multiple Members are there in one team, but one Member belongs to One Team only. This example is depicted in figure 3.6(c).

4. Many-to-Many (M:N) - Multiple records in Table A can relate to multiple records in Table B.

Example: One Student can enroll in multiple Courses, and each Course can have multiple Students. It is implemented using a junction table (e.g., Enrollment table linking Students and Courses). This example is depicted in figure 3.6(d).

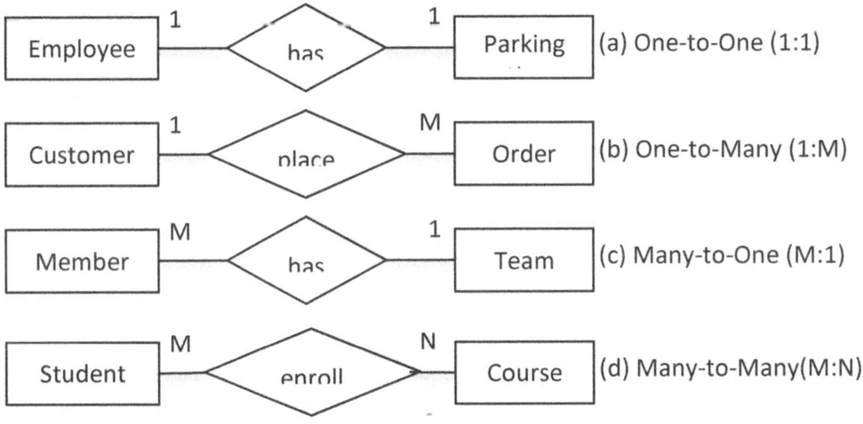

Figure 3.6: Types of Relationships in ERD

3.4. Data Modeling Examples

3.4.1. Example 1 – Banking System

Problem Statement: The banking system is a software which automates the general activities performed by a bank. The system is capable of creating new accounts of different types such as savings, fixed deposits etc. In order to create a new account, customers must be selected. If customer data is not available, new customers must be added before opening a new account. The system is also capable of editing existing customer data. The system keeps the record of each transaction for each and every account like – deposit, withdrawal, calculate interest etc. and later the transaction details can be viewed by the account holder and the banking personnel. The system also maintains account rules such as rate of interest, minimum and maximum balance, duration etc.

1. Conceptual Model

List of Entities: Customer, Account, Acc_Rule, Transaction

2. Logical Model

Attributes of Entities:

- Customer (cid, cname, email, phone, address, docs)

- Account (accno, atype, balance)

- Acc_Rule (atype, duration, roi, max_amt, min_amt)

- Transaction (tid, t_type, amount)

Relationships with Cardinality:

- A Customer can have multiple Accounts (1:M).

- Multiple Accounts of same type follow the same Acc_Rule (M:1).

- Each Account has multiple Transactions (1:M).

3. Entity Relationship Diagram

ER Diagram is shown in figure 3.7.

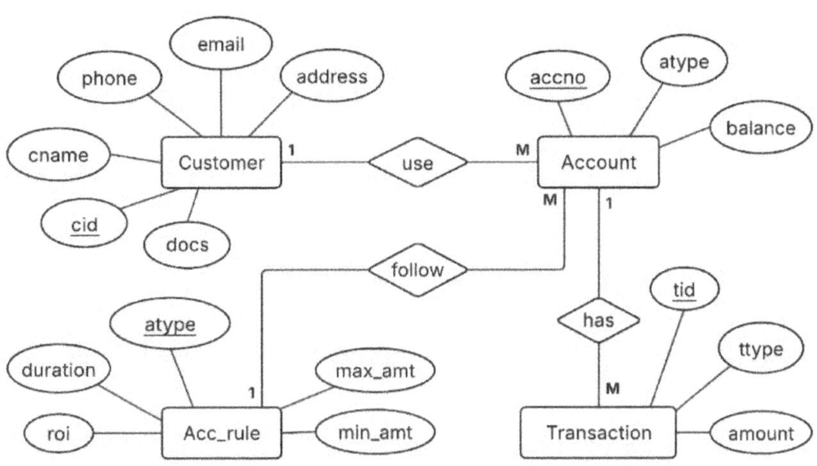

Figure 3.7: ERD for Banking System

4. Table Schema

Based on the ER diagram, here's a normalized relational schema (up to 3rd Normal Form) for the Banking System. The design avoids data redundancy and ensures data integrity.

A. Customer Table

Column	Data Type	Constraints
cid	INT	PRIMARY KEY
cname	VARCHAR	NOT NULL
phone	VARCHAR	UNIQUE
email	VARCHAR	UNIQUE
address	VARCHAR	
docs	TEXT	

B. Account Table

```
Column          Data Type           Constraints

-------         -----------         ------------

accno           INT                     PRIMARY KEY

atype            VARCHAR        FOREIGN KEY (Acc_rule.atype)

cid             INT                 FOREIGN KEY (Customer.cid)

balance         DECIMAL             NOT NULL
```

Note: Each customer can have multiple accounts, and an account belongs to one customer.

C. Transaction Table

```
Column          Data Type           Constraints

-------         -----------         ------------

tid             INT                     PRIMARY KEY

accno           INT             FOREIGN KEY (Account.accno)

ttype           VARCHAR         NOT NULL

                                (e.g., 'credit', 'debit')

amount          DECIMAL         NOT NULL
```

Note: One account can have many transactions, each transaction belongs to one account.

D. Acc_rule Table

```
Column          Data Type           Constraints

-------         -----------         ------------
```

atype	VARCHAR	PRIMARY KEY
duration	INT	(in months or years)
roi	DECIMAL	(Rate of interest)
min_amt	DECIMAL	
max_amt	DECIMAL	

Note: Each atype corresponds to one set of rules. This supports reusability and consistency.

5. Physical Model (SQL Statements for DDL - assuming DB is already created)

```sql
CREATE TABLE Customer (

    cid INT AUTO_INCREMENT PRIMARY KEY,

    cname VARCHAR(100) NOT NULL,

    phone VARCHAR(15) UNIQUE,

    email VARCHAR(100) UNIQUE,

    address VARCHAR(255),

    docs TEXT,

    created_at TIMESTAMP DEFAULT CURRENT_TIMESTAMP,

    updated_at TIMESTAMP DEFAULT CURRENT_TIMESTAMP

ON UPDATE CURRENT_TIMESTAMP

);

CREATE TABLE Acc_rule (

    atype VARCHAR(50) PRIMARY KEY,

    duration INT CHECK (duration >= 0),

    roi DECIMAL(5,2) CHECK (roi >= 0),
```

```sql
    min_amt DECIMAL(10,2) CHECK (min_amt >= 0),

    max_amt DECIMAL(10,2) CHECK (max_amt > min_amt),

    created_at TIMESTAMP DEFAULT CURRENT_TIMESTAMP,

    updated_at TIMESTAMP DEFAULT CURRENT_TIMESTAMP
ON UPDATE CURRENT_TIMESTAMP
);
CREATE TABLE Account (

    accno INT AUTO_INCREMENT PRIMARY KEY,

    atype VARCHAR(50),

    cid INT,

    balance DECIMAL(12,2)NOT NULL CHECK (balance >= 0),

    FOREIGN KEY (atype) REFERENCES Acc_rule(atype),

    FOREIGN KEY (cid) REFERENCES Customer(cid),

    created_at TIMESTAMP DEFAULT CURRENT_TIMESTAMP,

    updated_at TIMESTAMP DEFAULT CURRENT_TIMESTAMP
ON UPDATE CURRENT_TIMESTAMP
);
CREATE TABLE Transaction (

    tid INT AUTO_INCREMENT PRIMARY KEY,

    accno INT,

    ttype VARCHAR(20) NOT NULL
CHECK (ttype IN ('credit', 'debit')),

    amount DECIMAL(10,2) NOT NULL CHECK (amount > 0),

    FOREIGN KEY (accno) REFERENCES Account(accno),
```

```
created_at TIMESTAMP DEFAULT CURRENT_TIMESTAMP
);
```

6. Normalized Entity-Relationship Diagram (ERD)

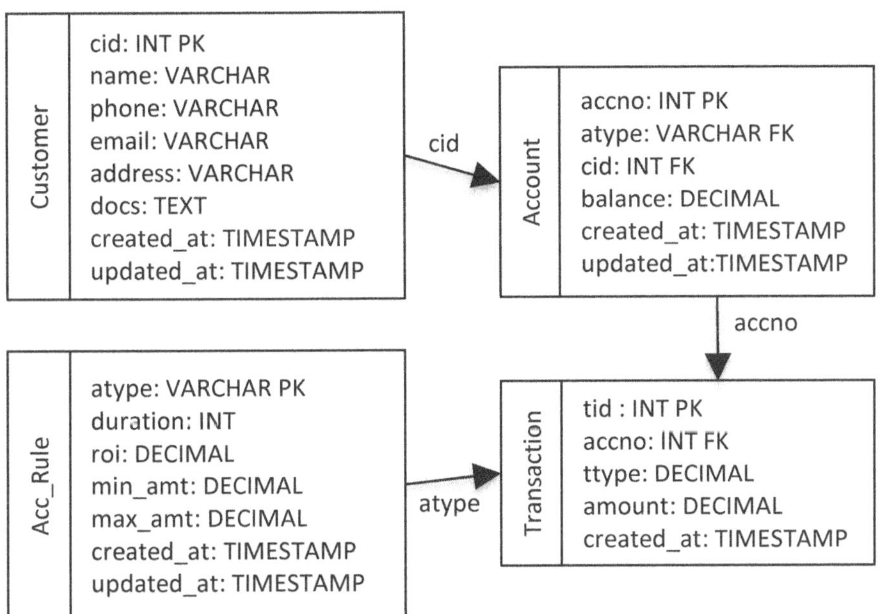

Figure 3.8: Normalized ERD for Banking System

3.4.2. Example 2 - Library Management System

Problem Statement: The library management system is created with an eye of making an automated library system instead of doing it manually. The system should maintain all the members' information, all the books' information. Maintain refers to add, edit and delete of the data. Make book issue and return must be performed by the system. The system also calculates fine if applicable.

1. Conceptual Model

List of Entities: Member, Book, Fine_Rule, Fine

2. Logical Model

Attributes of Entities:

- Member (mid, mname, email, phone, address)

- Book (bookid, title, author, publisher, edition)

- Fine_Rule (rule_id, duration, fine_rate)

- Fine (amount, pay_date)

Relationships with Cardinality:

- A Member can make multiple requisitions of Books (1:M).

- Multiple Members can issue multiple Books (M:N) which attracts Fine if not returned within date.

- Each Fine follows Fine_Rule (1:M).

3. Entity Relationship Diagram

ER Diagram is shown in figure 3.9

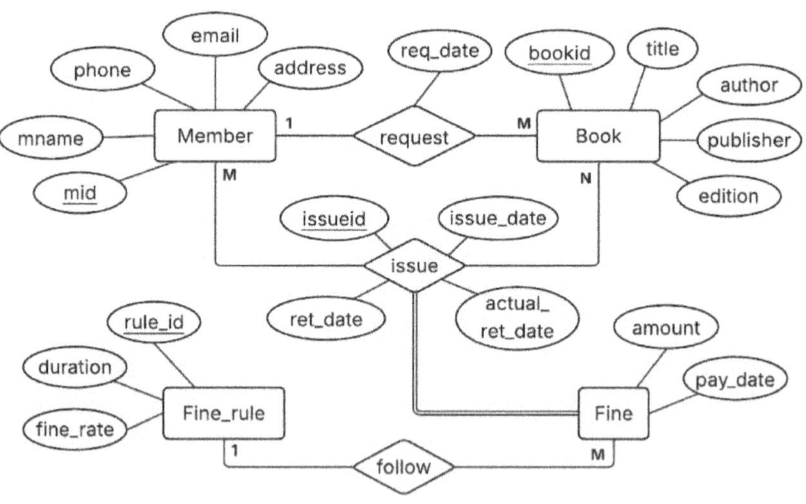

Figure 3.9: ERD for Library Management System

4. Physical Model (SQL Statements for DDL - assuming DB is already created)

```sql
CREATE TABLE Member (
    mid INT PRIMARY KEY,
    mname VARCHAR(100),
    phone VARCHAR(15),
    email VARCHAR(100),
    address TEXT
);
CREATE TABLE Book (
    bookid INT PRIMARY KEY,
    title VARCHAR(255),
    author VARCHAR(100),
    publisher VARCHAR(100),
    edition VARCHAR(50)
);
CREATE TABLE Fine_rule (
    rule_id INT PRIMARY KEY,
    duration INT,            -- in days
    fine_rate DECIMAL(5, 2) -- per day
);
CREATE TABLE Request (
    mid INT,
    bookid INT,
```

```sql
    req_date DATE,

    PRIMARY KEY (mid, bookid, req_date),

    FOREIGN KEY (mid) REFERENCES Member(mid),

    FOREIGN KEY (bookid) REFERENCES Book(bookid)
);
CREATE TABLE Issue (

    issueid INT PRIMARY KEY,

    mid INT,

    bookid INT,

    issue_date DATE,

    ret_date DATE,

    actual_ret_date DATE,

    rule_id INT,

    FOREIGN KEY (mid) REFERENCES Member(mid),

    FOREIGN KEY (bookid) REFERENCES Book(bookid),

    FOREIGN          KEY(rule_id)          REFERENCES
Fine_rule(rule_id)
);
CREATE TABLE Fine (.

    fineid INT PRIMARY KEY,

    issueid INT,

    amount DECIMAL(7,2),

    pay_date DATE,
```

```
    FOREIGN        KEY        (issueid)        REFERENCES
Issue(issueid)

);
```

Normalization Justification

- 1NF: All attributes are atomic (no multivalued or composite fields).

- 2NF: All non-key attributes are fully functionally dependent on the primary key.

- 3NF: No transitive dependencies (e.g., fine rate is kept in a separate rule table).

5. Normalized Entity-Relationship Diagram (ERD)

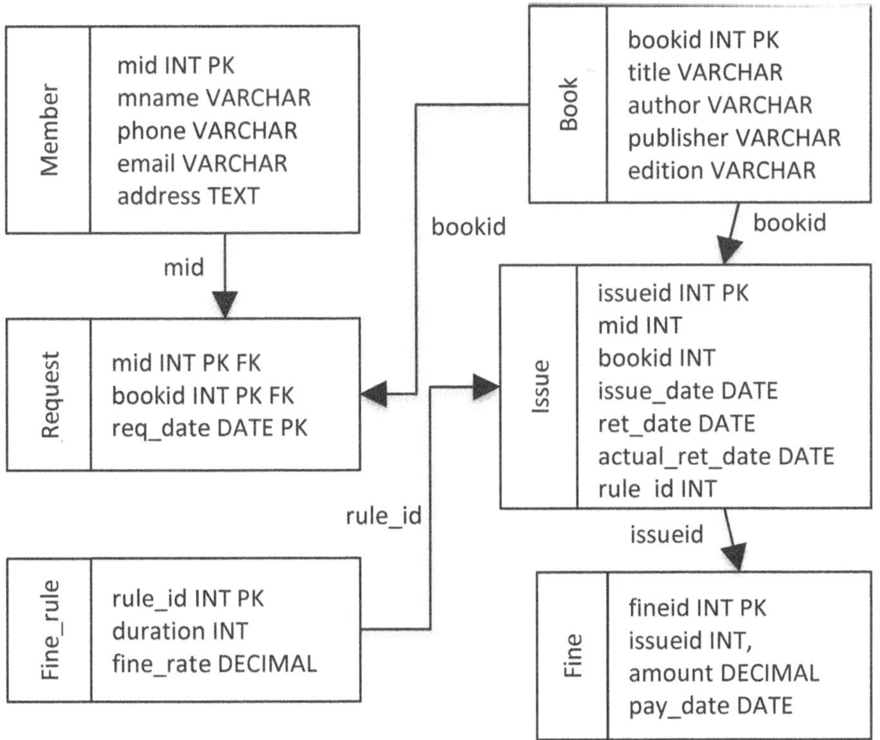

Figure 3.10: Normalized ERD for Banking System

3.4.3. Example 3 – Online Shopping System

Problem Statement: The Online Shopping System is designed to facilitate seamless interactions between customers and an e-commerce platform, allowing users to browse products, place orders, and make secure payments. The conceptual model identifies four core entities crucial to the system: Customer, Product, Order, and Payment. In this model, each customer has a unique identity and can place multiple orders over time. Products available in the catalog can be included in multiple orders, reflecting a many-to-many relationship between products and orders. Each order is linked to a single customer and includes one or more products. Once an order is placed, it must be associated with a corresponding payment record to confirm the transaction.

1. Conceptual Model

List of Entities: Customer, Product, Order, Payment

2. Logical Model

Attributes of Entities:

- Customer (CustomerID, Name, Email, Address)

- Product (ProductID, Name, Price, Stock)

- Order (OrderID, CustomerID, OrderDate, TotalAmount)

- Payment (PaymentID, OrderID, Amount, PaymentMethod)

Relationships with Cardinality:

- A Customer can place multiple Orders (1:M).

- An Order contains multiple Products (M:N).

- Each Order has multiple Payments (1:M).

3. Entity Relationship Diagram

ER Diagram is shown in figure 3.11

4. Table Schema (Normalization should be followed)

- The entity set Customer is converted to table named Customer

- The entity set Product is converted to table named Product

- The entity set Order is converted to table named Order

- The relationship "contain" is converted to table named OrderDetail

- The entity set Payment is converted to table named Payment

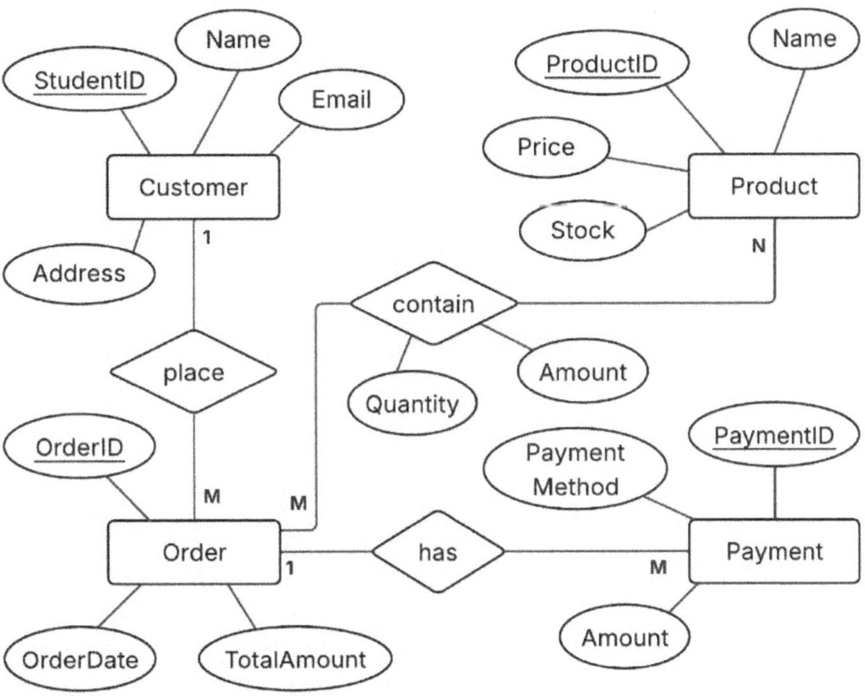

Figure 3.11: ERD for Online Shopping System

A. Table Name: Customer

Column Name	Data Type	Description
CustomerID	INT	PRIMARY KEY

```
Name                VARCHAR(100)

Email               VARCHAR(100)       UNIQUE

Address             TEXT
```

B. Table Name: Product

```
Column Name         Data Type          Description

-------------       ----------         ------------

ProductID           INT                PRIMARY KEY

Name                VARCHAR(100)

Price               DECIMAL(10,2)

Stock               INT
```

C. Table Name: Order

```
Column Name         Data Type          Description

-------------       ----------         ------------

OrderID             INT                PRIMARY KEY

CustomerID          INT                FOREIGN KEY

OrderDate           DATE

TotalAmount         DECIMAL(10,2)
```

D. Table Name: OrderDetail

```
Column Name         Data Type          Description

-------------       ----------         ------------

OrderID             INT                FOREIGN KEY
```

```
ProductID          INT                    FOREIGN KEY

Quantity           INT

Amount             DECIMAL(10,2)
```

E. Table Name: Payment

```
Column Name        Data Type              Description
-------------      ---------              ------------

PaymentID          INT                    PRIMARY KEY

OrderID            INT                    FOREIGN KEY

Amount             DECIMAL(10,2)

PaymentMethod      VARCHAR(50)
```

5. Physical Model (SQL Statements for DDL - assuming DB is already created)

```sql
CREATE TABLE Customer (
    CustomerID INT PRIMARY KEY,
    Name VARCHAR(100),
    Email VARCHAR(100) UNIQUE,
    Address TEXT
);
CREATE TABLE Product (
    ProductID INT PRIMARY KEY,
    Name VARCHAR(100),
    Price DECIMAL(10,2),
    Stock INT
```

```sql
);

CREATE TABLE Order (
    OrderID INT PRIMARY KEY,
    CustomerID INT,
    OrderDate DATE,
    TotalAmount DECIMAL(10,2),
    FOREIGN KEY (CustomerID)
REFERENCES Customers(CustomerID)
);

CREATE TABLE OrderDetail (
    OrderID INT,
    ProductID INT,
    Quantity INT,
    Amount DECIMAL(10,2),
FOREIGN KEY (OrderID)
REFERENCES Orders(OrderID),
FOREIGN KEY (ProductID)
REFERENCES Products(ProductID)
);

CREATE TABLE Payment (
    PaymentID INT PRIMARY KEY,
    OrderID INT,
    Amount DECIMAL(10,2),
    PaymentMethod VARCHAR(50),
```

```
    FOREIGN KEY (OrderID)

REFERENCES Orders(OrderID)

);
```

3.5. Conclusion

Best Practices in Data Modeling

- **Use Normalization** – Avoid duplicate data to improve consistency.

- **Define Relationships Clearly** – Use foreign keys to enforce relationships.

- **Ensure Scalability** – Design models that can handle future data growth.

- **Optimize Queries** – Use indexing and partitioning for better performance.

- **Regularly Review & Update** – Modify the model as business needs evolve.

Software data modeling is a fundamental step in designing robust, efficient, and scalable databases. It ensures that data is structured logically, relationships are well-defined, and the system performs optimally. Whether designing a banking system, e-commerce platform, or social media app, a well-planned data model is critical for success.

Tools to be used for Data Modeling

1. ER/Studio (Commercial)

Features: Logical and physical data modeling, Reverse engineering from databases, Support for collaboration and metadata management.

Best For: Enterprise data architecture

2. IBM InfoSphere Data Architect (Commercial)

Features: Integration with IBM databases, Complex data warehouse modeling, Support for data governance and metadata.

Best For: Large-scale IBM environments

3. Oracle SQL Developer Data Modeler (Free)

Features: Logical, relational, and physical modeling, Data type and constraint support, Integration with Oracle DB.

Best For: Oracle-based applications

4. MySQL Workbench (Free)

Features: Visual ER modeling, Forward and reverse engineering, SQL script generation.

Best For: MySQL databases

5. Lucidchart (Freemium – Cloud-based)

Features: Easy drag-and-drop ER diagrams, Real-time collaboration, Supports import/export of DB schemas.

Best For: Quick and collaborative modeling

6. Draw.io (diagrams.net) (Free)

Features: Simple drag-and-drop interface, Custom shapes and templates.

Best For: Quick visualizations and teaching

And many more …

Chapter 4

Function Oriented Software Design

4.1. Design Phase of the Waterfall Model

The Design Phase is the second stage of the Waterfall Model, following the Requirement Analysis phase. It plays a crucial role in transforming the gathered requirements into a structured plan that guides the development of the software system. This phase involves defining the system architecture, selecting technologies, designing databases, and preparing documentation to ensure a smooth implementation process.

Function-Oriented Software Design (FOSD) is a traditional approach to software development that focuses on decomposing a system into a set of interacting functions. This paradigm is widely used in structured programming and is primarily driven by data flow and process modeling techniques. It provides a clear, hierarchical representation of a system's operations, ensuring better organization and maintainability.

Function-oriented design techniques were introduced over four decades ago and remain widely used in software development today. These techniques initially conceptualize a system as a black-box, providing a set of services to its users. In the context of software applications, these services—such as "issue book" or "search book" in a Library Automation System—are known as high-level functions.

During the design process, these high-level functions undergo successive decomposition into more detailed functions, a process commonly referred to as top-down decomposition. Once this decomposition is complete, the identified functions are mapped to modules, forming a structured design that adheres to best design principles.

This text does not focus on any single design methodology. Instead, it presents a methodology that incorporates essential elements from several function-oriented design approaches. This broad perspective will enable readers to adapt to specific methodologies as needed, since different software development organizations may follow different techniques. However, these procedural design methodologies share fundamental similarities, differing primarily in terminology and notation rather than in core principles.

The methodology discussed here is known as Structured Analysis/Structured Design (SA/SD). It draws extensively from the methodologies proposed by:

- DeMarco and Yourdon (1978)

- Constantine and Yourdon (1979)

- Gane and Sarson (1979)

- Hatley and Pirbhai (1987)

4.2. Key Concepts in Function-Oriented Design

Function-Oriented Design is based on the following fundamental principles:

A. System Decomposition

The software system is broken down into smaller, manageable modules or functions, each performing a specific task. This hierarchical approach facilitates easier development and debugging.

B. Data Flow Representation

Data flow diagrams (DFDs) are commonly used in function-oriented design to represent the movement of data between different system components. DFDs provide a high-level overview of how data is processed within the system.

C. Data Dictionary

A data dictionary is a centralized repository that contains metadata (data about data) for a database or information system. It provides details about the structure, definitions, and constraints of data elements within the system. It lists all the elements composing the data appearing in data flow diagrams (DFDs).

D. Modularity

Functions are organized into modules to promote code reusability and maintainability. Each module should be designed to perform a well-defined task with minimal dependencies on other modules.

E. Cohesion and Coupling

Cohesion: Functions within a module should be closely related, working towards a common goal.

Coupling: Interaction between modules should be minimized to ensure independence and flexibility in the system.

4.3. Basic Concept of SA/SD Methodology

As the name suggests, the Structured Analysis/Structured Design (SA/SD) methodology consists of two distinct phases:

- Structured Analysis (SA)

- Structured Design (SD)

The relationship between these phases is illustrated schematically in the accompanying figure. Key observations include:

Structured Analysis (SA): This phase transforms the Software Requirements Specification (SRS) document into a Data Flow Diagram (DFD) model. During this process, functional decomposition is performed—breaking down each required function of the system into smaller, more detailed sub-functions.

Structured Design (SD): In this phase, the DFD model is further refined into a module structure, commonly referred to as the high-level design or software architecture. This structure is represented using a structure chart, which outlines how different modules interact within the system.

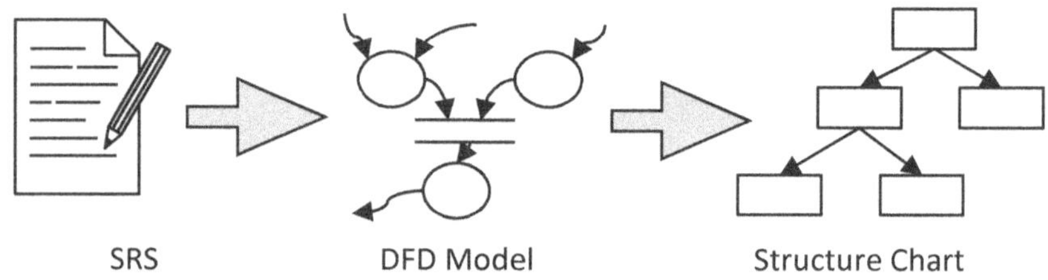

Figure 4.1: Structured analysis and structured design methodology

After completing the high-level design, the process moves into the detailed design phase. Here, the focus shifts to defining the algorithms and data structures for individual modules. This level of design serves as the foundation for direct implementation using a programming language.

It is essential to understand the distinction between these two phases:

- Structured Analysis captures the system's functional structure from the user's perspective.

- Structured Design translates this functional structure into an implementation-ready architecture that can be developed using a programming language.

4.4. Data Flow Diagram (DFD)

A Data Flow Diagram (DFD) is a visual representation of how data moves through a system. It shows the flow of information between processes, data stores, external entities, and data movement within a system.

Key Components of a DFD

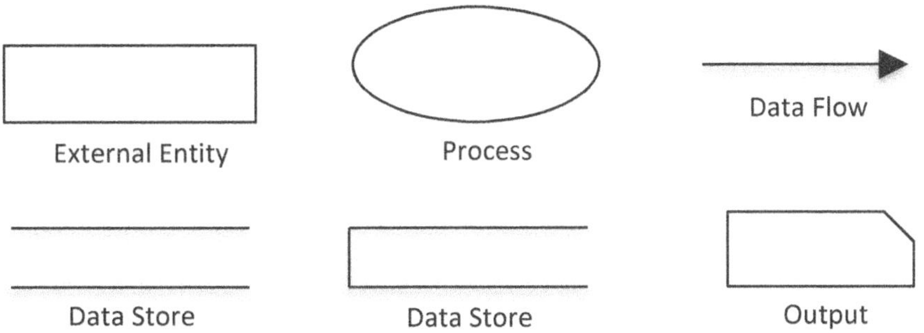

Figure 4.2: Key Components of DFD

1. Process (Circle or Oval)

   o   Represent actions or operations performed on data.

   o   Example: "Process Order" or "Validate Login."

2. Data Flow (Solid line with arrow on one end)

   o   Indicate the movement of data between elements.

   o   Example: "Customer Order Data" flowing from a user to a process.

3. Data Store (Open Rectangle / Three or Four sided Rectangle)

   o   Represent where data is stored for later use.

   o   Example: "Customer Database" or "Transaction Records" etc.

4. External Entity (Square or Rectangle)

   o   Represent sources or destinations of data outside the system.

   o   Example: "Customer" or "Bank" etc.

5. Output symbol (Truncated Rectangle)

- o The output symbol is used when a hard copy is produced.

- o Example: "Invoice" or "Prescription" etc.

Levels of DFDs

- Level 0 (Context Diagram) : Shows the entire system as a single process with external entities.

- Level 1 : Breaks down the main process into sub-processes.

- Level 2+ : Further decomposes complex processes into more detailed steps.

Rules for construction of DFD

- The context diagram i.e. level 0 diagram should represent the whole system together with the external entities.

- External entities can be presented only in the context diagram.

- The context diagram is broken down into 3 to 7 bubbles / processes each representing a functional sub system.

- The bubbles / processes are numbered as –

    - o Context level diagram is no. 0

    - o Level 1 diagram is numbered as 0.1, 0.2, … and so on

    - o Level 2 diagram which is obtained by breaking a particular bubble of level 1 diagram, is numbered as –

    - o For 0.1 (level 1) – 0.1.1, 0.1.2, 0.1.3, … and so on

    - o For 0.2 (level 2) – 0.2.1, 0.2.2, 0.2.3, … and so on

Synchronous and Asynchronous Operations in Data Flow Diagrams (DFD)

In Data Flow Diagrams (DFD), operations can be classified as synchronous or asynchronous based on how data is processed and how entities interact with each other.

A. Synchronous Operations

A synchronous operation requires an immediate response before the next step can proceed. The process must wait for the operation to complete before continuing.

B. Asynchronous Operations

An asynchronous operation does not require an immediate response. The sender can continue processing other tasks while waiting for a response.

Example 1 - Email Validation: In synchronous operation, Email entered by the user is directly validated in the next process. But in asynchronous operation, Email entered by the user is first stored in the user database. Later it is validated to produce output. The example is depicted below in figure 4.3.

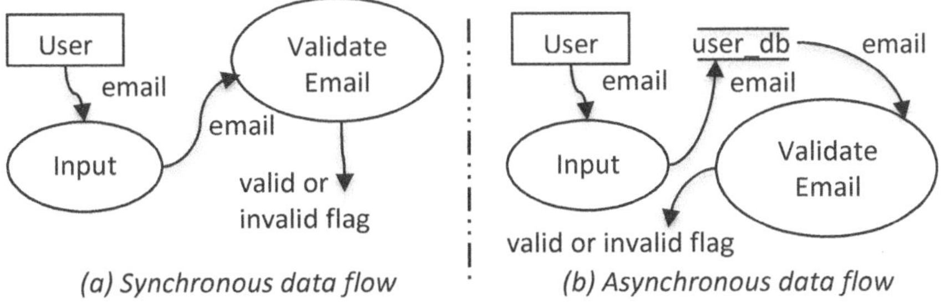

Figure 4.3: Simple example of Synchronous and Asynchronous data flow

Example 2 - Order Processing System: The customer places an order, the order is processed immediately and invoice is generated in synchronous operation. But in the asynchronous operation, the system does not process it immediately. First it stores the order request in the database, and processes it later to generate an invoice. The example is depicted below in figure 4.4.

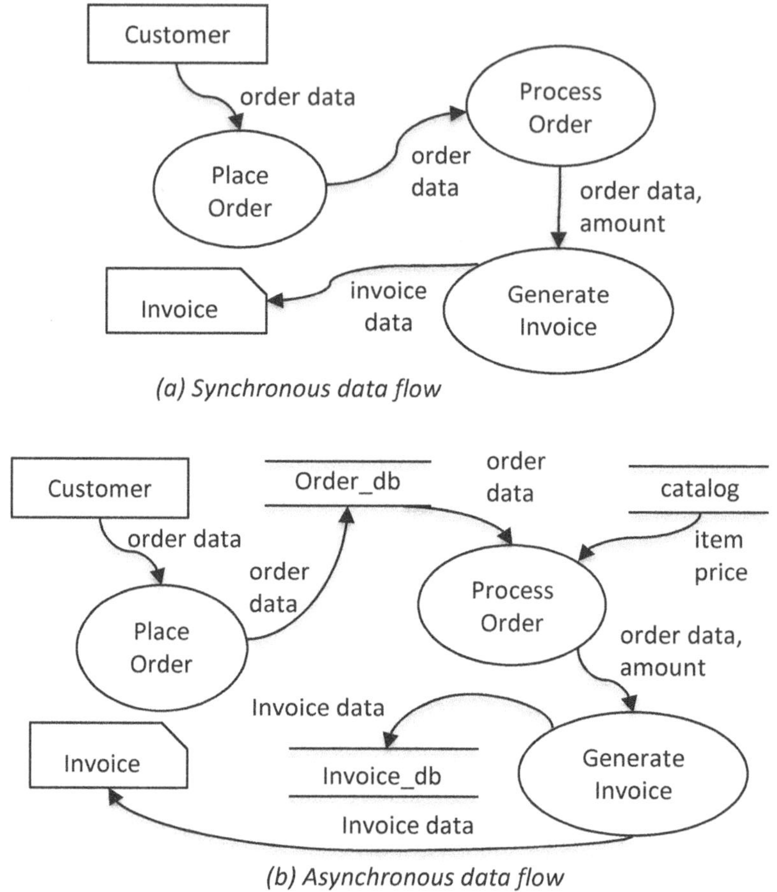

Figure 4.4: Advanced example of Synchronous and Asynchronous data flow

4.5. How to Create a Data Flow Diagram (DFD)

Creating a Data Flow Diagram (DFD) involves breaking down a system's data processes into different levels, illustrating how data flows between entities, processes, and data stores. Below is a step-by-step guide to creating a DFD.

Step 1: Identify the System Boundaries

- Define the scope of your system.

- Identify the inputs (data entering the system) and outputs (data leaving the system).

- Determine the external entities (users, systems, or organizations interacting with the system).

Step 2: Identify Key Components

A DFD consists of four main elements, It is very important step to identify them as follows -

- Identify and create the list of external entities

- Identify and create the list of activities

- Identify and create the list of data stores / repositories

- Identify and create the list of data flows

Step 3: Create a Context Diagram (Level 0 DFD)

- This is the highest-level DFD, showing the entire system as a single process.

- It connects external entities via data flows.

- Example: An Online Shopping System would have entities like Customer, Payment Gateway, and Inventory System, all interacting with the main system.

Step 4: Develop Level 1 DFD

- Break down the main process into sub-processes.

- Identify specific functions within the system (e.g., User Registration, Order Processing).

- Show data flow between these processes and data stores.

Step 5: Develop Level 2 and Beyond (If required)

- Further decompose complex processes into smaller functions.

- Add more details about how data is processed.

- An example of this scenario is shown in figure 4.5.

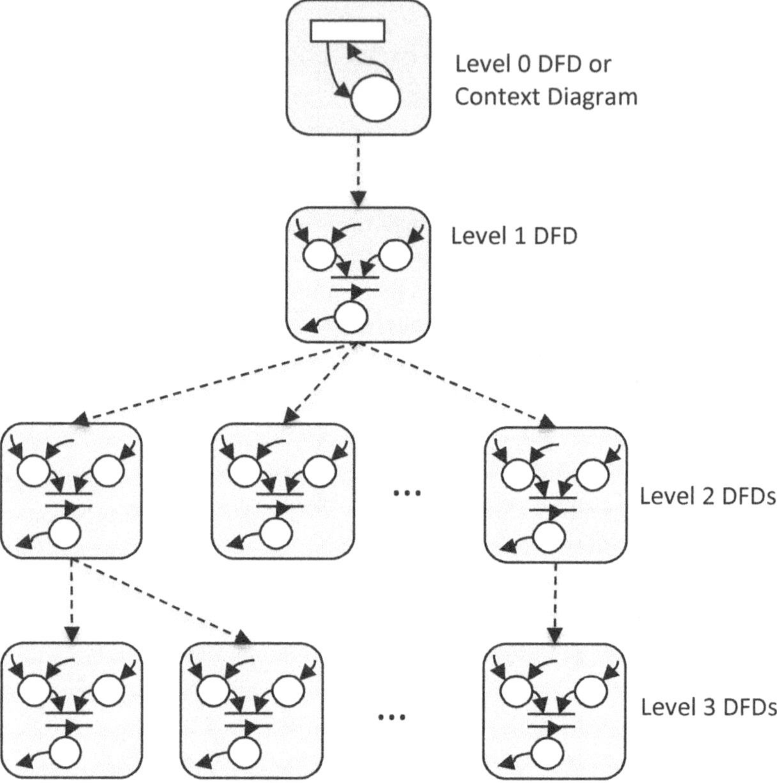

Figure 4.5: DFD model of a system consisting of a hierarchy of DFDs

Step 6: Verify and Refine the DFD

- Check for missing data flows or unnecessary elements.

- Ensure proper labeling for clarity.

- Validate with stakeholders to confirm accuracy.

The entire process of constructing a Data Flow Diagram (DFD) can be visualized collectively in Figure 4.6. This process typically begins with the creation of a Level 0 DFD, also known as the context diagram. At this initial stage, the system is represented as a single, high-level process. It includes all the external entities that interact with the system and defines the data flows between these entities and the system. The input-data refers to the data that flows from an external entity to the central process, while output-data refers to the data that flows from the central process back to an external entity.

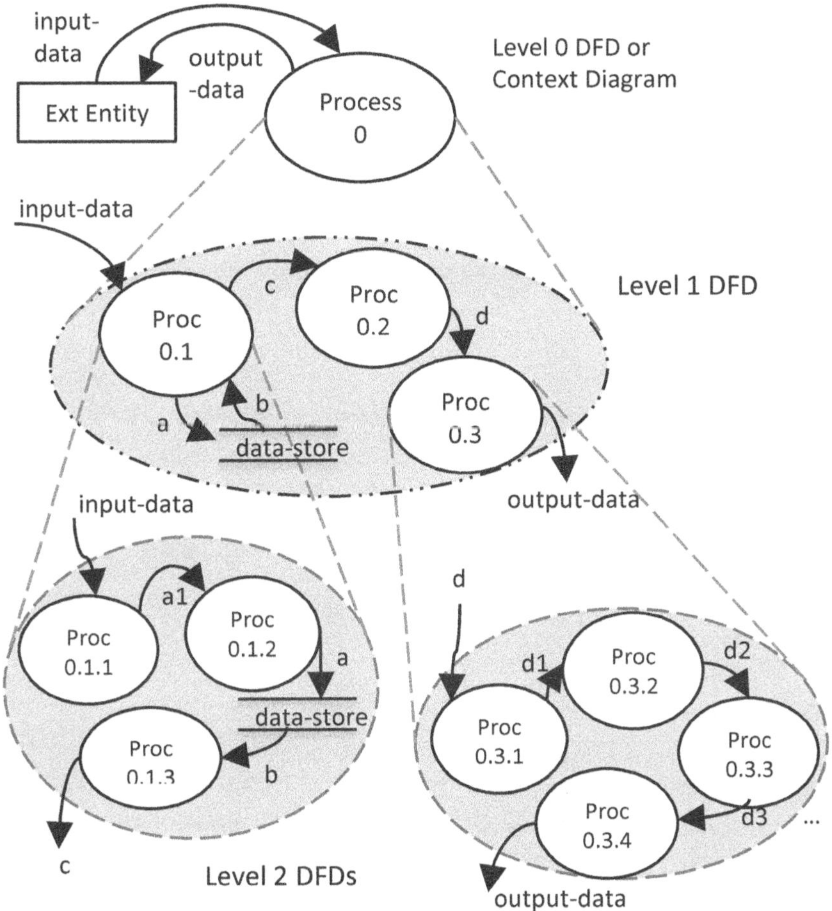

Figure 4.6: Anatomy of DFD model and decomposition of each level into its next level

Moving from Level 0 to Level 1

The next step is to develop the Level 1 DFD by decomposing the Level 0 diagram. In this phase, the single high-level process is broken down into multiple sub-processes (often represented as bubbles), which represent the system's main functional components. These sub-processes correspond to the activities or tasks previously identified in the system analysis. The input to the Level 1 DFD corresponds to the overall input data identified in Level 0. Similarly, the output of the Level 1 DFD represents the overall output data.

Typically, a Level 1 DFD contains between 3 to 7 processes, each with its own set of input and output data flows. Some processes may also interact with data stores, which are used to store and retrieve data as needed.

It's important to ensure that the data entering and exiting each process in Level 1 matches the data flow of the corresponding process in Level 0. This principle is known as DFD balancing, and it ensures consistency and correctness as you move between levels.

Expanding to Level 2 and Beyond

Depending on the complexity and requirements of the system, each Level 1 process can be further decomposed into a Level 2 DFD. However, drawing Level 2 diagrams is optional and should only be done when additional detail is necessary.

For example, in Figure 6, the process labeled 0.1 in Level 1 is further broken down into three sub-processes in Level 2. These are labeled 0.1.1, 0.1.2, and 0.1.3, forming the Level 2 DFD for process 0.1. Note that the overall input to process 0.1 is input-data, and its final output is c - both of which are preserved in the Level 2 diagram for consistency.

Similarly, process 0.3 in Level 1 is decomposed into its own Level 2 DFD in Figure 6. The input d and output output-data from process 0.3 are also maintained in its Level 2 representation.

Level 3 and Further Decomposition

If needed, you can continue to decompose complex processes from Level 2 into Level 3 diagrams. For instance, processes like 0.1.1 or 0.1.2 could be further expanded to show more granular details. However, such deep decomposition should only be pursued if it adds value or clarity to the system's understanding.

Now that we have discussed the structure and methodology of drawing DFDs, let us explore some real-life case studies in the next section to see how these principles are applied in practical scenarios.

4.6. Some worked-out Examples of DFD

4.6.1. Example 1 - Distance Calculator

Problem Statement: Draw DFD for calculating Euclidean distance between two points P1(x1,y1) and P2(x2,y2). Consider the values of x1, y1, x2, y2 to be integers and within a range from -500 to +500 only.

Solution:

Input to the system: x and y coordinates of two points referred here as point-data.

Output from the system: distance value.

List of external entities: User

List of activities: 1. Validate input, 2. Calculate distance between two points and 3. Display result

Now draw the level-0 DFD or context diagram. Just show a single process that contains the name of the overall system and number it with zero (0). Show the external entity User in a rectangle. Draw data flows in and out to the process connecting the external entity and name the data flows correctly. Data flows are shown in and out of each and every process.

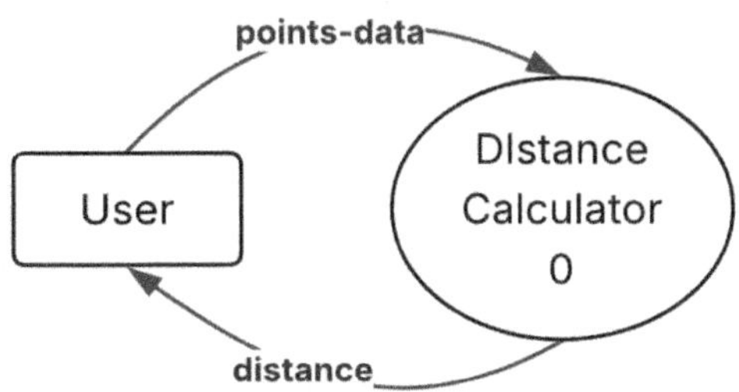

Figure 4.7: Distance Calculator Level-0 DFD

For the creation of level-1 DFD, create three processes according to the list of activities mentioned above. Name them accordingly and put numbers as 0.1, 0.2 and 0.3.

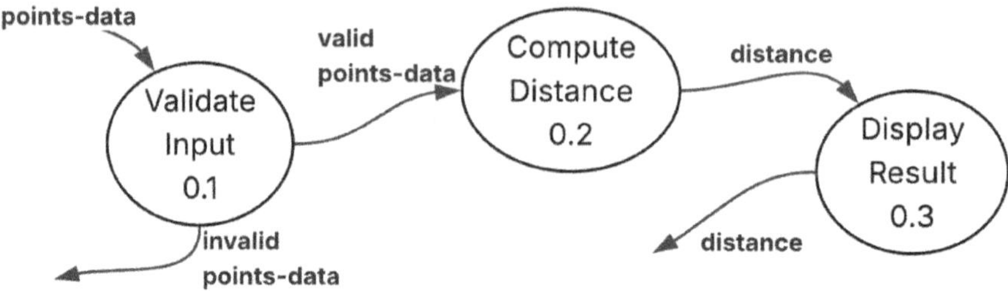

Figure 4.8: Distance Calculator Level-1 DFD

Next step is to draw the level-2 of 0.2 DFD (Compute Distance) as we feel that showing only compute distance may not be sufficient to demonstrate how the calculation is being performed. For this, we list the following sub activities for compute distance -

1.   Separate x and y values as x-val and y-val respectively

2.   Calculate x-value difference and square it (sqx)

3.   Calculate y-value difference and square it (sqy)

4.   Calculate the root of sum of sqx and sqy as distance

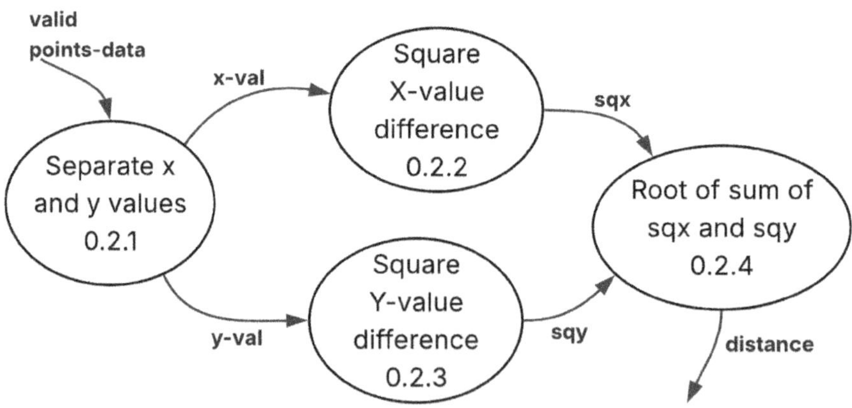

Figure 4.9: Distance Calculator Level-2 of 0.2 DFD

And now just draw the diagram using similar techniques as in previous levels.

4.6.2. Example 2 - Online Magazine System (DigiMag)

Problem Statement: Please go through Chapter 2 Section 2.5.1. For the detailed problem statement.

Solution:

We make the list of external entities and the list of activities for the SRS document done in section 2.5.1.

1. List all the external entities - there are four types of users – Admin, Reviewer, Submitter, and Viewer. Together they might be called "User".

2. List all the activities of the system

1.   Managing articles belonging to several categories

2.   Review articles by reviewer

3.   Subscription of articles

4.   View and feedback of articles

3. List all the data stores - User (may be separated as Admin, Reviewer, Submitter), Articles, Category, Feedback

Now draw the level-0 DFD or context diagram.

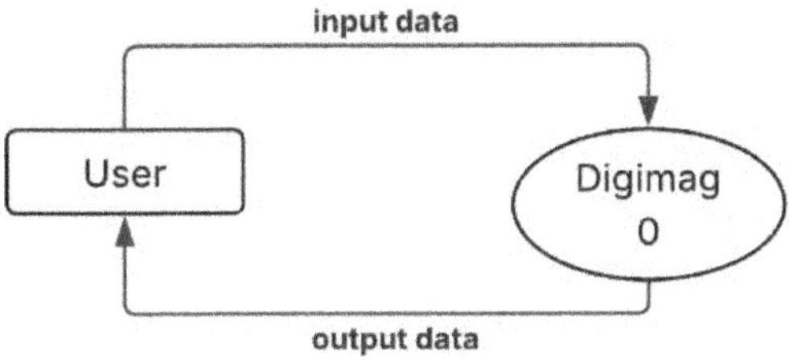

Figure 4.10(a): Digimag Level-0 DFD showing single external entity

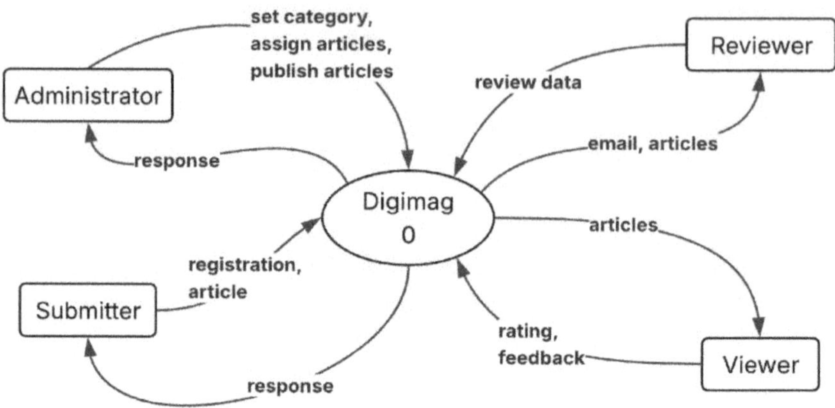

Figure 4.10(b): Digimag Level-0 DFD showing separate external entities

The next step is to use the list of activities to draw the level-1 DFD. Here we need to show all the data stores used in the system.

<u>Explanation of level-1 DFD for Digimag</u>

0.1 – Registration and Login

- Input: registration data and login credentials from the User.

- Validation:

    o   If valid, sends validated registration data to the User.

    o   If invalid, send an invalid input response.

- Output: Directs valid users to specific roles: Admin, Reviewer, or Submitter.

- These roles determine what functionalities the user can access next.

0.2 – Manage Articles

- Accessible only after a valid Admin login.

- Handles category data and article publish data.

- Output:

o   Sends valid category data to the Category data store.

o   Publishes or manages articles.

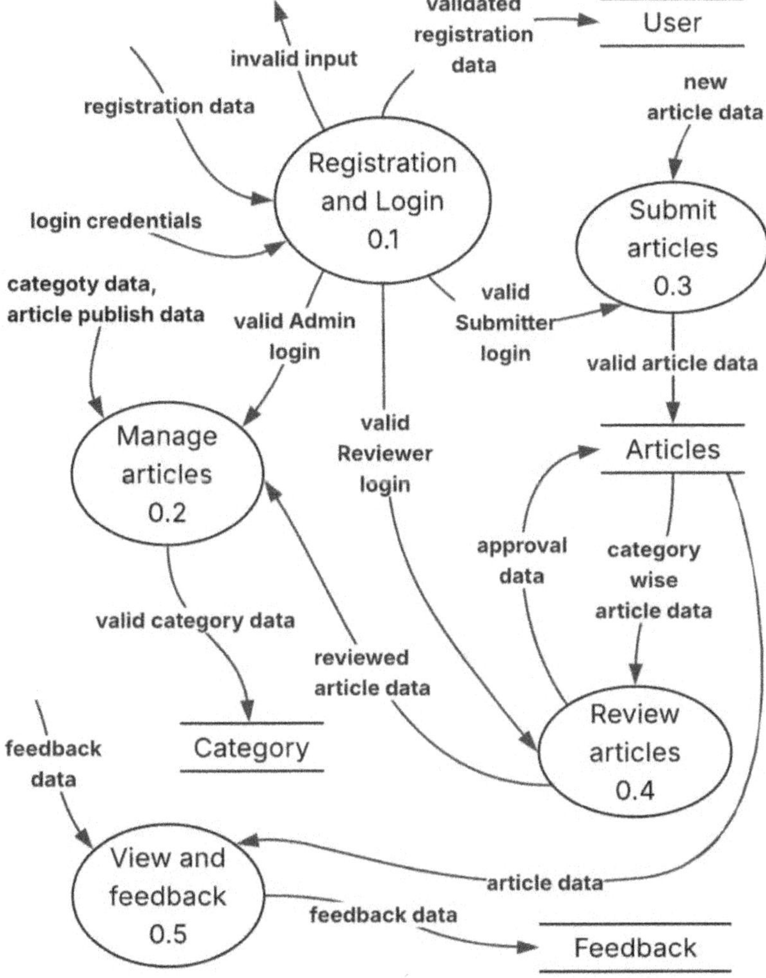

Figure 4.11: Digimag Level-1 DFD

0.3 – Submit Articles

- Accessed by users with valid Submitter login.

- Users send new article data which is validated.

- Output: Validated articles are stored in the Articles data store.

0.4 – Review Articles

- Handled by users with Reviewer login.

- Input: Gets article data from the Articles data store.

- Reviews articles based on category.

- Sends approval data back to the Articles store and reviewed article data to the Manage Articles process.

0.5 – View and Feedback

- Allows users to view articles and give feedback.

- Input: Retrieves category-wise article data from Review Articles.

- Output: Sends feedback data to the Feedback data store and also returns feedback data to the system for possible display.

Data Flows Summary

- Bi-directional flows like login credentials, feedback data, and article data are used between processes and data stores.

- Each role (Admin, Reviewer, Submitter) is directed to a corresponding functionality through the login validation step.

Level-2 DFDs can also be drawn from the above Level-1 DFD. For example, now we shall draw the Level-2 of 0.2 (Manage articles). The list of sub activities are listed as follows -

- add and edit category

- open and close portal

- assign articles to reviewers

- publish articles

Explanation of level-2 DFD of 0.2 (Manage articles) for Digimag

0.2.1 – Add and Edit Category

This process allows an admin to input or update category data. The result of this process is valid category data, which is stored in the Category data store. This categorization helps organize the articles and supports further processes such as review and publication.

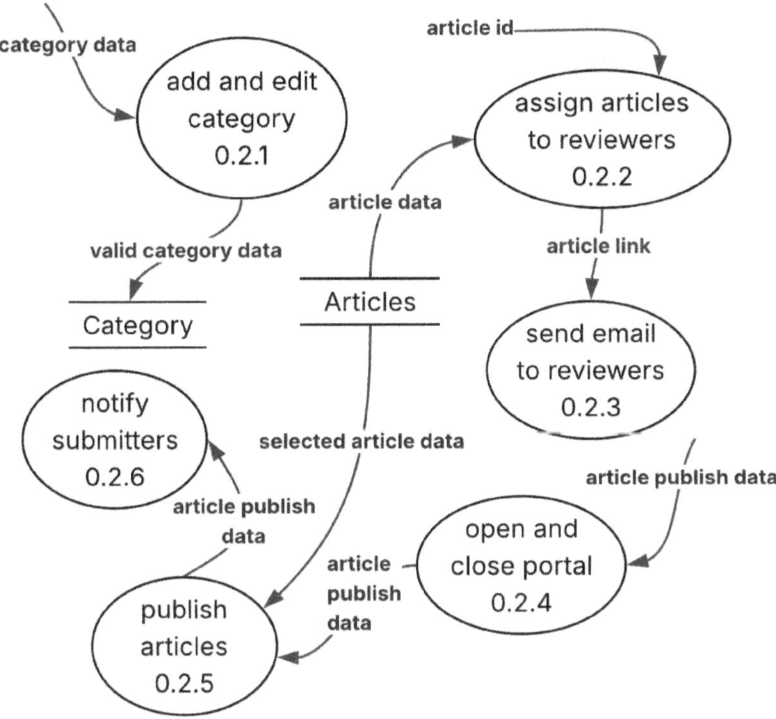

Figure 4.12: Digimag Level-2 DFD of 0.2 (Manage articles)

0.2.2 – Assign Articles to Reviewers

This process takes article data from the Articles store and allows the admin or editor to assign a specific article (identified by article ID) to a reviewer. This step ensures that each article is sent to an appropriate reviewer for evaluation.

0.2.3 – Send Email to Reviewers

Once articles are assigned, this process generates an article link and sends it via email to the reviewers. This step ensures that reviewers are notified and can access the article for review.

0.2.4 – Open and Close Portal

This process manages the availability of the submission/review portal. Using article publish data, it decides when the portal should be open or closed for submissions and reviews. This is crucial for managing deadlines and article cycles.

0.2.5 – Publish Articles

This process receives selected article data (approved and finalized articles) from the Articles store. It then uses this data to complete the publication workflow, marking articles as published and possibly pushing them to a live environment.

0.2.6 – Notify Submitters

After articles are published, the system uses this process to inform the original submitters about the status of their articles. Article publish data is used to notify users via email or system notification about acceptance, rejection, or publication.

Data Flows Summary

- Category data flows into system and is validated before storage.

- Article data is passed between assigning, notifying, and publishing processes.

- Article publish data is key in linking multiple steps: closing portals, publishing, and notifying users.

- Notifications go out to both reviewers (via email) and submitters.

4.6.3. Example 3 - Banking System

Problem Statement: The banking system is a software which automates the general activities performed by a bank. The system is capable of creating new accounts of different types such as savings, fixed deposits etc. In order to create a new account, customers must be selected. If customer data is not available, new customers must be added before opening a new account. The system is also capable of editing existing customer data. The system keeps the record of each transaction for each and every account like – deposit, withdrawal, calculate interest etc. and later the transaction details can be viewed by the account holder and the banking personnel. The system also maintains account rules such as rate of interest, minimum and maximum balance, duration etc. List of data sources can be considered as Customer, Account, Rule and Transaction.

Solution:

As per the problem statement, followings are the key considerations -

List of External Entities – Customer, Banker

List of Activities –

1. Add new customer

2. Edit customer

3. Create new account

4. Make transaction

5. View transaction details

6. Maintain account rules

List of Data Stores (taken from Chapter 3 Example 3.4.1.) – Customer, Account, Acc_Rule, Transaction

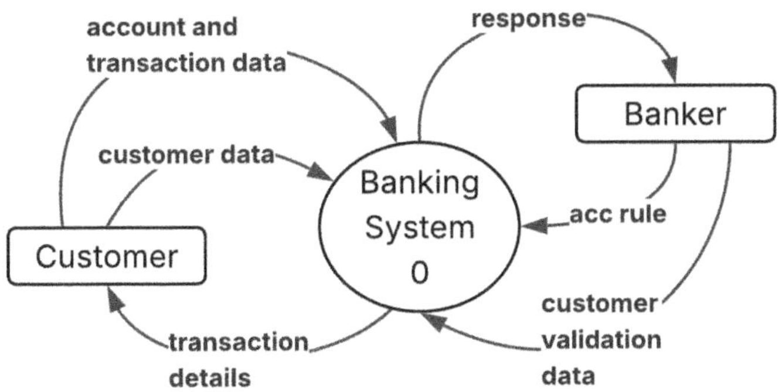

Figure 4.13: Banking System Level-0 DFD

Now draw the level-0 DFD or context diagram (see figure 4.13).

The next step is to use the list of activities to draw the level-1 DFD. Here we need to show all the data stores used in the system.

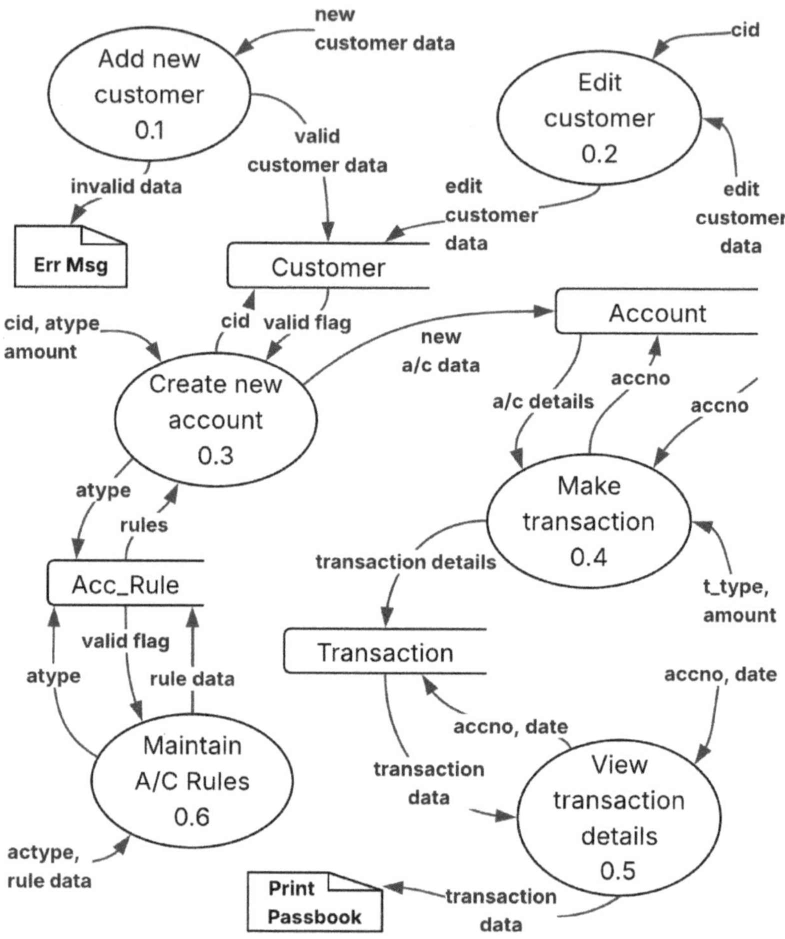

Figure 4.14: Banking System Level-1 DFD

Explanation of level-1 DFD for Banking System

0.1 Add New Customer

- Input: New customer data.

- Process: Validates the data to register a new customer.

- Output: Stores valid customer data in the Customer data store. If data is invalid, send an error message to Err Msg.

0.2 Edit Customer

- Input: Customer ID (cid) and edit customer data.

- Process: Updates existing customer details.

- Output: Updated data stored in the Customer data store.

0.3 Create New Account

- Input: cid, atype (account type), and amount.

- Process: Verifies customer and account rules. Creates a new account if validation is successful.

- Output: Stores new a/c data in the Account data store. Retrieves rules from the Acc_Rule store to validate account type.

0.4 Make Transaction

- Input: accno, transaction type (t_type), and amount.

- Process: Performs deposit, withdrawal, or transfer operations.

- Output: Stores transaction details in the Transaction store. Updates a/c details in the Account store.

0.5 View Transaction Details

- Input: accno, date.

- Process: Retrieves transaction history for a given account and date.

- Output: Fetches transaction data from Transaction data store. Optionally used for Print Passbook.

0.6 Maintain A/C Rules

- Input: actype, rule data.

- Process: Adds or updates rules for specific account types (e.g., minimum balance).

- Output: Stores rules in Acc_Rule data store. Helps validate account creation during process 0.3.

Messages

Err Msg: Used for sending feedback when customer data is invalid.

Print Passbook: Uses transaction data to generate passbook entries.

Flow of Activities

- A new customer is added or an existing one is edited.

- Once validated, the customer can open a new account.

- Account rules are checked before account creation.

- Customers can make transactions, which are stored.

- Customers can view their transactions or print their passbook.

- Admin can maintain rules for different account types.

Some of the Level-2 DFDs are drawn from the above Level-1 DFD. For example, now we shall draw the Level-2 of 0.1 (Add new customer) and Level-2 of 0.4 (Make transaction). The list of sub activities are listed as follows -

Sub activities for Level-2 of 0.1 (Add new customer)

1. validate input

2. generate customer id (cid)

3. store customer data in database

Sub activities for Level-2 of 0.4 (Make transaction)

1. validate input

2. check account status

3. determine transaction type (deposit or withdrawal)

4. update transaction database

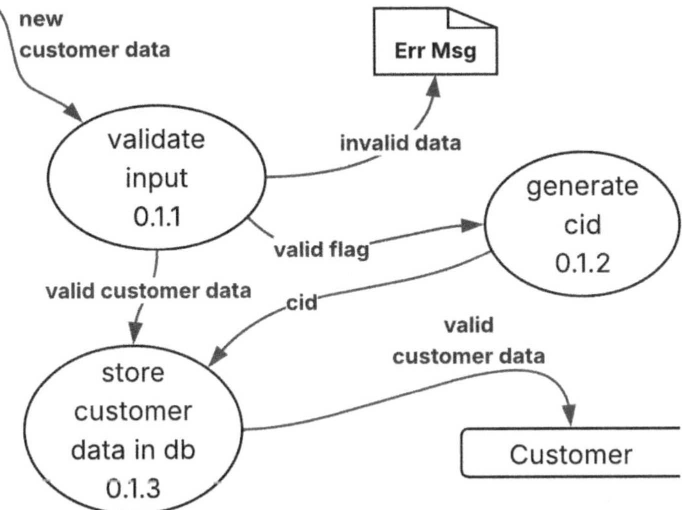

Figure 4.15: Banking System Level-2 DFD of 0.1 (Add new customer)

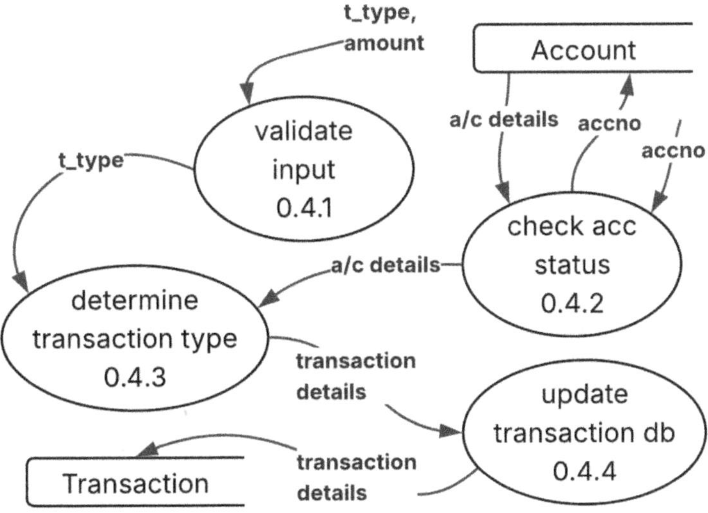

Figure 4.16: Banking System Level-2 DFD of 0.4 (Make transaction)

4.6.4. Example 4 - Library Management System

Problem Statement: The library management system is created with an eye of making an automated library system instead of doing it manually. The system should maintain all the members' information, all the books' information. Maintain refers to add, edit and delete of the data. Make book issue and return must be performed by the system. The system also calculates fine if applicable.

Solution:

As per the problem statement, followings are the key considerations -

List of External Entities – Librarian, Member

List of Activities

1. Manage Book Information (add, edit/update, delete)

2. Manage Member Information (add, edit/update, delete)

3. Search Book

4. Issue and Return of Book

List of Data Stores (taken from Chapter 3 Example 3.4.2.) – Book_record, Member_record, Book_Requsition, Issue_record, Fine_rule

Now draw the level-0 DFD or context diagram.

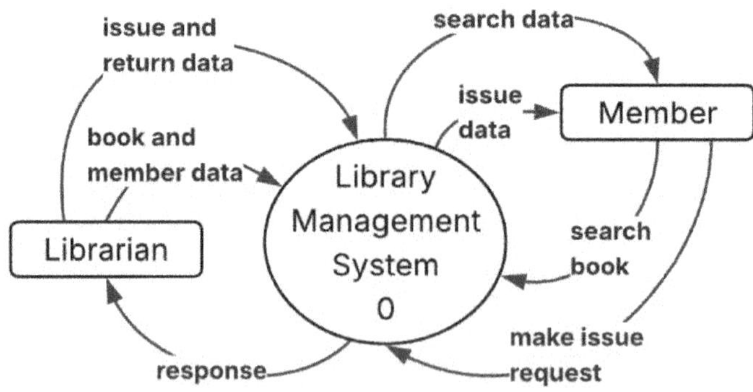

Figure 4.17: Library Management System Level-0 DFD

The next step is to use the list of activities to draw the level-1 DFD. Here we need to show all the data stores used in the system.

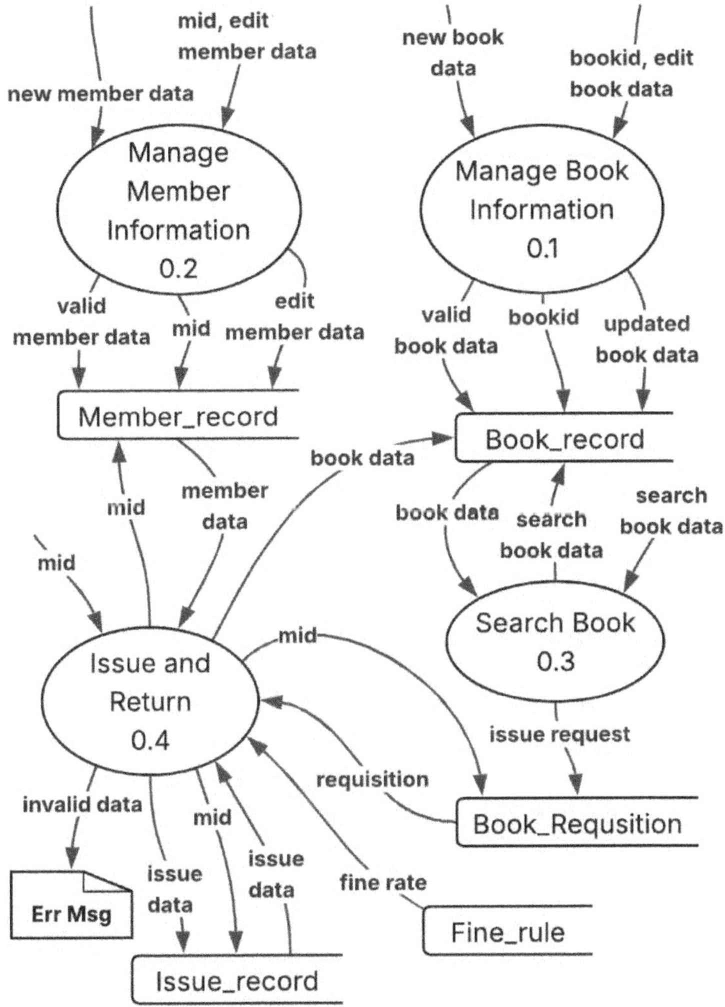

Figure 4.18: Library Management System Level-1 DFD

Some of the Level-2 DFDs are drawn from the above Level-1 DFD. For example, the Level-2 of 0.1 (Manage Book Information) is given below. The list of sub activities are listed as follows -

Sub activities for Level-2 of 0.1 (Manage Book Information)

1. Get new book data

2. Generate bookid

3. Add new book

4. Get bookid (for edit / update)

5. Update book data

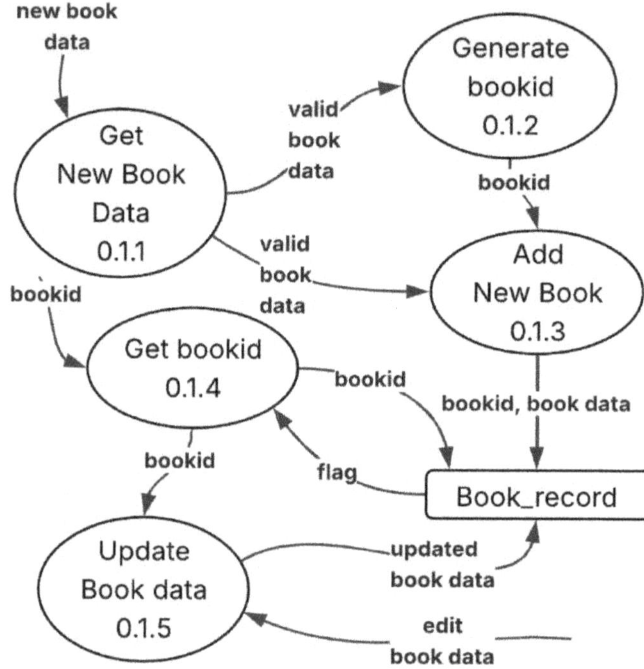

Figure 4.19: Library Management System Level-2 DFD of 0.1

Now we create the Level-2 of 0.4 (Issue and Return). Sub activities for Level-2 of 0.4 (Issue and Return) -

1. Validate member

2. Get requisition (for book issue)

3. Issue book

4. Return book

5. Calculate fine (if any)

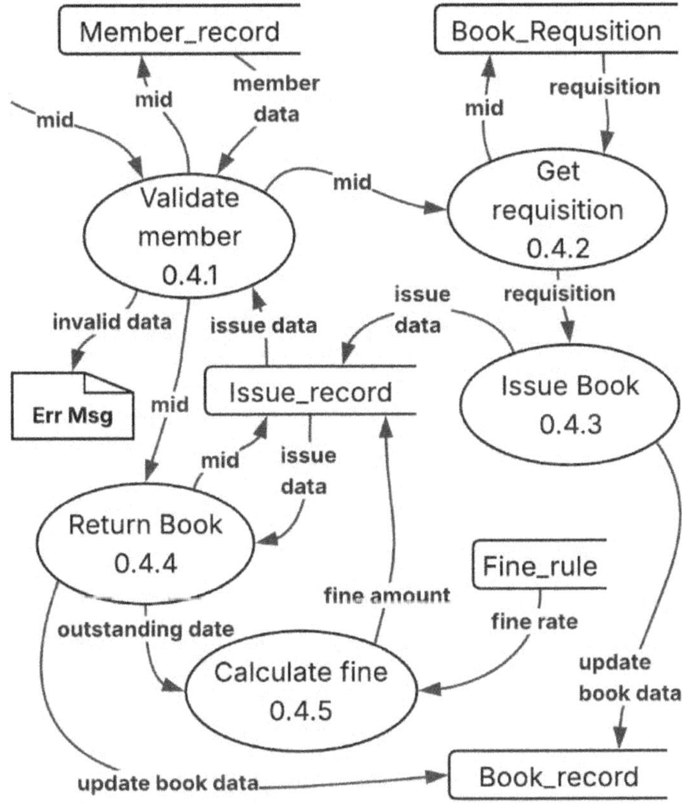

Figure 4.20: Library Management System Level-2 DFD of 0.4

4.6.5. Example 5 – Online Shopping System

Problem Statement: Problem Statement: The Online Shopping System is designed to facilitate seamless interactions between customers and an e-commerce platform, allowing users to browse products, place orders, and make secure payments. The conceptual model identifies four core entities crucial to the system: Customer, Product, Order, and Payment. In this model, each customer has a unique identity and can place multiple orders over time. Products available in the catalog can be included in multiple orders, reflecting a many-to-many relationship between products and orders. Each order is linked to a single customer and includes one or more products. Once an order is placed, it must be associated with a corresponding payment record to confirm the transaction.

Solution:

As per the problem statement, followings are the key considerations -

List of External Entities – Customer, Payment System

List of Activities

1. Customer Authentication

2. Search Product

3. Cart Management

4. Purchase Product

5. Provide Feedback

List of Data Stores (taken from Chapter 3 Example 3.4.5.) – Customer, Product, Order, OrderDetail, Payment

Now draw the level-0 DFD or context diagram.

Figure 4.21: Online Shopping System Level-0 DFD

The next step is to use the list of activities to draw the level-1 DFD. Here we need to show all the data stores used in the system. Please note that the external entity Payment System is shown here in level-1 DFD for better understanding of the payment process.

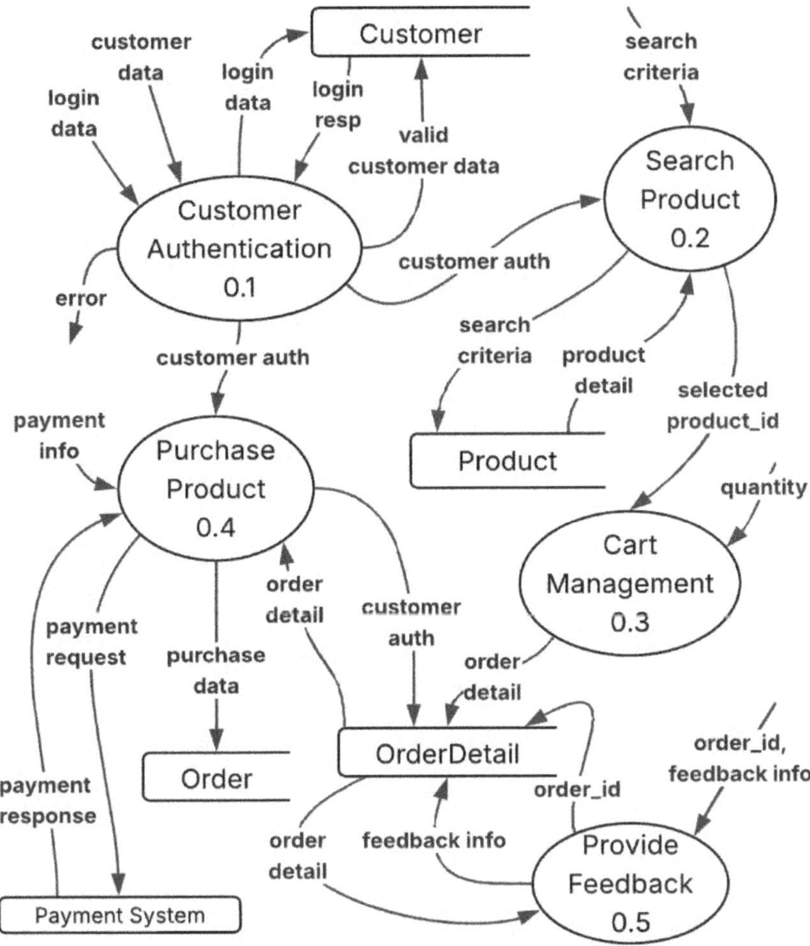

Figure 4.22: Online Shopping System Level-1 DFD

<u>Explanation of level-1 DFD</u>

0.1 Customer Authentication

- Input: Login data from the customer.

- Process: Validates the login credentials.

- Output: If valid: Sends valid customer data and login response. If invalid: Sends an error message.

- Data Store Accessed: Customer for verifying credentials.

0.2 Search Product

- Input: Search criteria entered by the customer.

- Process: Retrieves product details based on the search query.

- Output: Sends relevant product details to the customer.

- Data Store Accessed: Product.

- Requires: Customer must be authenticated (customer auth).

0.3 Cart Management

- Input: Selected product ID and quantity.

- Process: Adds the selected products to the shopping cart.

- Output: Generates order detail for future purchase.

- Data Store Accessed: OrderDetail.

- Requires: Customer authentication.

0.4 Purchase Product

- Input: Payment info and order detail.

- Process: Sends a payment request to the Payment System. On receiving payment response, confirm the order.

- Output: Saves the purchase data in the Order data store. Also updates the OrderDetail store.

- Requires: Valid customer auth.

Level-2 of 0.4 (Purchase product) is given in figure 4.23. The list of sub activities are listed as follows -

Sub activities for Level-2 of 0.4 (Manage Book Information)

1. Validate customer

2. Fetch order detail

3. Make payment

4. Interact with payment system

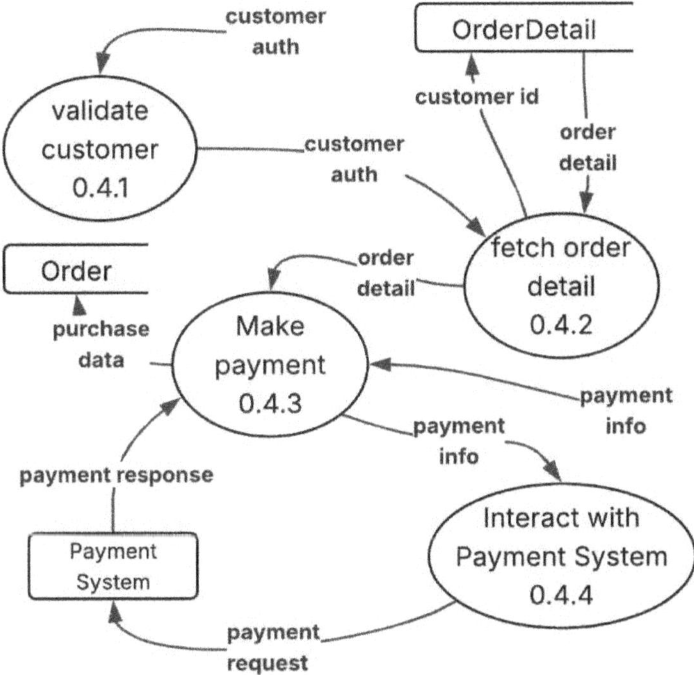

Figure 4.23: Online Shopping System Level-2 DFD of 0.4

4.7. Data Dictionary

A data dictionary is a centralized repository that contains metadata (data about data) for a database or information system. It provides details about the structure, definitions, and constraints of data elements within the system.

Key Components of a Data Dictionary

Table Names – Names of all tables in the database.

Column Names – Names of fields/attributes in each table.

Data Types – The type of data stored in each field (e.g., INTEGER, VARCHAR, DATE).

Field Descriptions – Explanation of what each field represents.

Constraints – Rules applied to the data (e.g., PRIMARY KEY, NOT NULL, UNIQUE).

Relationships – Links between tables (e.g., foreign key relationships).

Default Values – Predefined values for fields if no data is entered.

Allowed Values – Specific values a field can take (e.g., ENUM types).

Data Source – Where the data originates from.

Indexes – Indexes that improve query performance.

Types of Data Dictionaries

Active Data Dictionary – Automatically updated when changes occur in the database.

Passive Data Dictionary – Manually maintained and updated separately from the database.

Importance of Data Dictionary

Standardization – Ensures data consistency across an organization.

Improved Communication – Helps developers, analysts, and stakeholders understand data definitions.

Data Integrity & Quality – Helps enforce rules and constraints.

Documentation – Serves as a reference for database users and administrators.

Note: Example of Data Dictionary are given along with the examples of Data Flow Diagrams.

Symbols used in Data Dictionary

[a | b] : represents selection, i.e. either a or b

( ) : denotes item appears within () may or may not present

a + (b) : either a or a + b

{ } : represents iterative definitions

{ }* : represents many examples an iterative definition

{ }5 : represents 5 examples of an iterative definition

= : represents equivalence

/* */ : comment

E.g. : Payslip = {Employee + Month + Salary} + /* ORG-NAME */

Example of Data Dictionary

Consider the following Data Flow Diagram (figure 4.24) for an Order Processing System.

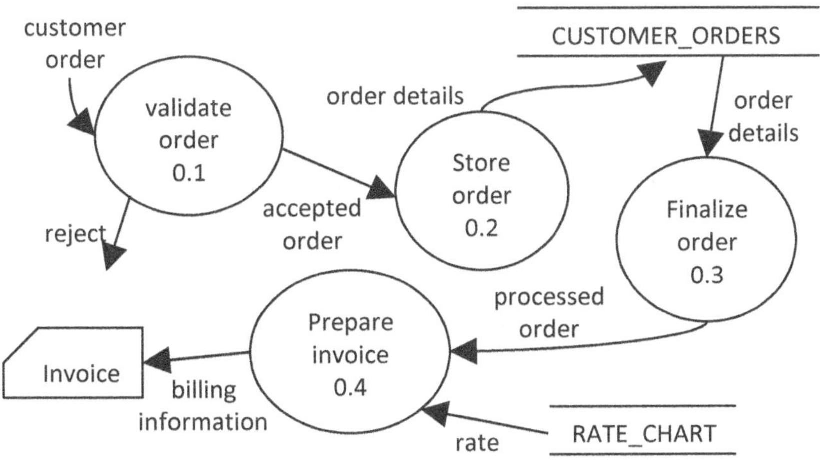

Figure 4.24: Order Processing System Level-1 DFD

In the Order Processing System, Customer makes an order. The order is first validated. It the order has any discrepency, it is rejected. Otherwise it is accepted and stored into CUSTOMER_ORDER data store. Then the order is precessed and finalized and an invoice is prepared by collecting the rates of items from the RATE_CHART data store. Finally an invoice is generated and sent to the Customer.

Let's have a look on how the data from DFD can be defined.

Rate_Chart = {item_id + item_name + unit_price + date_of_update}*

Customer_Order = Item_list + {order_no + date_of_order + cid + amount}*

Item_list = {item_id + quantity}*

Invoice = Order_Record + [cash | cheque | card]

date_of_order = {date + month + year}

Now, followings are the examples of the elements appeared Rate_Chart in the Data Dictionary above -

item_id	
DATA ELEMENT	item_id
DESCRIPTION	Unique identification for each item
TYPE	String
LENGTH	10
ALIASES	itemid, i_id
RANGE	NA

item_name	
DATA ELEMENT	item_name
DESCRIPTION	Name of the item
TYPE	String
LENGTH	50
ALIASES	itemname, i_name
RANGE	NA

unit_price	
DATA ELEMENT	unit_price

DESCRIPTION	Rate of the item per unit
TYPE	Double
LENGTH	6, 2
ALIASES	price, price_per_unit, item_price
RANGE	0.00 to 9,999.99

date_of_update	
DATA ELEMENT	date_of_update
DESCRIPTION	date + month + year
TYPE	Integer
LENGTH	2 + 2 + 4
ALIASES	upd_date, updated_at
RANGE	1 to 31, 1 to 12, 2000 to 2099

Figure 4.25: Definition of each Data Element for Rate Chart

Other data elements which appear in the data dictionary defined previously, can also be defined in similar manner.

From the DFD, the definition of each data is not clear. If the DFD is sent to the coding team without proper definition of data, they may not write the proper code as the definition of each data is unknown to them. Here the Data Dictionary plays an important role. The Data Dictionary bridges the gap between designer and the programmer.

4.8. Decision Tree and Decision Table

Decision Tree

A Decision Tree is a flowchart-like structure used for decision-making. Each internal node represents a test on an attribute, each branch represents the outcome of that test, and each leaf node represents a class label (decision taken after computing all attributes). It is commonly used in Machine Learning, Business Decision Analysis, and Software Engineering.

The order of conditions and actions can be obtained by decision tree. It is also a method showing the relationship between different conditions. Nodes of the tree represent conditions. Leaves of the tree are the actions.

Example: Decision Tree

Scenario: Suppose you're building a system that advises whether to play tennis based on weather conditions.

Outlook	Temperature	Humidity	Wind	Play Tennis
Sunny	Hot	High	Weak	No
Sunny	Hot	High	Strong	No
Overcast	Hot	High	Weak	Yes
Rain	Mild	High	Weak	Yes
Rain	Cool	Normal	Weak	Yes
Rain	Cool	Normal	Strong	No
Overcast	Cool	Normal	Strong	Yes
Sunny	Mild	High	Weak	No
Sunny	Cool	Normal	Weak	Yes

Table 4.1: Weather Data for playing tennis

Figure 4.26 shows the Decision Tree Based on Outlook:

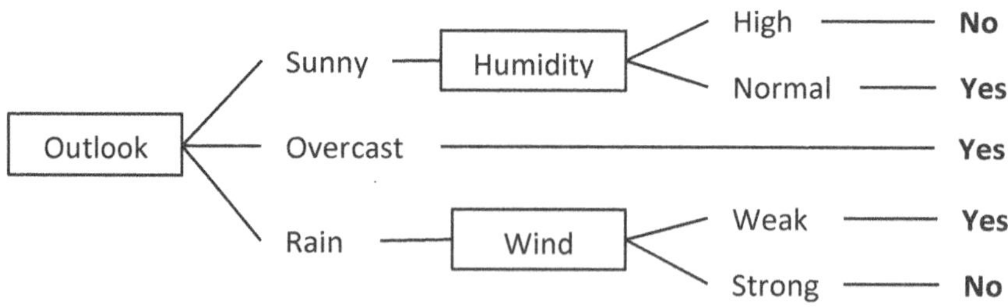

Figure 4.26: Decision Tree Based on Outlook

Decision Table

A Decision Table is a tabular method for representing and analyzing decision rules. It includes conditions, rules, and actions. It is especially useful when dealing with a large number of combinations of conditions. This helps visualize all combinations in a structured format.

A decision table defines a logical procedure by means of said conditions and actions. It is a matrix of rows and columns, rather than a tree. It is made up of mainly four sections –

1. Condition Statements identify relevant statements.

2. Condition Entry tells which value (if any) applies for a particular condition.

3. Action Statements list the set of all steps that can be taken when a certain condition occurs.

4. Action Entry shows what specific action is to be taken.

The rules are formed by the combination of the condition statements. The structure of the Decision Table is shown in table 4.2.

Header (H)	Rules (R)
Condition Statements (CS)	Condition Entry (CE)
Action Statements (AS)	Action Entry (AE)
Notes (if any)	

Table 4.2: Structure of Decision Table

Example: Decision Table

Scenario: Online store discount policy

If a user is a member and purchases above $100, they get a 20% discount. If the user is not a member but spends above $100, they get a 10% discount. If the user is a member and purchases below $100, then a 5% discount is given. Otherwise, no discount is given.

Online Store Discount Policy		**Rules**			
		R1	**R2**	**R3**	**R4**
C1	User is a member?	Y	Y	N	N
C2	Purchase above $100?	Y	N	Y	N
A1	Get a 20% discount	X			
A2	Get a 10% discount			X	
A3	Get a 5% discount		X		
A4	No discount				X

Table 4.3: Decision Table Example

Complete Examples of Decision Tree and Decision Table

4.8.1. Example 1: Application for admission to an extension course are screened using following rules - For admission, the candidate should be sponsored by the employer and he should possess prescribed minimum qualifications. If his fee is paid, he is sent a letter of admission. If the fee is not paid, a letter of provisional admission is sent. In all other cases, a letter of regret is sent.

Solution:

Conditions

- C1: Is the candidate sponsored by an employer?

- C2: Does the candidate possess prescribed minimum qualifications?

- C3: Is the candidate's fee paid?

Actions

- o A1: Send a letter of admission

- o A2: Send a letter of provisional admission

o   A3: Send a letter of regret

Decision Tree is shown in figure 4.27 and the Decision Table is shown in table 4.4.

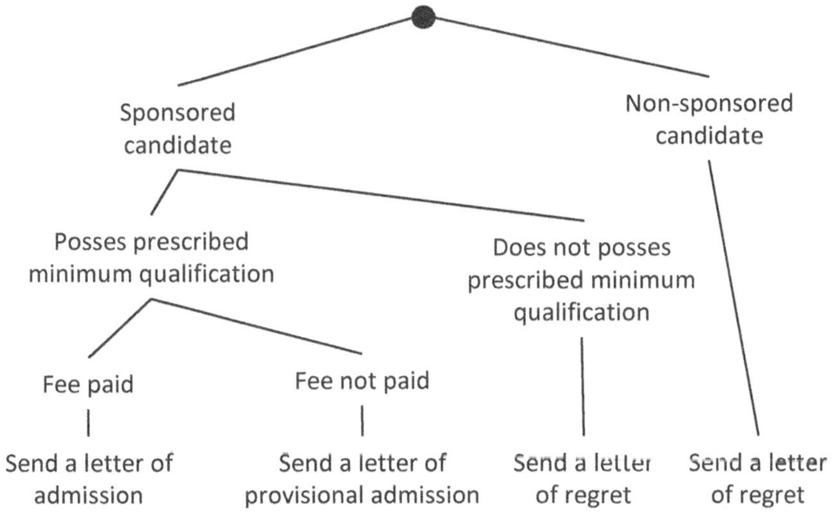

Figure 4.27: Decision Tree for Example 1

Admission to an Extension Course		Rules			
		R1	**R2**	**R3**	**R4**
C1	Is the candidate sponsored by employer?	Y	Y	Y	N
C2	Does the candidate possess prescribed minimum qualifications?	Y	Y	N	Y
C3	Is the candidate's fee paid?	Y	N	-	-
A1	Send a letter of admission	X			
A2	Send a letter of provisional admission		X		
A3	Send a letter of regret			X	X

Table 4.4: Decision Table for Example 1

4.8.2. Example 2: A university has the following rules to qualify for a degree with physics as main subject and maths as subsidiary subject. He should get 50% or more in physics and 40% or more in maths to qualify. If he gets <50% marks in physics, he should get 50% or more in maths. He should however get 40% or more in physics. If he gets <40% in maths and 60% or more in physics, he is allowed to reappear in the maths paper so that he can qualify. Otherwise, he does not qualify.

Solution:

Notation used –

- For maths: M

- For physics: P

Decision Table is shown in table 4.5 and the Decision Tree is shown in figure 4.28.

	Qualify for a Degree Of University	Rules					
		R1	**R2**	**R3**	**R4**	**R5**	**R6**
C1	Maths >= 40	Y	Y	N	Y	N	Y
C2	Maths >= 50	-	Y	-	-	-	N
C3	Physics >= 40	-	Y	-	N	-	Y
C4	Physics >= 50	Y	N	-	-	-	N
C5	Physics >= 60	-	-	Y	-	N	-
A1	Qualify for Degree	X	X				
A2	Reappear for Maths paper			X			
A3	Does not Qualify				X	X	X

Table 4.5: Decision Table for Example 2

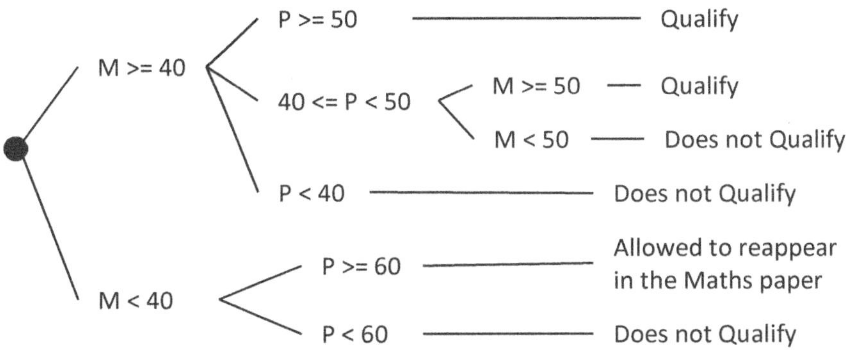

Figure 4.28: Decision Tree for Example 2

4.9. Conclusion

In this chapter, we explored two fundamental tools for system analysis and design — Data Flow Diagrams (DFDs) and the Data Dictionary.

Data Flow Diagrams provide a graphical representation of how data moves through a system, highlighting the processes, data stores, data sources, and destinations. By creating DFDs at various levels, analysts can systematically refine system requirements and design logical workflows without focusing on technical details.

Complementing the DFDs, the Data Dictionary serves as a centralized repository that defines all the data elements, structures, and relationships within the system. It ensures consistency, clarity, and accuracy across all stages of system development, facilitating better communication between developers, analysts, and stakeholders.

Together, DFDs and the Data Dictionary form the backbone of structured system analysis, enabling the creation of well-organized, efficient, and maintainable information systems.

Chapter 5

Object Oriented Software Design

5.1. Overview of OOSD

Object-Oriented Software Design (OOSD) is a methodology for designing software using the principles of Object-Oriented Programming (OOP). It focuses on breaking down software into objects, which encapsulate data and behavior in a structured and reusable way.

Key Concepts of OOSD

- Encapsulation – Hiding internal details and exposing only necessary functionality.

- Abstraction – Simplifying complex systems by modeling only relevant details.

- Inheritance – Reusing properties and behaviors from parent classes.

- Polymorphism – Allowing different classes to be treated as the same type via interfaces or inheritance.

OOSD Process

- Requirement Analysis – Understanding what the software should do.

- System Design – Identifying major components (classes, modules).

- Object Design – Defining relationships between objects (association, aggregation, composition).

- Implementation – Writing the actual code based on the design.

- Testing & Maintenance – Ensuring functionality and making improvements.

Benefits of OOSD

- Modularity – Code is organized into independent, reusable objects.

- Scalability – Easy to extend and modify.

- Maintainability – Code is easier to debug and update.

- Reusability – Objects and classes can be used across projects.

Modeling in Software Design

A model is an abstract representation of a system, constructed to understand the system before actually creating the system. Modeling is a very important mechanism to system design. The success of a system depends heavily on modeling.

A modeling language must include –

1. Model elements

2. Notation

3. Guidelines

Visual notation of a model can provide several benefits such as –

- Clarity – it is easier to understand and check errors in visual representation rather than description in language

- Familiarity – modeling approach is the most common technique used by most of the developers / designers

- Maintenance – visual representation can improve the maintainability of the system

- Simplification – higher level of representation results in fewer but more general constructs, which leads to simplicity and conceptual understanding

Model can be of two types –

1. Static Model

A static model can be viewed as a snapshot of the system parameters at a specific point of time. Static models are needed to represent the structural or static aspect of the system.

Eg. – Class Diagram

2. Dynamic Model

A dynamic model can be viewed as a collection of procedures or behaviors that reflect the behavior of the system over a given time.

Eg. – Sequence Diagram, Collaboration Diagram

Advantages of Modeling

- Models make it easier to express complex ideas

- Models break the system into smaller parts so that important and unimportant part become separated

- Models enhance and reinforce learning and training

- The cost of modeling is less than actual experiment

- Manipulation in model is much easier than manipulation in real system

5.2. UML Diagrams in OOSD

Unified Modeling Language (UML) is a standardized visual language used to design and document software systems. It helps in understanding, designing, and communicating system architecture. UML is widely used in Object-Oriented Software Design to represent objects, relationships, and behaviors in a system.

The current version of the Unified Modeling Language (UML) is UML 2.5, which was released in June 2015 [UML 2.5 Specification]. The UML specification is maintained and updated by the Object Management Group (OMG), the official standards body for UML.

The original versions of UML were developed by the renowned "Three Amigos":

1.   Grady Booch, known for the Booch method

2.   Ivar Jacobson, creator of Object-Oriented Software Engineering (OOSE)

3.   Jim Rumbaugh, who introduced the Object Modeling Technique (OMT)

Formation of UML

The Unified Modeling Language (UML) is the primary modeling language used for analyzing, specifying, and designing software systems. The History of UML Formation is shown in figure 5.1.

In the late 1980s and throughout the 1990s, various methodologies emerged in the software development field, each offering unique strengths and weaknesses. These methodologies were continually modified and refined over time to address different challenges and needs in system design.

In the mid-1990s, Grady Booch, James Rumbaugh, and Ivar Jacobson— three pioneers in object-oriented modeling—came together at Rational Software Corporation. They combined their individual methodologies to create a unified approach that would eventually become the first version of UML, known as Booch '93.

In November 1997, the Object Management Group (OMG) officially adopted UML as a standardized language, solidifying its role as the de facto standard for software modeling.

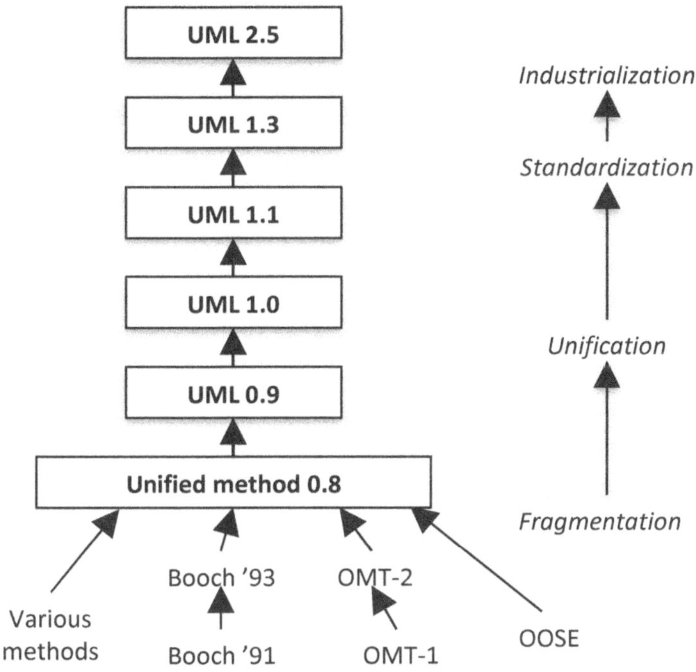

Figure 5.1: History of UML Formation

UML 2.5 Diagrams Overview and Classification

A UML diagram is a graphical representation—or a specific view—of a system model that may be under design, in development, or already deployed. It consists of graphical elements (symbols), typically nodes connected by edges (also called paths or flows), which represent various elements in the UML model of the system. In addition to diagrams, a UML model can also include supporting documentation, such as use cases written in a structured textual format.

The type of a UML diagram is determined by the primary symbols it contains. For example, if the main elements are classes, the diagram is a Class Diagram. If it illustrates use cases and actors, it is a Use Case Diagram. A Sequence Diagram focuses on the chronological exchange of messages between lifelines (objects or components).

Although UML defines specific types of diagrams, the specification does not prohibit mixing elements from different diagram types. For instance, it is valid to combine structural and behavioral elements—such as embedding a state machine within a use case diagram. As a result, the boundaries between diagram types are flexible, though some UML tools may limit the elements available within a specific diagram type for consistency or simplicity.

According to the UML specification, there are two primary categories of UML diagrams:

1. Structure Diagrams

These depict the static architecture of a system, including its components, their relationships, and levels of abstraction. Structure diagrams represent both conceptual and implementation-level elements, which may be abstract concepts, real-world entities, or software components.

2. Behavior Diagrams

These illustrate the dynamic behavior of a system over time. They capture how objects interact, change states, and respond to events - essentially showing how the system evolves during execution.

Brief Description of Each Diagram

Use Case Diagrams are used to represent the functional requirements of a system, capturing both internal and external influences. These diagrams are instrumental in illustrating user interactions and expectations, helping to define the system's intended behavior from the user's perspective.

Activity Diagrams model the flow of control from one activity to another within a system. Each activity represents an operation or step in the process. These diagrams are particularly useful for capturing the dynamic behavior of a system by showing workflows and the order in which activities occur.

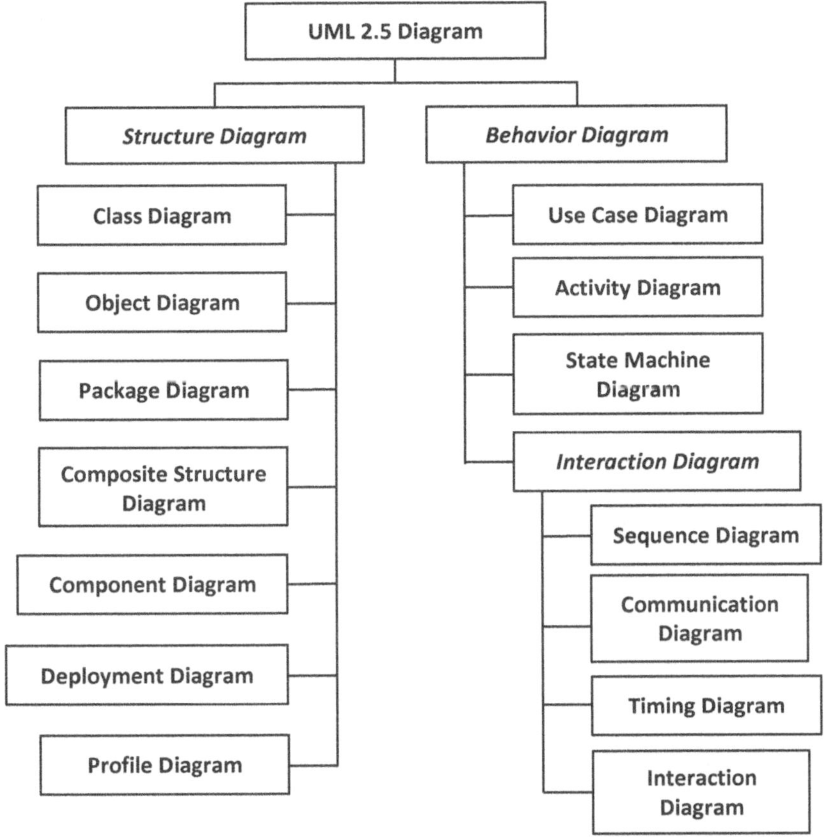

Figure 5.2: Overview of UML 2.5 Diagrams

State-Chart Diagrams (or state machine diagrams) describe the various states an object can occupy during its lifetime, along with the transitions between those states. They are used to model the life cycle of system elements and show how an object responds to events over time.

Sequence Diagrams depict the chronological sequence of messages exchanged between objects. They are used to model the temporal behavior of a system by highlighting how interactions unfold in a time-ordered manner.

Communication Diagrams, on the other hand, focus on the spatial structure of interactions. They show how objects are connected and how messages are passed between them, emphasizing the structural organization of the participants involved in an interaction.

Timing Diagrams represent changes in object states or values over time and show how events influence these changes. These diagrams are especially useful for modeling the behavior of real-time systems, where precise timing of state changes is critical.

Interaction Overview Diagrams provide a high-level view of interaction flow within the system by combining elements of sequence, activity, and communication diagrams. They help visualize control flow across various interactions, offering a comprehensive view of system behavior.

Class Diagrams model the static structure of a system, identifying key abstractions such as classes, attributes, operations, and relationships. They serve as a foundational blueprint during the analysis and design phases and evolve as more details are added to each abstraction.

Object Diagrams capture a snapshot of the system at a specific point in time by illustrating instances of classes and their relationships. They offer a concrete view of the system's structure during execution.

Package Diagrams are used to organize and encapsulate the major components of a system into packages. These diagrams help visualize the dependencies and organization of high-level modules, making them useful for large-scale systems.

Composite Structure Diagrams depict the internal structure of a class or component, including its sub-parts, ports, and connectors. These diagrams help in modeling the internal configuration and interactions within a structured classifier.

Component Diagrams illustrate the physical components of a system and their interrelationships. They represent the implementation view by showing how software components (e.g., executables, libraries) fit together.

Deployment Diagrams describe the hardware environment of a system and show how software components are deployed across various hardware nodes. These diagrams are essential for modeling the hardware topology and deployment architecture.

Profile Diagrams provide a lightweight extension mechanism to UML by allowing the definition of custom stereotypes, tagged values, and constraints. They enable the UML meta-model to be tailored for specific domains or platforms, enhancing flexibility and adaptability in modeling.

The classification of all UML diagrams are depicted in figure 5.2.

We shall discuss the following UML diagrams in detail in the next sections:

1. Use Case Diagram

2. Class Diagram

3. Sequence Diagram

4. Communication Diagram

5. Activity Diagram

5.3. Use Case Diagram

Overview

Use Case Diagrams are an essential part of the Unified Modeling Language (UML) and are primarily classified as behavioral diagrams. They are used to represent the functional behavior of a system from the perspective of its external users, known as actors. These diagrams illustrate the various use cases - that is, specific actions or services that the system is capable of performing in response to interactions with these actors. The actors can be human users, other systems, hardware devices, or any external entities that interact with the system.

Each use case depicted in the diagram represents a distinct functionality that the system provides. Importantly, these use cases must result in an observable and meaningful outcome for the actor or other stakeholders involved. The purpose is to model the system's functionality in a way that is easy to understand, even for non-technical stakeholders, thereby facilitating requirements gathering, validation, and communication throughout the development lifecycle.

Interestingly, use case diagrams exhibit both behavioral and structural characteristics, making them a hybrid form in the UML diagram taxonomy. While their primary role is to describe dynamic behavior, they also share traits of structural diagrams, specifically as a specialized variant of class diagrams. In this context, the system's functional components (use cases) and external entities (actors) are treated as classifiers, which are connected using associations to indicate interaction or participation.

This dual nature allows use case diagrams to serve as a bridge between system structure and user behavior, making them particularly valuable during the early stages of software analysis and design. They not only highlight what the system should do, but also provide insight into who interacts with which parts of the system, ensuring a user-centric approach to system design.

Components of Use case Diagrams

The use case diagram is composed of

- System boundary
- Actors
- Use cases and their specifications
- Relationships among Use cases and Actors

System Boundary

The system boundary is a rectangular area that defines the scope of the system being modeled. It visually separates the system from its external environment. Anything written or drawn inside the rectangle, becomes internal to the system. The items which are written or drawn outside the system boundary are considered to be external to the system.

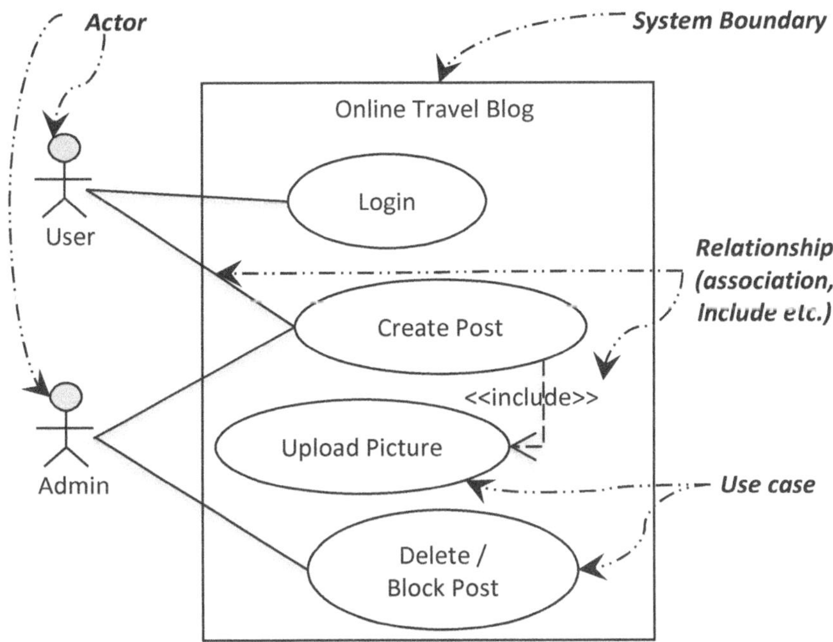

Figure 5.3: Components of Use case Diagrams

Actors

Actors are the entities that interact with the system. They can be users, external systems, or other entities that initiate actions within the system. Actors are typically represented by stick figures or icons.

Please note that these stick figures are used as stereotypes to depict many models at the same time like process, thread, meta-class, power-type etc. labelled with guillemets <<>>. The roles the actors play in the system is important, not their real world identity.

Classification of Actors

Actors can be classified into the following categories:

- human: e.g. novice/trained user; system administrator

- non-human: e.g., fax, e-mail

- primary: ultimate user of the system

- secondary: ensures the correct functionality of the system

- active: initiates use cases

- passive: corresponding use case is initiated by the system

Identification of Actors in a system

To find out Actors in a system, we need to ask the following questions with respect to the system to be designed:

- Who uses the essential use cases?

- Who needs system support in order to fulfill the daily tasks?

- Who is responsible for system administration?

- What are the external devices/software systems the system has to communicate with?

- Who is interested in the results of the system?

Use Cases

Use cases represent the specific actions or services the system provides. They describe what the system does in response to an actor's interaction. Use cases are typically represented as ovals, can contain short descriptions of events in the system from a user's perspective.

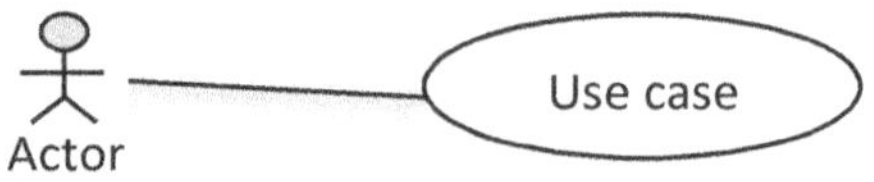

Figure 5.4: Actor and Use Case in Use case Diagrams

Identification of Use Cases in a system

The Use Cases can be identified by answering some questions –

- What function does the actor require from the system?

- Does the actor need to manipulate any information to the system?

- Does the actor need to be notified about some events in the system or vice-versa?

- Can the actor's daily job be simplified?

- What input output does the system need and where from they come or go?

Relationships

Relationships show how actors and use cases interact. Common relationships include:

1. **Association**: A simple connection between an actor and a use case, indicating they interact (as shown in figure 5.4).

2. **Include**: One use case includes the functionality of another, meaning it uses the other use case as part of its process.

3. **Extend**: One use case can extend the functionality of another, meaning it adds optional behavior.

4. **Generalization**: In UML modeling, a generalization relationship is a relationship in which one model element (the child) is based on another model element (the parent). It involves a child entity inheriting the functionality of a parent entity, applied to both actors and use cases.

Relationships among Use Cases

Use Cases share various kinds of relationships. A relationship between two Use Cases is basically a dependency between the two Use Cases. Defining the relationship between two Use Cases is the decision of the modeler of the use case diagram.

The following three relationships are there among Use Cases

1. Include

The include relationship involves one Use Case including the behavior of another Use Case in its sequence of events and actions. Thus, the include relationship explores the issue of reuse by factoring out the commonality across Use Cases.

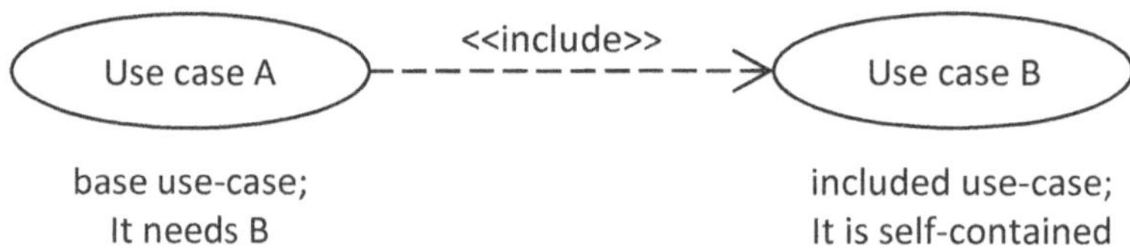

Figure 5.5: Include relationship between Use Cases

Figure 5.5 shows that the behavior of Use Case B is included into Use Case A where the included use case B is necessary to ensure the functionality of the base use case A.

Example: In an admission system, if a candidate is selected by the use case Select Candidate, the candidates will be notified of selection by included use case Notify Candidate. The included use case Notify Candidate is necessary to ensure the functionality of the base use case Select Candidate. Figure 5.6 shows the scenario.

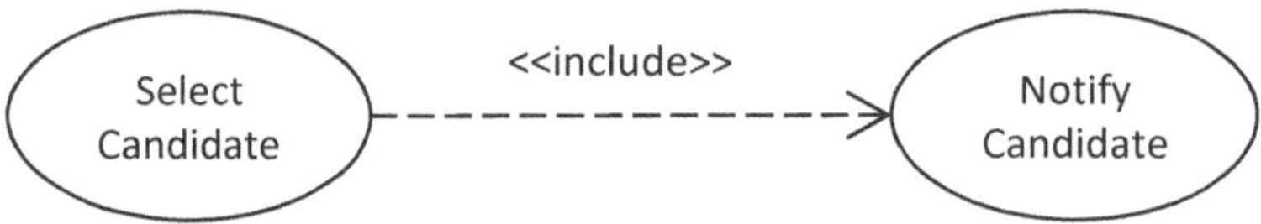

Figure 5.6: Example of Include relationship between Use Cases

The Use Case Notify Participants may be included in other Use Cases, for example, in Cancel Appointment.

2. Extend

The <<extend>> relationship among the Use Cases is used to show optional system behaviour. An optional system behavior is extended only under certain conditions, known as Extension Points.

Figure 5.7 shows that the behavior of B may be incorporated into A. The extending Use Case B may be (but need not be) activated by the base Use Case A. Extension points specify the location where the extending Use Cases extends the base Use Case. The condition under which the extending Use Case is incorporated has to be specified. More than one extension point can be specified for each Use Case. The names of extension points have to be unique. The names of extension points need not be equal with the names of the extending Use Cases.

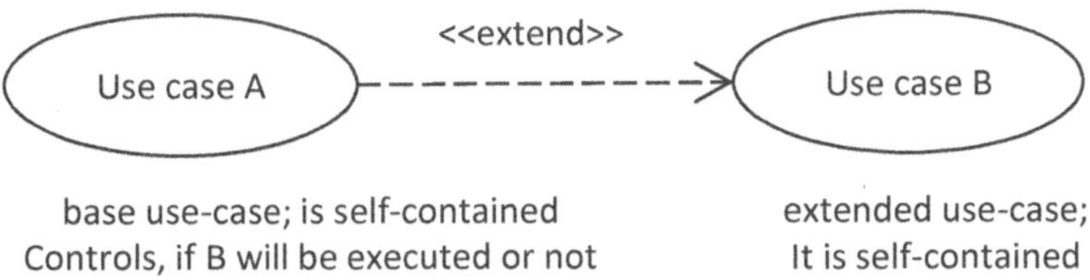

Figure 5.7: Extend relationship between Use Cases

Example: In a shopping system, discount is provided only if the purchase amount is above Rs. 2,000 or the customer is a prime customer. The behavior of Calculate Discount may be incorporated into Purchase Item, at extension point: purchase amount above Rs. 2,000, customer = Prime. The scenario is depicted in figure 5.8.

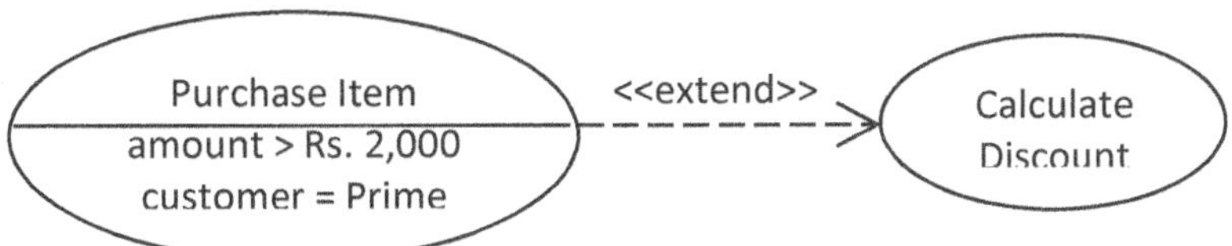

Figure 5.8: Example of Extend relationship between Use Cases

3. Generalization

Generalization works the same way with Use Cases as it does with classes. The child Use Case inherits the behavior and meaning of the parent Use

Case. Generalization helps us to depict the hierarchy present between Use Cases.

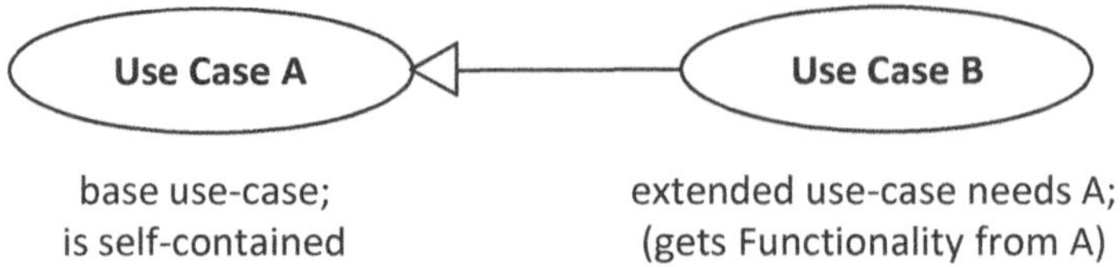

Figure 5.9: Generalization relationship among Use Cases

It is similar to the generalization relationship between classes. Use case B inherits the behavior of use case A and is allowed to override and extend it. B inherits all relationships of A. Modeling of abstract Use Cases is also possible.

Example 1: Authentication by PIN Use Case will inherit the base Use Case Authentication, to include the basic algorithm, but it adds on features like PIN matching (see figure 5.10(a)).

Example 2: Customers can Make Payment in two ways, either by card, or through the UPI (see figure 5.10(b)).

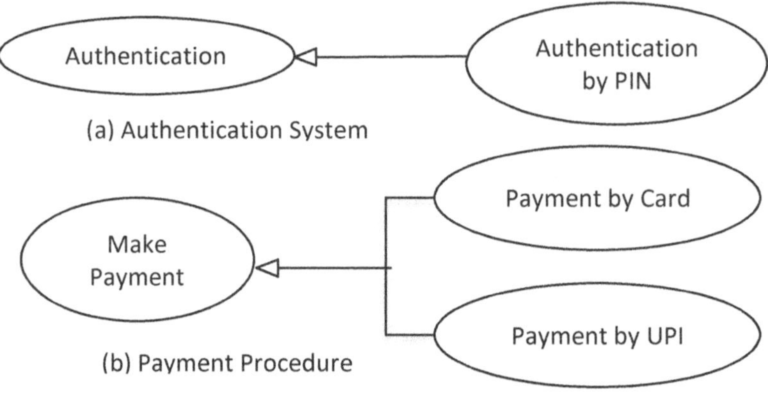

Figure 5.10: Example of Generalization relationship among Use Cases

Relationships among Actors

There can be hierarchy among the actors. That is the base actor will execute some use cases, and the specialized actors will execute extra Use Cases.

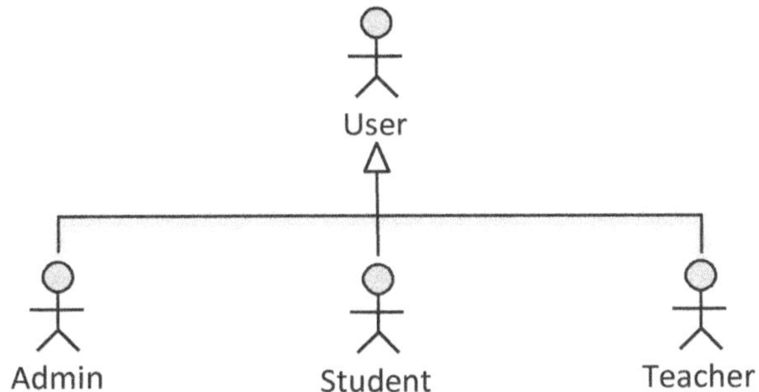

Figure 5.11: Example of Generalization relationship among Actors

Example: In a School Management System, there types of User - Admin, Teacher and Student. This scenario is depicted in figure 5.11.

Example of Complete Use Case Diagram

5.3.1. Mobile Payment System: Consider a mobile service providing system that provides services for regular phone calls and internet facilities. A customer has to login into the system. In the first login attempt, the customer has to register himself/herself. A logged in customer can pay money to the mobile service providing system for the service the customer enjoys on a monthly basis. Payment may be done either by credit card or by net banking. The customer may optionally get a print of the money receipt after payment. The money is paid by the customer through an external banking system.

Solution:

List of Actors - 1. Customer, 2. External Banking System

List of Use cases – 1. Register, 2. Login, 3. Make Payment, 3a. Payment by Credit Card, 3b. Payment by Netbanking, 4. Get printout of the money receipt

List of Relations -

- Register associated with Customer

- Login associated with Customer

- Make Payment associated with Customer

- Payment by Credit Card and Netbanking are associated with External Banking System

- Make Payment extends Get printout of the money receipt

- Make Payment has two sub use cases - Payment by Credit Card and Payment by Netbanking

Now we draw the diagram as follows -

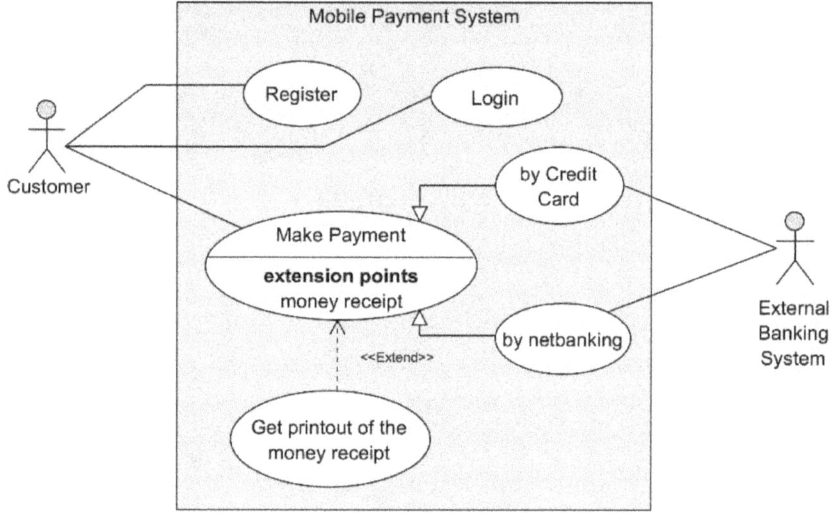

Figure 5.12: Use Case Diagram of Mobile Payment System

5.4. Class Diagram

Overview

A Class Diagram is one of the most commonly used diagrams in the Unified Modeling Language (UML). It is a type of static structure diagram that describes the structure of a system by showing the system's classes, their attributes and operations (methods), and the relationships among the classes.

Class diagrams are essential in both object-oriented analysis and design, as they provide a blueprint of the system's classes before actual implementation.

What is a Class?

A class is a set of objects that share a common structure, common behavior, and common semantics.

A single object is simply an instance of a class, whereas an object is a concrete entity that exists in time and space, a class represents only an abstraction, the "essence" of an object, as it were. For a class Book, objects may be:

{"ANSI C", "Byron Gottfried", 575.50}

{"JavaScript", "David Flanagan", 775.00}

{"Digital Image Processing", "R C Gonzalez", 699.99}

Class Book abstracts – Title, Author, and Price

Representation of class in a class Diagram is shown in figure 5.13.

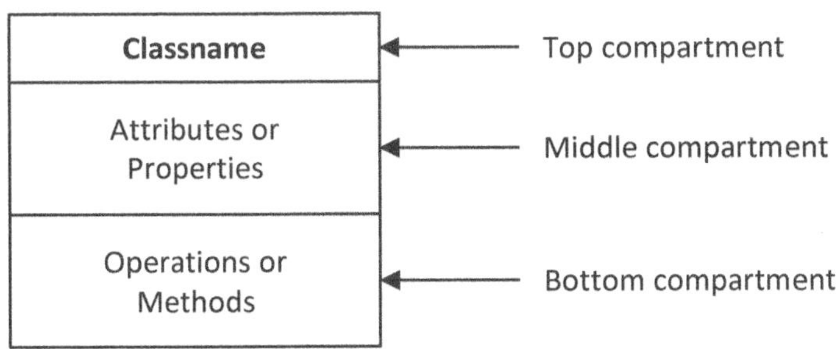

Figure 5.13: Representation of class in a class Diagram

Core Components of a Class Diagram

In Class Diagram, a class is represented as a rectangle divided into three compartments:

a. Class Name

The top compartment contains the name of the class, which is typically written in bold and centered to clearly distinguish it. If the class is abstract, meaning it cannot be instantiated directly, the class name is shown in italicized text to indicate this special characteristic. This naming convention allows viewers to immediately recognize the type and nature of the class within the system.

b. Attributes (Properties)

The middle compartment lists the attributes of the class, which define the data or properties associated with that class.

Property (Attributes) specification format:

Visibility PropertyName : Type [Multiplicity] = DefaultValue {Property string}

The visibility of the properties are denoted by +(public), #(protected) and -(private).

- PropertyName is underlined if the Property is static.

- A property may be Read Only, Static, Ordered, Unique or Optional (to indicate allowable null value).

- Property could have multiplicity. The multiplicity bounds constrain the size of the collection of property values. By default the maximum bound is 1.

- The default-value option is an expression for the default value or values of the property.

- A derived Property, designated by a preceding /, is one that can be computed from other properties, but doesn't actually exist.

Example of Attributes (Properties) of a Class in a Class Diagram is shown in figure 5.14.

<table>
<tr><td align="center">Student</td></tr>
<tr><td>#name: String
+date of birth: Date
-roll no: String {unique}
-/age: Integer
+subject: Subject[1..*]</td></tr>
</table>

Figure 5.14: Example of Attributes of a Class

Explanation of figure 5.14 –

- **name** is protected and of type String.

- **dateofbirth** is public and of type Date.

- **rollNo** is private, of type int, and must be unique.

- **age** is derived (maybe calculated from dateofbirth) and of type int.

- **subject** is public and refers to one or more (1..*) instances of Subject class.

c. Operations (Methods/Functions)

The bottom compartment of the class rectangle is used to define the class's operations or methods, which describe the behaviors the class can perform. Like attributes, operations follow a structured format that includes visibility, the method name, a list of parameters (if any), and the return type.

Operation (Methods) specification format:

Visibility OperationName (ParameterName : Type) : ReturnType
{Property string}

- The visibility of the operations are denoted by +(public), #(protected) and -(private).

- OperationName is underlined if it is Static, and is italic if it is Abstract.

- Return type is optional.

- An operation may be Read Only, Static, Ordered, Unique, Abstract, Sequential, Guarded or Concurrent.

<table>
<tr><td colspan="1" align="center">Student</td></tr>
<tr><td>#name: String
+date of birth: Date
-roll no: String {unique}
-/age: Integer
+subject: Subject[1..*]</td></tr>
<tr><td>#recordAttendance(): bool
+getCertificates(): Certificates[*] {unique, ordered}
-changeSubject(Subject s): bool
+calculateAge(): Integer
+bookMusicClassSlots (): bool {concurrent}</td></tr>
</table>

Figure 5.15: Example of Operations of a Class

Example of Operations (Methods/Functions) of a Class in a Class Diagram is shown in figure 5.15.

Note: Class name (top compartment) is mandatory but attributes and operations (middle and bottom compartments) are completely optional. They are shown as per requirement.

Relationships among classes

In UML class diagrams, various types of relationships are used to depict how classes are connected and interact with each other. The relationships are as follows -

a) Association

One of the most common is the association, which represents a general link between two or more classes. This connection is shown using a solid line and may include multiplicity indicators such as 1, 0..*, or 1..* to specify how many instances of one class can be associated with instances of another. Associations can be unidirectional, meaning only one class is aware of the relationship, or bidirectional, meaning both classes are aware and interact with each other.

- An association icon (a line connector with label - association name) connects multiple classes and denotes a logical connection.

- Associations can be binary or N-ary.

- A class may have association to itself (Reflexive).

The concept of association is shown in figure 5.16.

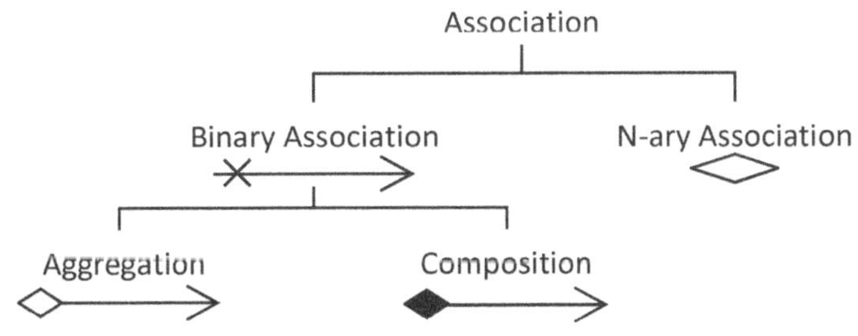

Figure 5.16: Classification of Associations of Classes

We show an association below (figure 5.17) between Artist and Painting-

Figure 5.17: Example of Binary Association of Classes

An association has three main concepts

1. Association End

2. Navigability

3. Association Arity

Association end is a connection between the line depicting an association and the icon depicting the connected classifier. The association end name is commonly referred to as a role name. The role name is optional and suppressible. Artist is playing the role of a creator associated with the artwork end typed as Painting. Association end could be owned either by the end class or association itself.

<u>Navigability in Association</u>

End property of association is navigable from the opposite end(s) of association if instances of the classes at this end of the link can be accessed efficiently at run-time from instances at the other ends of the link. Navigable end is indicated by an open arrowhead on the end of an association. Not navigable end is indicated with a small x on the end of an association. All types of navigability are shown in figure 5.18.

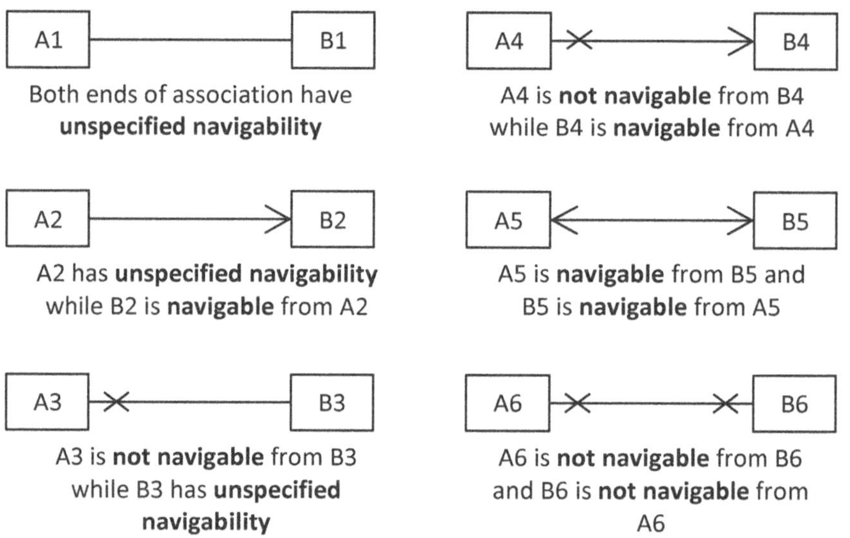

Figure 5.18: Navigability in Association

Example of Navigability in Association: An object of class Car can call methods of Driver object. But the object of class Driver cannot call the methods of Car object. This scenario is shown in figure 5.19.

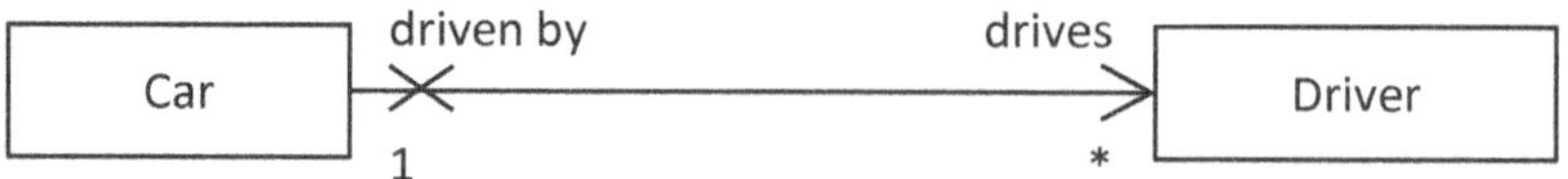

Figure 5.19: Example of Navigability in Association

b) *Aggregation (Has-A Relationship)*

A more specific form of association is aggregation, also known as a "has-a" relationship. Aggregation illustrates a whole-part relationship where the part can exist independently of the whole. For example, a Library may contain multiple Books, but those books can still exist even if the library is removed. Aggregation is depicted using a hollow diamond at the end of the association line pointing toward the "whole" class.

Example: A Library has Books

Figure 5.20: Example of Aggregation

c) *Composition (Strong Aggregation)*

Composition is a stronger form of aggregation, representing a relationship in which the part cannot exist independently of the whole. For instance, a House is composed of Rooms, and if the house is destroyed, the rooms cease to exist as well. This relationship is shown using a filled (black) diamond symbol and emphasizes strong ownership.

Example: A House has Rooms

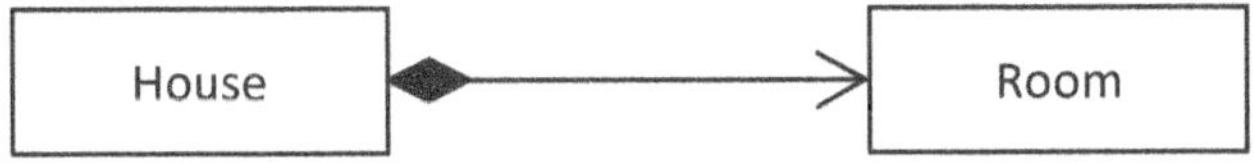

Figure 5.21: Example of Composition

Note: Aggregation could be depicted together with navigability and association end ownership. Similarly, composition is depicted as a binary association decorated with a filled black diamond at the aggregate (whole) end.

For example, a Rectangle has a 'sides' collection of four unique Line Segments. Line Segments are navigable from the Rectangle. Association end 'sides' is owned by Rectangle, not by association itself. Figure 5.22(a) shows the scenario. In the second example, Folder could contain many files, while each File has exactly one Folder parent. If Folder is deleted, all contained Files are deleted as well. This is depicted in figure 5.22(b).

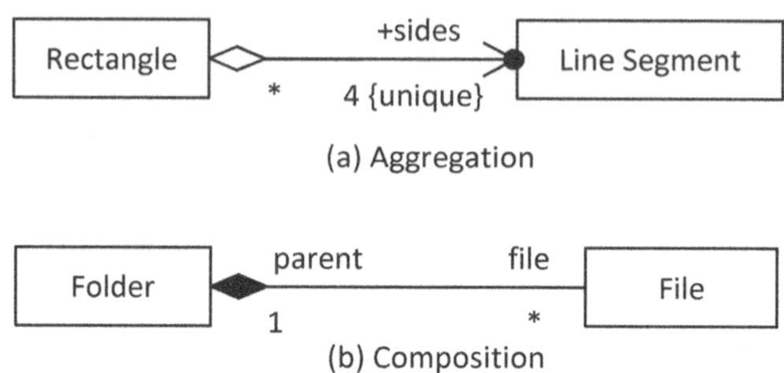

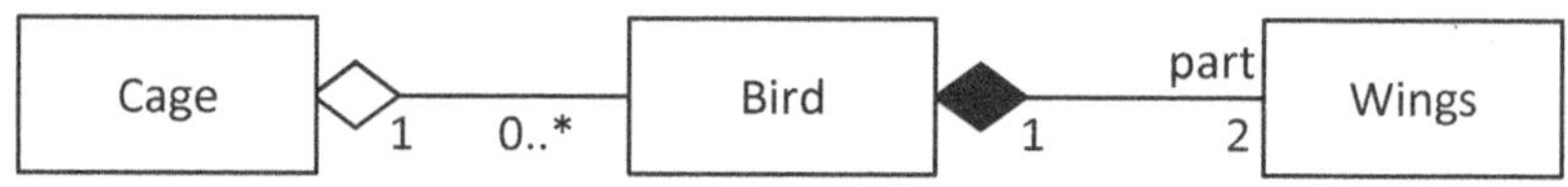

Figure 5.22: Example of Aggregation and Composition

Another Example: Draw class diagram for the following problem - A Bird has exactly two Wings. A Cage contains zero or more Birds. Strong aggregation lies between Bird and Wings while weak aggregation lies between Cage and Bird. The corresponding class diagram is shown in figure 5.23.

Figure 5.23: Example of Class Diagram

d) Generalization (Inheritance)

Another key relationship is inheritance, or generalization, which shows an "is-a" relationship between a subclass and a superclass. This indicates that the subclass inherits the properties and behaviors of the superclass. Inheritance is illustrated with a hollow triangle arrow pointing toward the parent (superclass). For example, a Dog class may inherit from an Animal class, indicating that a dog is a kind of animal.

Example: Dog "is-a" Animal as depicted in figure 5.24.

Figure 5.24: Example of Generalization

A generalization is shown as a line with a hollow triangle as an arrowhead. It can be shown using two styles - separate target style and shared target style. This is shown in figure 5.25.

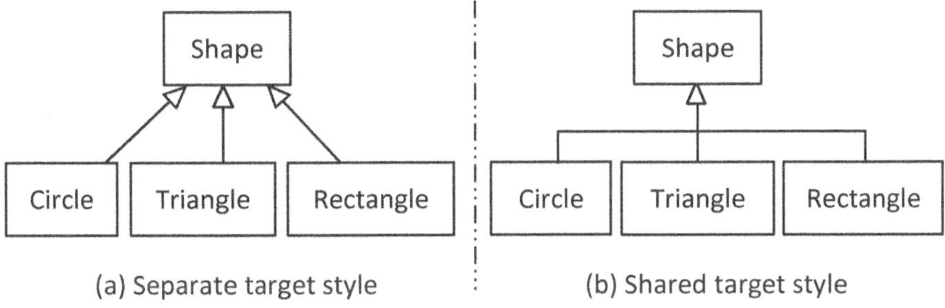

Figure 5.25: Different style of showing Generalization

e) Realization (Interface Implementation)

Realization is a relationship that exists between a class and an interface it implements. It signifies that the class provides concrete implementations for the methods defined in the interface. This is depicted using a dashed line with a hollow triangle pointing toward the interface.

Example: Let's say we are modeling a payment system. There's an interface called PaymentMethod with a method processPayment(). Two classes, CreditCard and Netbanking, implement this interface.

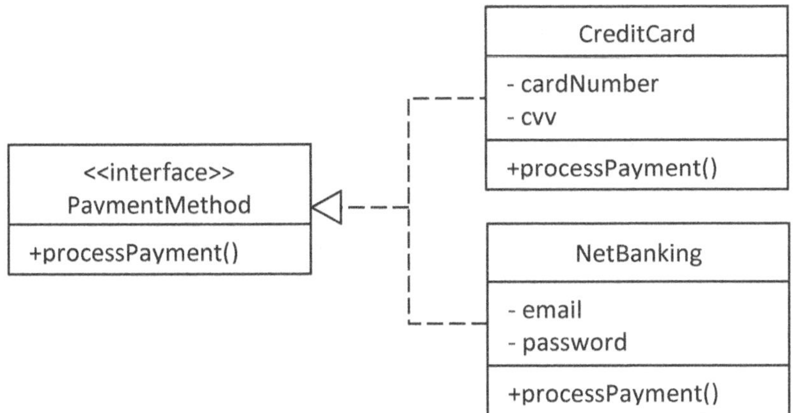

Figure 5.26: Example of Realization in Class Diagram

PaymentMethod is an interface with a method processPayment(). Both CreditCard and Netbanking realize this interface. That means they implement the processPayment() method. The dashed line with a hollow triangle pointing from CreditCard and PayPal to PaymentMethod represents the realization relationship. This scenario is shown in figure 5.26.

f) Dependency

Dependency represents a temporary relationship where one class depends on another to perform a certain function, typically using it as a method parameter or a local variable. This is a weaker link than association and is shown using a dashed line with an arrow pointing from the dependent class to the class it uses.

Steps to draw Class Diagram

Step 1. Identify the Classes –

Start by determining the main entities in the system (e.g., User, Order, Product).

Step 2. Define Attributes and Methods –

Each class has Attributes / Fields (e.g., name, email, price etc. for User).

Each class has Methods / Functions (e.g., login(), calculateTotal() etc.)

UML Notation:

+ public   - private   # protected   ~ package

Step 3. Draw Class Boxes –

Each class is represented in a box divided into three parts as discussed earlier.

Step 4. Add Relationships Between Classes. Determine their multiplicity.

All the Relationships are discussed earlier.

Example of Complete Class Diagram

5.4.1. Mobile Payment System: Please go through the problem statement in section 5.3.1.

Solution:

Here's an explanation of each class and the relationships between them:

1. Customer - This class represents a user of the system.

Attributes:

- email: string — private

- password: string — private

- fullname: string — private

- phone: string — private

Methods:

- +register(em, p, fn, ph): void — registers a new customer

- +login(em, pw): boolean — authenticates a customer

Relationships -

- Aggregation with Usage: A customer makes 0 or more usages (1..*) — shown by the diamond symbol.

2. Usage - This class represents service usage (e.g., data usage, calls, etc.).

Attributes:

- email: string — private

- utype: char — usage type (like call, data, etc.)

- date: Date — date of usage

- amount: double — cost incurred

Methods:

- +generatebill(): Usage – generates a usage bill

Relationships:

- Connected to Customer via aggregation: A customer makes many usages.

- Generates an Invoice – many usages (0..*) generate an invoice (1).

3. Invoice - Represents a bill generated from usage.

Attributes:

- invoiceid: int

- email: string

- monthyear: Date — for which the invoice is generated

- totalamount: double

Methods:

- +generateinvoice(): Invoice — creates an invoice

- +genInvID(): int — generates invoice ID

Relationships:

- One Invoice has one or more Payments

- One Invoice is generated from multiple Usage records

4. Payment - Represents a payment made for an invoice.

Attributes:

- paymentid: int

- invoiceid: int – which invoice it's paying

- dateofpayment: Date

- mode: char — mode of payment (e.g., 'C' for card, 'U' for UPI, etc.)

Methods:

- +makepayment(): boolean — process the payment

Relationships:

- Connected to Invoice: One invoice has one or more payments (1..*)

Summary of Relationships

1. Customer ↔ Usage: Aggregation, 1 customer can have many usages.

2. Usage ↔ Invoice: Many usage entries generate 1 invoice.

3. Invoice ↔ Payment: 1 invoice can be linked to multiple payments.

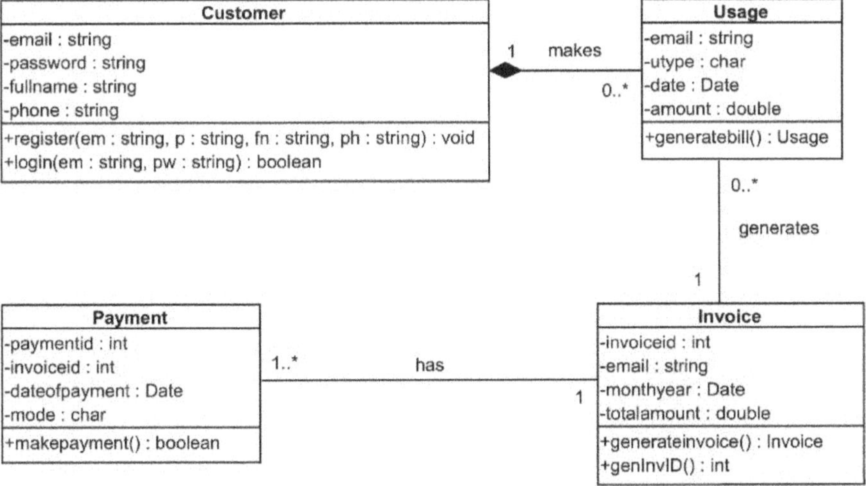

Figure 5.27: Class Diagram of Mobile Payment System

5.5. Sequence Diagram

Overview

A Sequence Diagram is a type of interaction diagram that shows how objects interact in a particular scenario of a use case. It focuses on the order of messages exchanged between different objects to accomplish a specific task.

The sequence diagram is used to model the dynamic behavior of a system. It visualizes how objects collaborate over time. It is also used to capture the time order of message flow. It helps identify responsibilities and object interactions.

Major components of Sequence Diagram

The major components of a Sequence Diagram are Lifeline, Messages and Interaction Fragments.

a) Lifeline

A lifeline is a fundamental element in a UML sequence diagram that represents an individual participant involved in the interaction. Each lifeline corresponds to a single instance of an entity or object that takes part in the communication.

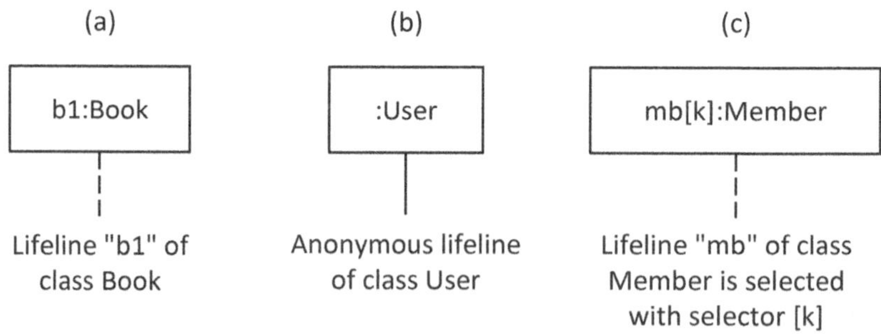

Figure 5.28: Different style of showing Lifeline

If the associated element has a multiplicity greater than one (i.e., it is a multi-valued or collection-type element), the lifeline may include a selector expression. This selector specifies which particular instance or subset of the element the lifeline is referring to during the interaction.

Visually, a lifeline is represented by a rectangle at the top—known as the lifeline's head, which is labeled with its identifier. Extending downward from the rectangle is a vertical line (solid or dashed) that illustrates the lifetime of the participant throughout the interaction.

The typical notation used to identify a lifeline is:

ObjectName[selector] : ClassName

Where:

- ObjectName is the name of the specific instance,

- selector (optional) is used when selecting a part of a collection,

- ClassName is the type or class of the object being represented.

b) Messages

A message in a sequence diagram represents a specific form of communication between the lifelines (objects or participants) involved in an interaction. It illustrates how one lifeline sends information to another during a system process.

There are two primary classifications of messages in sequence diagrams –

1. Messages by Action Type

2. Messages by Presence of Events

I. Messages by Action Type

A message can indicate the invocation of an operation (method call and execution) or the sending and receiving of a signal between objects. These messages define the nature of the interaction occurring between lifelines.

The various types of Messages by Action type are:

1. synchronous call

A synchronous call typically represents an operation call where the sender sends a message and then waits for a response before continuing execution. This behavior models tightly coupled interactions.

Notation: A solid line with a filled arrowhead pointing toward the receiving lifeline as shown in figure 5.29(a).

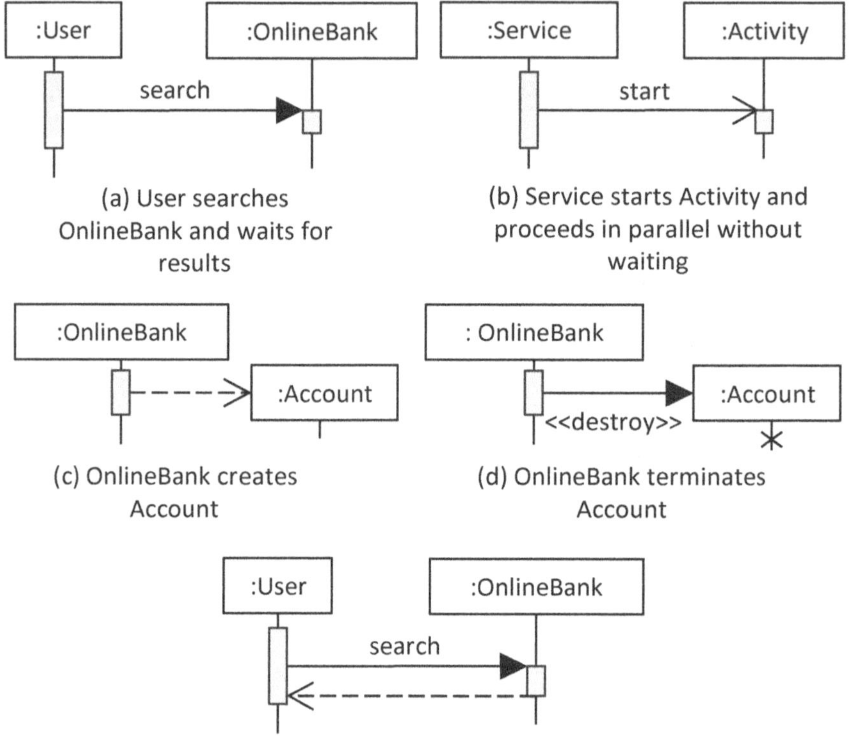

(a) User searches OnlineBank and waits for results

(b) Service starts Activity and proceeds in parallel without waiting

(c) OnlineBank creates Account

(d) OnlineBank terminates Account

(e) User searches OnlineBank and waits for results to be returned

Figure 5.29: Different Messages by Action Type

2. asynchronous call / signal

An asynchronous call allows the sender to send a message and immediately continue its execution without waiting for a return value. This type of message reflects loosely coupled or event-driven interactions.

Notation: A solid line with an open arrowhead as shown in figure 5.29(b).

3. create

A create message is used to indicate the creation of a new lifeline (object). It is sent to a lifeline that is being instantiated during the interaction.

Notation: A dashed line with an open arrowhead, pointing to the object being created as shown in figure 5.29(c).

4. delete

A delete message signals the termination of a lifeline. The receiving lifeline ends at that point in the diagram.

Notation: The lifeline ends with a large "X" symbol at the bottom as shown in figure 5.29(d).

5. reply

A reply message represents the return of a result or response to a previous synchronous operation call.

Notation: A dashed line with an open arrowhead, pointing back to the calling lifeline.as shown in figure 5.29(e).

II. Messages by Presence of Events

Messages may also be classified depending on whether the send event, the receive event, or both are explicitly defined. This classification influences how the message is interpreted within the timing and structure of the sequence diagram.

The various types of Messages by Presence of Events are:

complete message: The semantics of a complete message is the trace <sendEvent, receiveEvent>. Both sendEvent and receiveEvent are present.

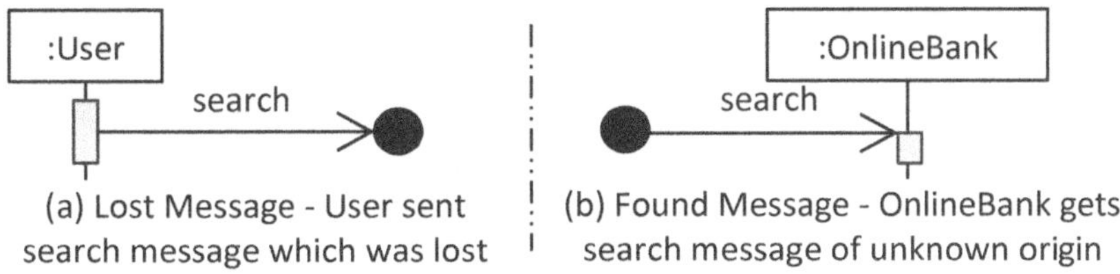

Figure 5.30: Lost and Found Message

lost message: It is a message where the sending event is known, but there is no receiving event.

found message: It is a message where the receiving event is known, but there is no (known) sending event.

unknown message (default): both sendEvent and receiveEvent are absent (should not appear)

c) Interaction Fragments

An interaction fragment is a named element that represents the most fundamental unit of interaction within a UML sequence diagram. Conceptually, each interaction fragment can be thought of as a self-contained interaction, capable of expressing a specific aspect of communication between lifelines.

There is no universal notation for a generic interaction fragment. Instead, its various subtypes define their own specific notations and semantics, allowing for a wide range of expressive capabilities in modeling dynamic behavior.

Some common types of interaction fragments include:

Occurrence: This type of fragment represents a specific point in time—an event that occurs either at the start or end of a message, or at the beginning or end of an execution. It helps pinpoint critical moments in the sequence of interactions.

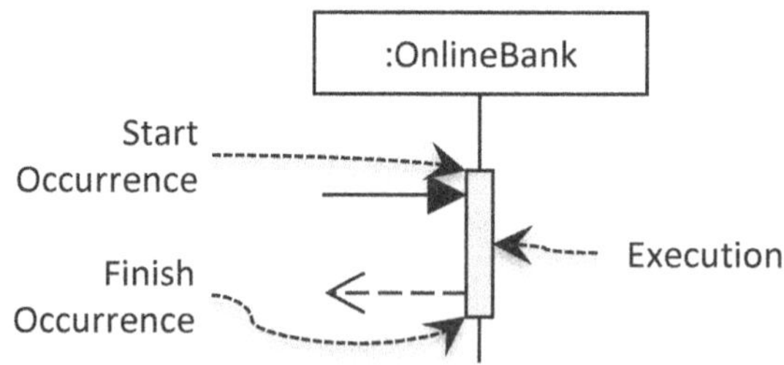

Figure 5.31: Occurrence and Execution of Interaction Fragments

Execution (also called Activation): This fragment signifies a period during which a participant (object or lifeline) is performing an operation or behavior. It may represent the execution of an internal action, the process of sending a message, or a state of waiting for a response from another participant. Visually, executions are shown as narrow rectangles ("activation bars") on a lifeline. These are depicted in figure 5.31.

Example of Complete Sequence Diagram

5.5.1. Mobile Payment System: Please go through the problem statement in section 5.3.1.

Solution:

In the Mobile Payment System, we can divide the whole system into three interaction fragments, namely authorization, invoice generation and payment. Each fragment is shown as a frame in the sequence diagram. Each frame has a set of interactions which are taken from the methods of the corresponding class diagram (shown in the example at section 5.4.1). The Sequence Diagram of Mobile Payment System is shown in figure 5.32.

Explanation of the diagram

- Actors and Objects:

- Customer (Actor) – initiates actions

- c:Customer – the customer object

- inv:Invoice – invoice object

- u:Usage – usage object

- p:Payment – payment object

sd authorization - This interaction fragment models customer registration and login.

> 1. register(em, p, fn, ph) - The customer invokes the register method on the Customer class with email, password, fullname, and phone number.

2. login(em, pw) - The customer calls login with email and password to authenticate.

2.1. Login status is returned (dashed return line).

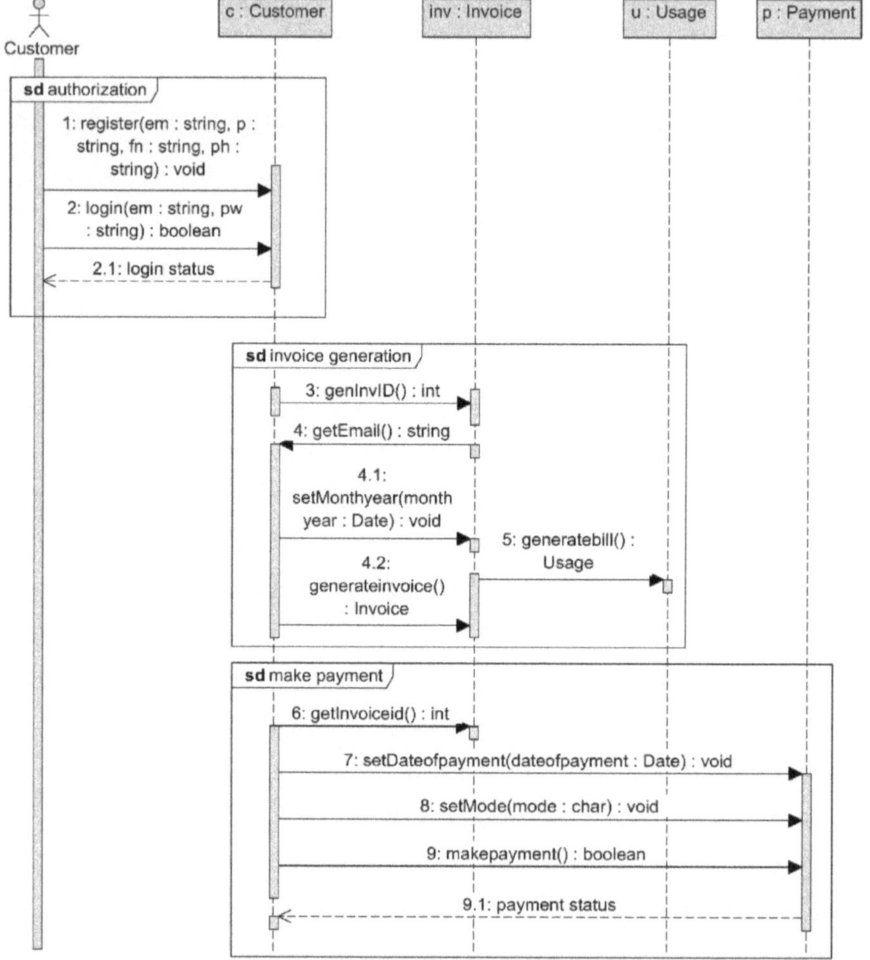

Figure 5.32: Sequence Diagram of Mobile Payment System

sd invoice generation - This models how an invoice is generated from usage.

3. genInvID() - The customer requests the system to generate a new invoice ID.

4. getEmail() - Email is fetched (possibly from the session or usage records).

4.1. setMonthyear(Date) - The invoice's billing month is set.

4.2. generateinvoice() - The actual invoice is generated.

5. generatebill() - The usage object generates the billing details to be included in the invoice.

sd make payment - This models the process of making a payment for an invoice.

6. getInvoiceid() - The invoice ID is retrieved for which payment will be made.

7. setDateofpayment(Date) - The date of the payment is recorded.

8. setMode(mode) - Payment mode is set (e.g., cash, card, UPI).

9. makepayment() - The payment is executed.

9.1. Payment status is returned (e.g., success/failure).

5.6. Communication Diagram

Overview

A Communication Diagram (formerly called a Collaboration Diagram) is a type of interaction diagram in UML that shows how objects interact to perform a specific behavior. Unlike sequence diagrams (which emphasize time order), communication diagrams emphasize the structural organization of objects and the messages passed between them.

It is best used when you want to visualize how different parts of a system collaborate and how objects are connected.

Purpose of Communication Diagrams

- To show object interactions based on their relationships.

- To describe message flow between objects.

- To focus on collaboration and context, rather than just time sequencing.

Key Components

a) Frame

Communication diagrams are typically presented within a rectangular frame, which includes a name compartment in the upper-left corner. While there is no unique long-form heading specifically designated for communication diagrams, the general term interaction (commonly used for all interaction diagrams) is often applied. Similarly, there is no specific short-form label reserved for communication diagrams. Instead, the abbreviation sd, which generally stands for sequence diagram, is frequently used as a generic shorthand for interaction diagrams, including communication diagrams. However, this can lead to confusion, as "sd" is more commonly associated with sequence diagrams. These are shown in figure 5.33.

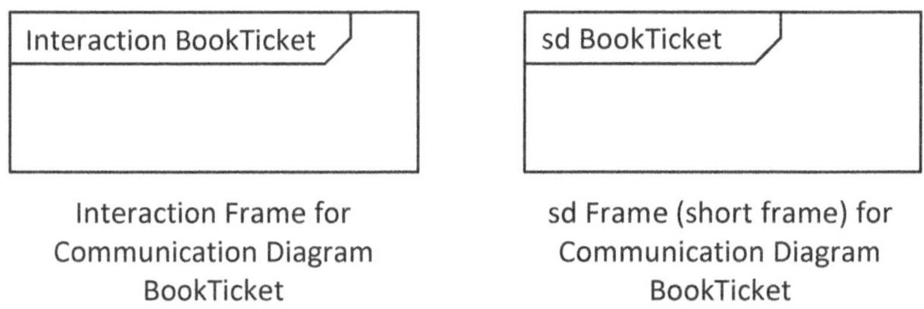

Figure 5.33: Frame in Communication diagram

b) Lifeline

A Lifeline is a specialized type of named element that represents an individual participant involved in an interaction. In UML diagrams, a lifeline typically symbolizes an object or an entity that takes part in the message exchange.

In sequence diagrams, a lifeline is visualized as a rectangle (the head) connected to a vertical dashed line (the tail) that represents the passage of time and the object's lifespan during the interaction. However, in communication diagrams, the lifeline is depicted only as the head (a rectangle) - there is no vertical tail shown.

The standard notation used to identify a lifeline is:

objectName[selector] : ClassName

Here, objectName represents the instance name, selector is optional and used for identifying a particular element in a collection, and ClassName refers to the class or type of the lifeline.

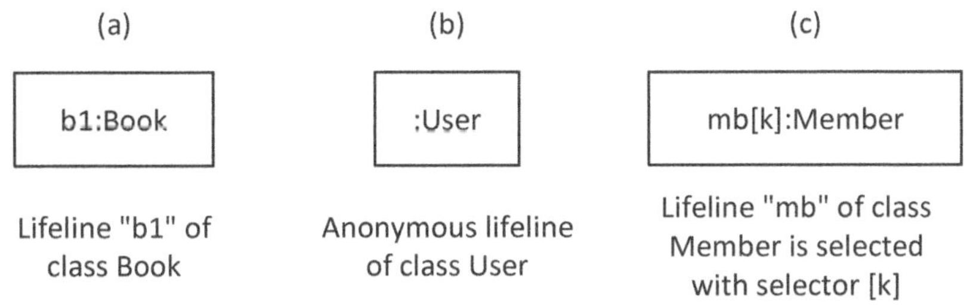

Figure 5.34: Lifelines in Communication diagram

c) Message

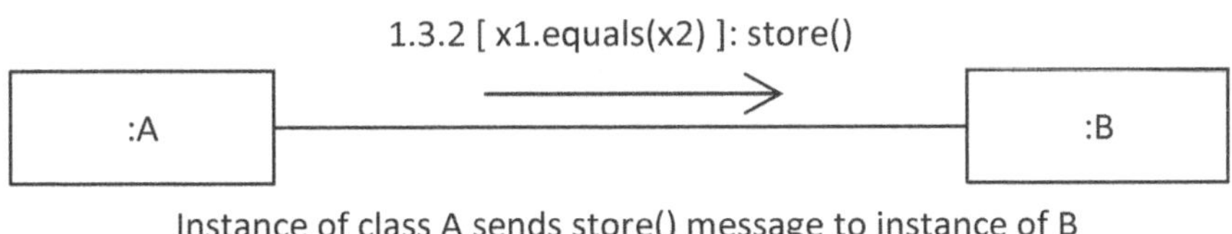

Figure 5.35: Message passing in Communication Diagram

In a Communication Diagram, a message is represented by a line connecting two lifelines, with a sequence expression and arrow placed above the line. The arrow indicates the direction of communication—from the sender to the receiver.

<u>Sequence Expression</u>

The sequence expression is a dot-separated series of sequence terms, followed by a colon (:) and then the message name. It defines the order in which messages are exchanged during the interaction.

Syntax: sequence-expression ::= sequence-term '.' ... ':' message-name

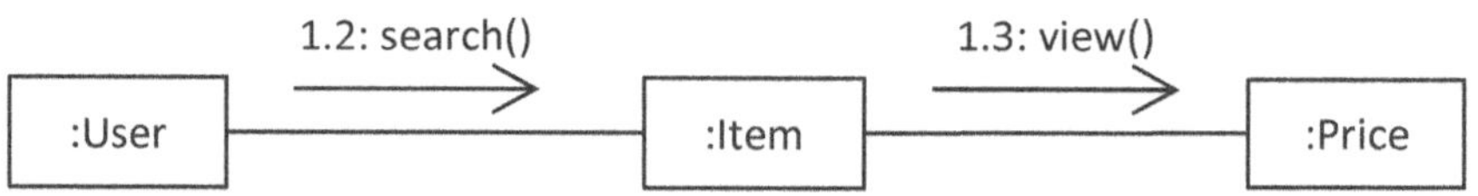

Instance of User sends search() message to instance of Item, and after that Item sends view() to Price

Figure 5.36: Sequential Order in Sequence Expression

<u>Sequence Term</u>

A sequence term can include:

sequence-term ::= [integer [name]] [recurrence]

The integer part represents the order of the message within a procedural or nested call. An optional name or recurrence (like loops or conditions) may be added to reflect more complex message flows.

This structure helps in clearly organizing and understanding the flow of messages, especially in complex interactions where multiple objects and nested operations are involved.

Figure 5.37(a) shows the Concurrent Thread, 5.37(b) Guard, 5.37(c) Recurrence and 5.37(d) Iteration in Sequence Expression.

Note: The interaction between the objects is shown in both the Sequence and the Communication diagrams. However, the selection of Sequence Diagram and the Communication Diagram is decided by the following factors –

- o If the time is the most important aspect to emphasize, then the Sequence Diagram is chosen.

- o If the context is the most important aspect to emphasize, then the Communication Diagram is chosen.

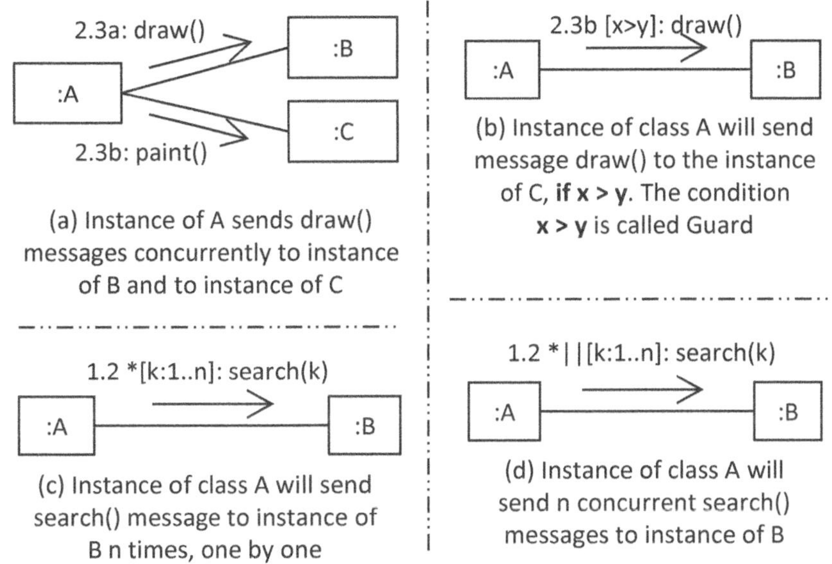

Figure 5.37: Concurrent Thread, Guard, Recurrence and Iteration

Example of Complete Communication Diagram

5.6.1. Example 1: Order Management System - A customer wants toplace order an e-commerce system. The system will verify the customer's payment through a payment service and then confirm the order.

Solution:

Participants (Objects) – :Customer, :OrderSystem, :PaymentService, :Order

Interactions (Messages) -

 1: addCustomer()

 2: requestOrder()

 3: validatePayment()

 4: confirmOrder()

 5: sendConfirmation()

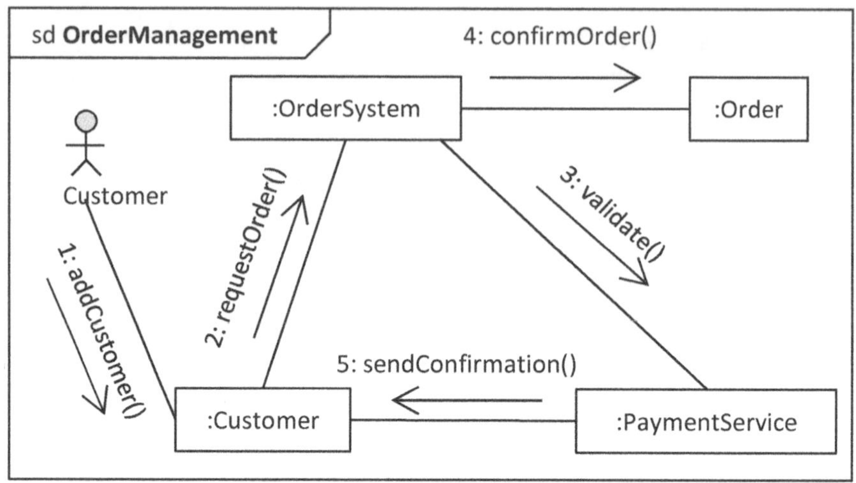

Figure 5.38: Communication Diagram for Online Book Purchase

Explanation:

- The communication diagram shows how objects interact by passing messages, which are numbered to indicate order.

- Each message is labeled with the sequence number, message name, and the direction of the call.

- Unlike sequence diagrams (which focus on time), communication diagrams focus on the structural organization of objects and their relationships.

-

5.6.2. Example 2: Printer Server - An accounts office has a single printer which is accessible by all the employees of that office. The printer is controlled by a printer server. All employees' computers are connected to the printer server. An employee can send a print request at any time to the printer server. If the printer is busy, the file is stored in a queue and a message is sent to the employee's computer. When the print job is completed, another status message is sent. All the messages are displayed on the employee's computer monitor.

Solution:

Participants (Objects)- :EmployeeComputer, :PrinterServer, :Printer, :PrintQueue

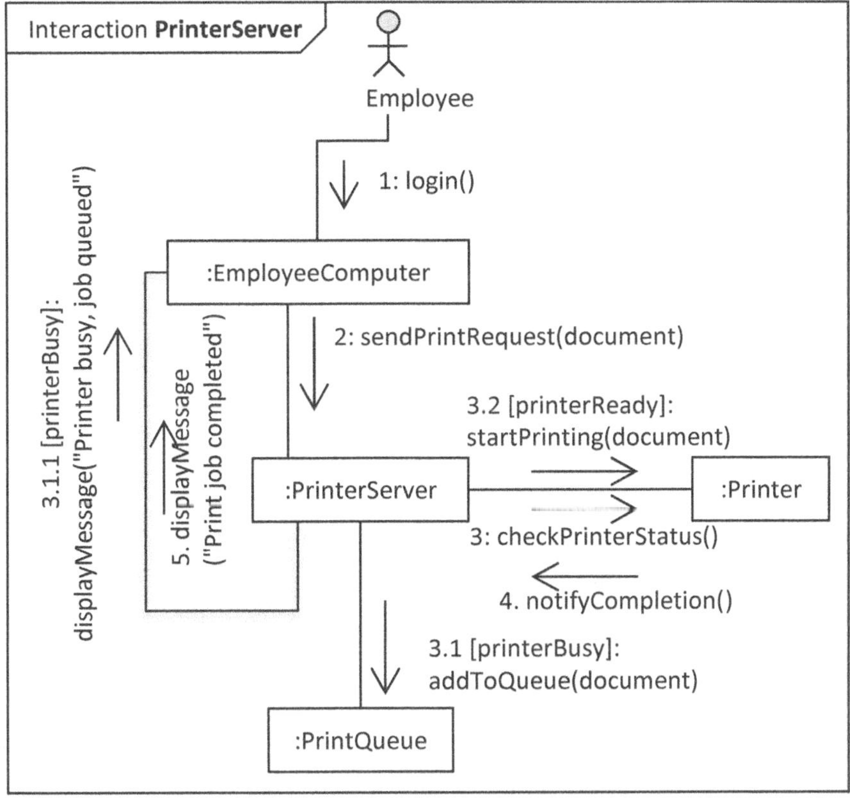

Figure 5.39: Communication Diagram for Printer Server

Interactions (Messages): Let us find messages from the problem statement and list them.

1: login() - Employee (Actor) → :EmployeeComputer

2: sendPrintRequest(document) –

               :EmployeeComputer → :PrinterServer

3: checkPrinterStatus() - :PrinterServer → :Printer

3.1: if busy, addToQueue(document) - :PrinterServer → :PrintQueue

3.1.1: displayMessage("Printer busy, job queued") –

:PrinterServer → :EmployeeComputer

3.2: if ready, startPrinting(document) - :PrinterServer → :Printer

4: notifyCompletion() - :Printer → :PrinterServer

5: displayMessage("Print job completed") -

:PrinterServer → :EmployeeComputer

Now create a frame named "Interaction PrintServer" and draw all the components inside the frame accordingly. The required diagram is shown in figure 5.39.

5.7. Activity Diagram

Overview

An Activity Diagram is a type of UML behavior diagram that illustrates the flow of control or object flow within a system. It emphasizes the sequence, decisions, and conditions that guide the flow of activities.

Activity diagrams are visually similar to traditional flowcharts, making them easy to understand and interpret.

They are commonly used to:

- Represent algorithms (both sequential and parallel),

- Describe the realization of a use case,

- Or model complex workflows involving multiple steps and conditions.

Activities in the diagram can be triggered by:

- The completion of other actions,

- The availability of specific objects or data,

- Or the occurrence of external events outside the defined flow.

Key Components of an Activity Diagram

1. Activity – The overall process being modeled.

2. Partition (Swimlane) – Divides responsibilities among different actors or components.

3. Activity Edge – Connects nodes and indicates the direction of flow.

4. Control – Includes decisions, merges, forks, joins, etc., to manage flow logic.

5. Objects – Represent data or entities involved in the process.

6. Actions – Atomic steps or operations performed during the activity.

1. Activity

An activity is a parameterized behavior that represents a coordinated flow of actions. It models the execution flow using activity nodes connected by activity edges. Each node can represent:

- The execution of a specific task (e.g., a calculation or operation call)

- Object manipulation

- Or control flow constructs such as decisions, synchronization, and concurrency.

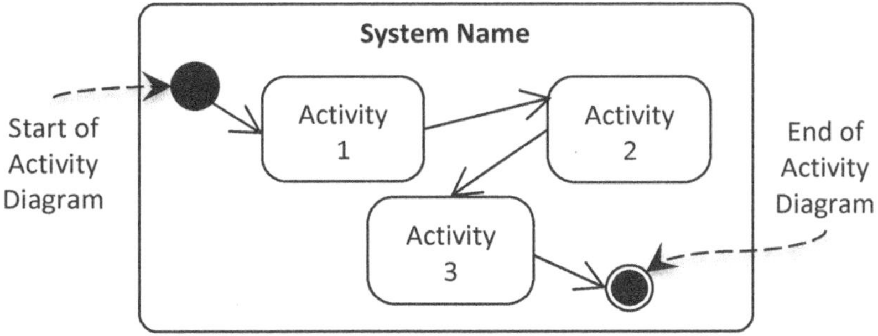

Figure 5.40: Activity with start and end in Activity Diagram

Activities can be hierarchical—invoking other activities down to individual actions. In object-oriented systems, activities are typically invoked indirectly through methods associated with operations.

An activity can include different types of nodes, such as:

- Action nodes – perform specific tasks

- Object nodes – represent data flow

- Control nodes – manage flow of control

2. Partition (Swimlane)

An activity partition is a grouping of actions within an activity that share a common characteristic. These partitions often represent organizational units, roles, or business actors in a business process model.

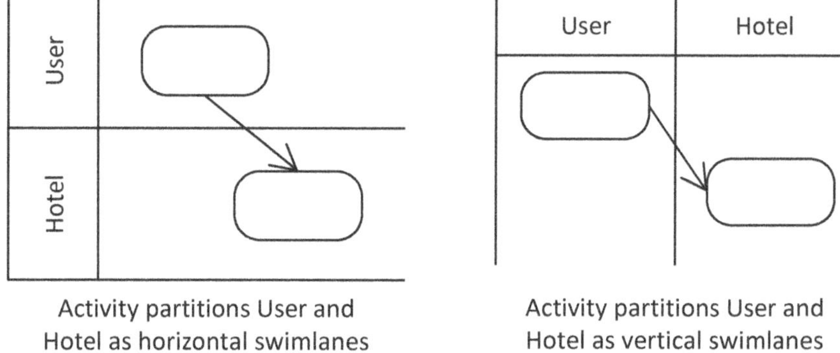

Figure 5.41: Swimlane in Activity Diagram

A partition may also represent an attribute, with its subpartitions corresponding to specific values of that attribute. For example, a partition could represent the location where a behavior occurs, with subpartitions indicating specific locations.

Activity partitions are commonly depicted using swimlane notation, which consists of two parallel lines (horizontal or vertical) with a labeled box indicating the partition's name. Any activity nodes - such as actions or control flows - placed within these lines are considered to belong to that partition.

3. Activity Edge

An Activity Edge is an abstract element that represents a directed connection between activity nodes, along which tokens or data objects flow during execution. There are two main types of activity edges:

a.   Control edges – manage the flow of control

b.   Object flow edges – carry data between nodes

Each activity edge can have a guard condition, which is a logical expression evaluated at runtime. The edge is only traversed if the guard statement evaluates to true. Guard conditions are shown in square brackets, e.g., $[x > 0]$.

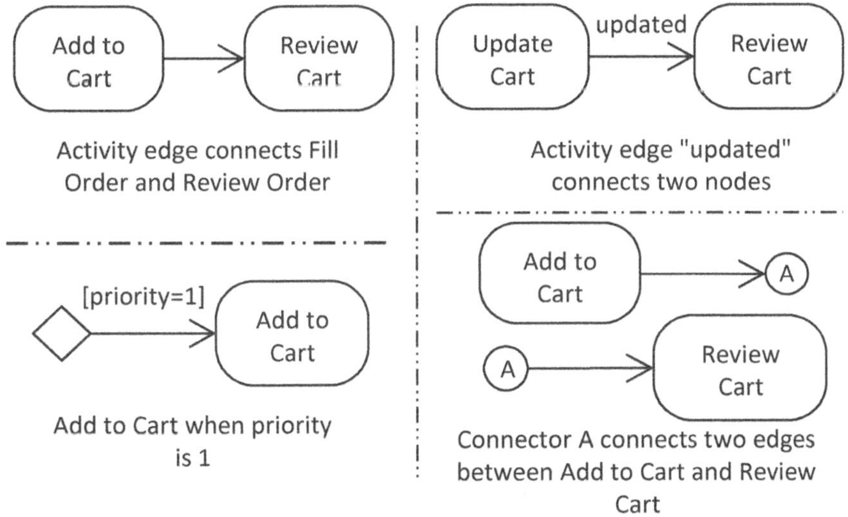

Figure 5.42: Different Activity Edges in Activity Diagram

Activity edges can also be notated using a connector, which appears as a small circle labeled with a name to represent the flow between non-adjacent parts of the diagram.

4. Object Flow Edge

Object flow edges are a type of activity edge used to represent the flow of data or objects between action nodes within an activity. They illustrate how object tokens move through the system during execution. The weight attribute of an object flow edge specifies the minimum number of tokens that must pass through the edge simultaneously for the flow to occur.

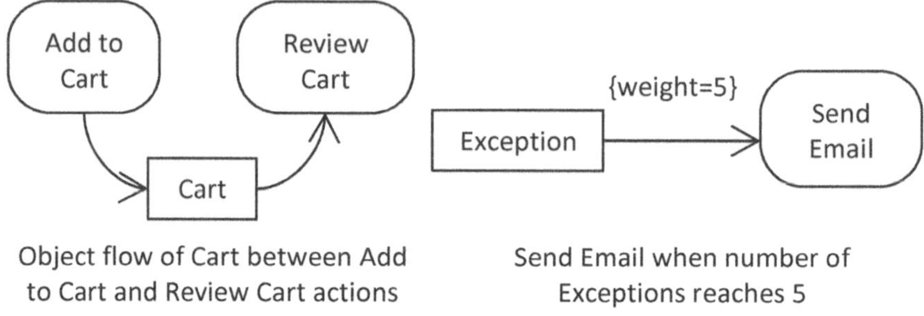

Figure 5.43: Object Flow Edges in Activity Diagram

5. Control Node

A control node is a type of activity node used to coordinate the flow of control and data between other nodes in an activity. There are several types of control nodes, each with a specific role:

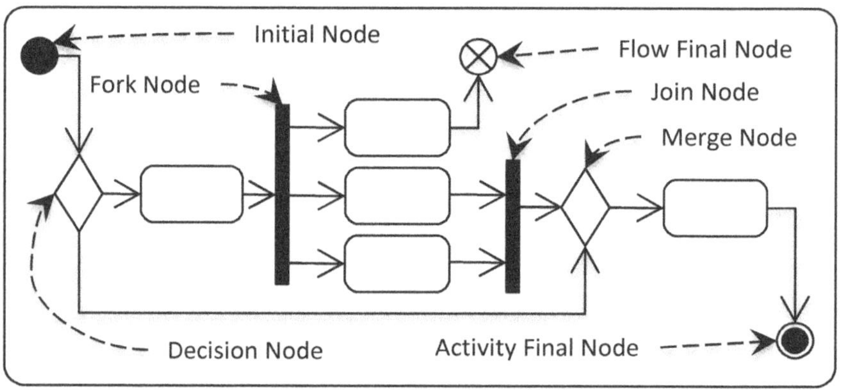

Figure 5.44: All types of Control Nodes in Activity Diagram

i. Initial Node

- Marks the starting point of the activity.

- When the activity begins, a control token is placed at the initial node.

- Tokens are immediately offered to all outgoing edges.

- Note: Initial nodes within structured nodes (e.g., loops) behave differently and don't receive a token when the outer activity starts.

- Notation: A filled black circle.

ii. Flow Final Node

- Terminates only the flow that reaches it.

- Destroys tokens arriving at it without affecting other ongoing flows in the activity.

- Notation: A small circle with an X inside.

iii. Activity Final Node

- Terminates the entire activity when reached.

- Stops all ongoing flows and executing actions in the activity.

- Destroys all tokens in object nodes (except output activity parameter nodes).

- An activity can have multiple final nodes, but reaching any one of them ends the activity.

- Notation: A circle with a bold outline and a filled black circle inside.

iv. Decision Node

- Represents a branching point where a token is sent along one of several possible paths based on conditions.

- Can have one or two incoming edges and multiple outgoing edges.

- All incoming and outgoing edges (except decision input) must be either all control or all object flows.

- Used for: Modeling conditionals (like if statements).

- Notation: A diamond-shaped symbol.

v. Merge Node

- Combines alternative flows into a single outgoing path.

- Does not synchronize tokens—only one token is accepted at a time.

- Should not be used for parallel flows.

- Notation: Diamond shape (same as decision node, but used differently).

vi. Fork Node

- Splits a single incoming flow into multiple concurrent flows.

- Used to introduce parallel execution.

- Notation: A thick horizontal or vertical bar with one incoming edge and multiple outgoing edges.

vii. Join Node

- Synchronizes multiple concurrent flows into a single outgoing flow.

- Waits for all incoming tokens before proceeding.

- Also used to support parallelism in activities.

- Notation: A thick horizontal or vertical bar with multiple incoming edges and one outgoing edge.

6. *Actions*

An Action is a named element that represents a single, indivisible step within an activity. It performs a specific task and is not broken down further within the same activity.

Activities are composed of these individual actions, which collectively define the behavior of the system. While an action may appear simple within an activity, it can reference more complex behavior - for example, a call behavior action can invoke another activity. In such cases, the action itself remains atomic in the current context, even though the behavior it triggers may be complex.

Activities can be reused across different parts of a system by being referenced in multiple actions.

Notation: Actions are depicted as rounded rectangles, with the action's name or description written inside the shape.

Steps to Draw a UML Activity Diagram

1. Understand the Use Case or Process

   a. Clearly define what process or behavior you want to model.

   b. Identify the start and end points, key actions, decisions, and actors or systems involved.

2. Identify Activity Nodes

   a. Break down the process into individual steps or actions.

   b. Determine: Actions (e.g., "Submit Form"), Object Nodes (e.g., data passed between actions) and Control Nodes (e.g., start, decisions, forks, joins, end)

3. Identify Control Flow

   a. Determine how the process flows from one step to another.

   b. Include conditions, alternatives, and parallel paths if needed.

4. Draw Swimlanes (Optional but Recommended)

   a. Use vertical or horizontal swimlanes to represent different: Roles (e.g., Customer, System, Admin), Departments or components. This clarifies who or what performs each action.

5. Place the Initial Node

    a. Use a filled black circle to mark the start of the activity.

6. Add Actions and Object Nodes

    a. Represent each action using a rounded rectangle.

    b. If data flows between actions, show it using object nodes (rectangles with names).

7. Add Control Nodes

    a. Decision Node: Diamond shape for branching paths.

    b. Merge Node: Diamond shape to bring alternative flows together.

    c. Fork Node: Thick bar to split flow into parallel paths.

    d. Join Node: Thick bar to synchronize parallel flows.

    e. Final Node: Circle with a bold border and a black dot inside (to end the activity).

    f. Flow Final Node: Small circle with an "X" inside (to end just one path).

8. Connect Nodes with Activity Edges

    a. Use arrows to show the direction of flow.

    b. Optionally add guards (conditions in square brackets, e.g., [valid]) on decision branches.

9. Review and Refine

    a. Make sure that all actions are connected, flow logic is correct, parallel and conditional flows are clearly represented.

10. Label Clearly

a. Add labels to actions, decision outcomes, object flows, and swimlanes for clarity.

Example of Complete Activity Diagram

5.7.1. Online Examination System: First of all students have to enter credentials for login (userid and password) in order to login into the exam system. In case of incorrect credentials, the students will be asked to enter them again. On successful login, the exam system will do the following – Select course code, Start exam, Finish exam. Examiners will be responsible for setting pass marks and negative marking rules. Also they will make the evaluation after the exam is over. Exam system will generate an exam report after the exam is finished. Final results can be displayed by the exam system only after completion of both generation of exam report and evaluation. Now students can take printouts of the result.

Solution: Activity Diagram of Online Examination System is shown in figure 5.45.

<u>Explanation of the Diagram</u>

This UML Activity Diagram illustrates the Exam Registration and Evaluation System and its flow of actions between three main entities: Student, Exam System, and Examiner. It uses vertical swimlanes to show responsibility and flow across components.

Swimlane Breakdown

1. Student - Handles login, test selection, taking the exam, and receiving results.

2. Exam System - Performs authentication, handles exam logic, and generates results.

3. Examiner - Defines exam rules and evaluates completed exams.

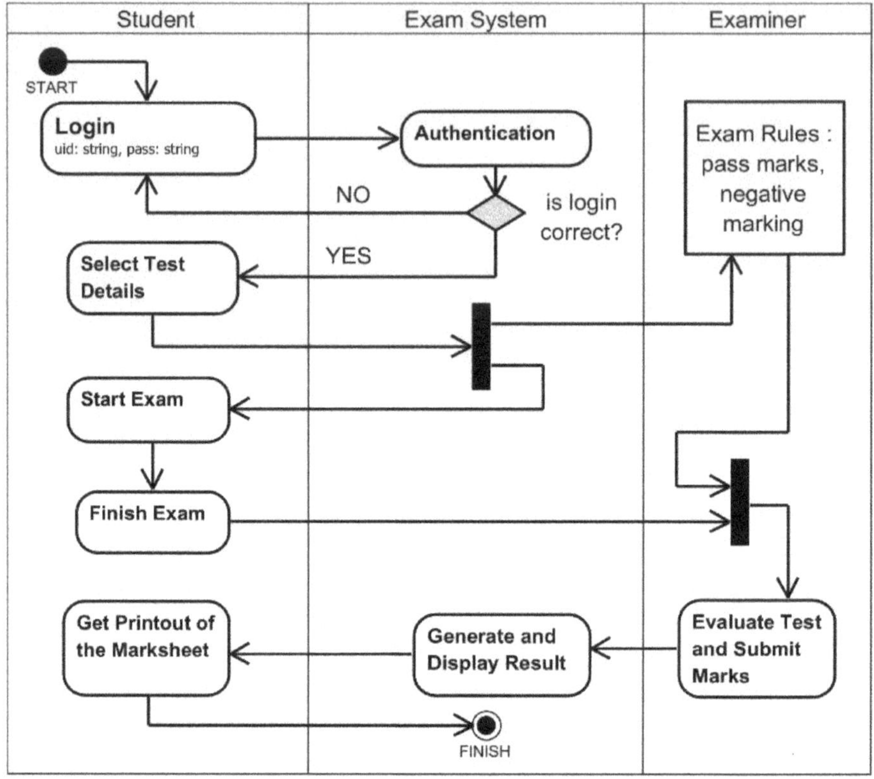

Figure 5.45: Activity Diagram of Online Examination System

Step-by-Step Flow Explanation

Start Node - The diagram starts with a filled black circle, indicating the start of the process.

Login - The Student logs in by providing uid and password.

Authentication - Login credentials are passed to the Exam System. The system performs authentication.

Decision Node: Is login correct? If NO, control returns to the Student to try logging in again. If YES, the process continues to test selection.

Select Test Details - The Student selects which test to take.

Fork Node (Parallel Paths) - Once the test is selected, two parallel activities happen: Student prepares to start the exam. Examiner sets the exam rules (e.g., pass marks, negative marking).

Start Exam & Finish Exam - The Student begins and completes the exam.

Evaluate Test and Submit Marks - After the exam, the Examiner evaluates the test and submits the results.

Join Node - The result evaluation and completion of the exam are synchronized using a join node.

Generate and Display Result - The Exam System generates and displays the result to the student.

Get Printout of the Marksheet - Student may choose to print the marksheet.

Final Node - The process ends here with a final node (bold circle with another black circle inside).

Key UML Symbols Used

- Rounded rectangles: Action nodes (e.g., Login, Start Exam)

- Diamond: Decision node (e.g., is login correct?)

- Thick bars: Fork and join nodes (parallelism)

- Vertical swimlanes: Represent roles (Student, Exam System, Examiner)

- Arrows: Flow of control

5.8. Other UML Diagrams

There are some other UML diagrams which are used when they are really needed to execute. Some of them are as follows -

5.8.1. Object Diagram

An object diagram is a graphical representation of specific instances, including objects and their data values. Essentially, it is a snapshot of the system at a particular moment, capturing the detailed state of various elements. As an instance of a class diagram, a static object diagram reflects how objects interact and relate at a specific point in time, providing a concrete view of the system's structure during execution.

This is a variant of the class diagram. Uses almost identical notations like class diagrams. It shows actual objects instead of actual class. It is an example of a class diagram.

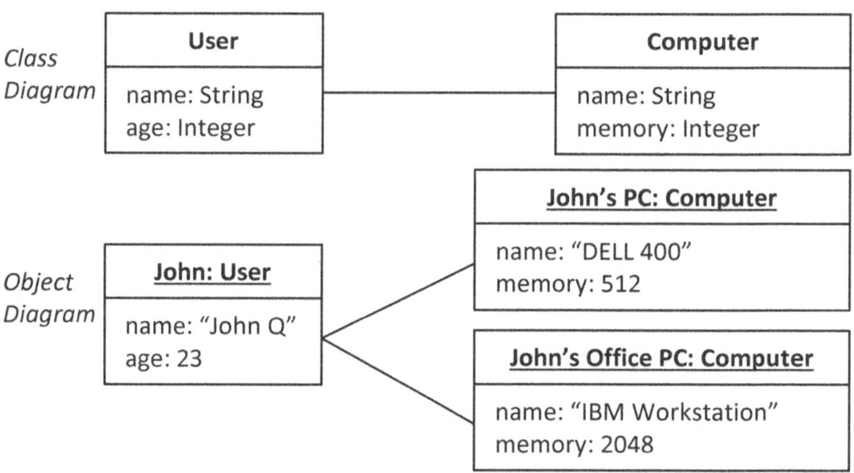

Figure 5.46: Example of Object Diagram

The diagram shown in figure 5.46 compares a class diagram and its corresponding object diagram. The class diagram defines two classes: User with attributes name and age, and Computer with attributes name and memory, along with an association between them. The object diagram represents real-world instances of these classes. John: User is an instance of User with the name "John Q" and age 23, and he is associated with two Computer objects: John's PC, a "DELL 400" with 512 MB memory, and John's Office PC, an "IBM Workstation" with 2048 MB memory. This illustrates how abstract models (classes) relate to concrete examples (objects).

Note: UML 2.5 specification simply provides no definition of object diagram.

5.8.2. Package Diagram

A package diagram is a type of UML structure diagram that illustrates the organization of a system at the package level. It typically includes elements such as packages, packageable elements, dependencies, element imports, package imports, and package merges. This diagram helps in organizing large and complex systems by grouping related elements into packages and showing their relationships.

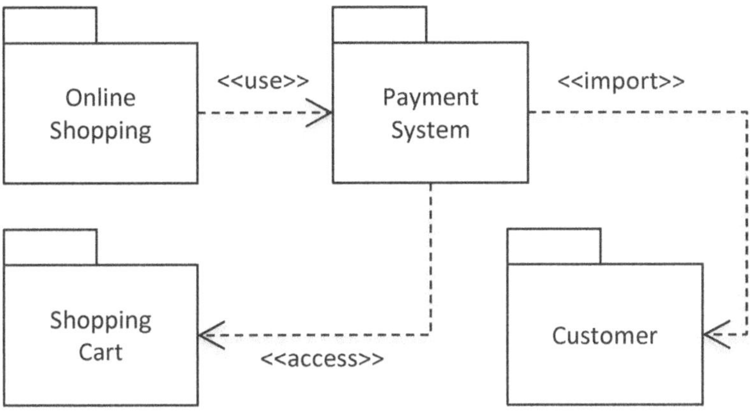

Figure 5.47: Example of Package Diagram

The UML Package Diagram in figure 5.47 illustrates the relationships and dependencies between different components of a shopping system. The Online Shopping package uses the Payment System package, indicating a functional dependency. The Payment System imports the Customer package, meaning it can directly use its public elements. Additionally, the Shopping Cart package accesses the Payment System and the Customer package, implying it interacts with their exposed interfaces. These relationships help define how the system's modules communicate and depend on one another in terms of functionality and structure.

5.8.3. Model Diagram

A model diagram is an auxiliary UML structure diagram used to represent a specific abstraction or perspective of a system. It is often used to depict architectural, logical, or behavioral aspects, offering a high-level view of the system. For instance, it can illustrate the architecture of a multi-layered or multi-tiered application, providing clarity on the structure and interaction between different system layers.

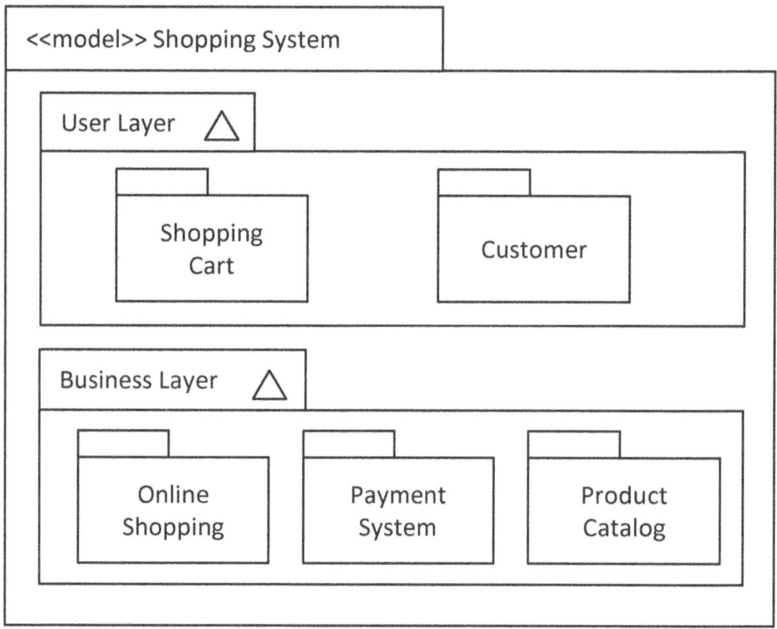

Figure 5.48: Example of Model Diagram

The UML Model Diagram shown in figure 5.48 represents the structure of a Shopping System model, organized into two main layers: the User Layer and the Business Layer. The User Layer includes packages for Shopping Cart and Customer, representing user-facing components. The Business Layer contains core service packages such as Online Shopping, Payment System, and Product Catalog, which handle the main business logic and backend operations of the system. This layered architecture clearly separates user interface components from business logic, promoting modularity and maintainability.

5.8.4. Component Diagrams

It shows the physical structure of the system in terms of code components. A component can be – source component, binary component, system component or executable component. A component class creates a mapping from the logical view to the component view. Dependency among the components are shown in order to analyze how other components are affected by change in one component.

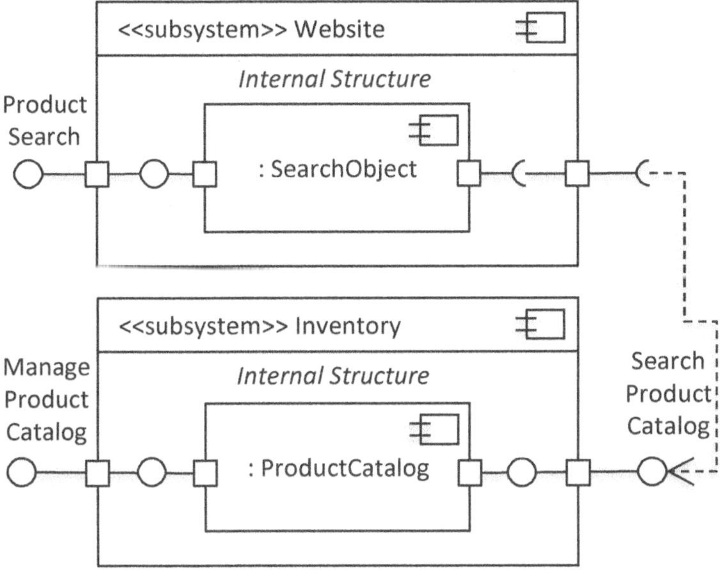

Figure 5.49: Example of Component Diagram

The UML Component Diagram depicted in figure 5.49 shows the internal structure and interaction between two subsystems: Website and Inventory. The Website subsystem contains a SearchObject component responsible for handling product search, while the Inventory subsystem includes a ProductCatalog component for managing the product catalog. The solid and dashed lines with ports represent connectors and interfaces, indicating how components communicate internally within each subsystem and externally between subsystems. Specifically, the SearchObject in the Website subsystem interacts with the ProductCatalog in the Inventory subsystem to perform catalog searches, illustrating component collaboration in a service-oriented architecture.

5.8.5. Deployment Diagram

This diagram shows the physical architecture of the hardware and software in the system. It also shows the actual component devices as nodes along with the connection they have to each other inside the nodes. Executable components and objects are allocated to show which software units are executed on which nodes.

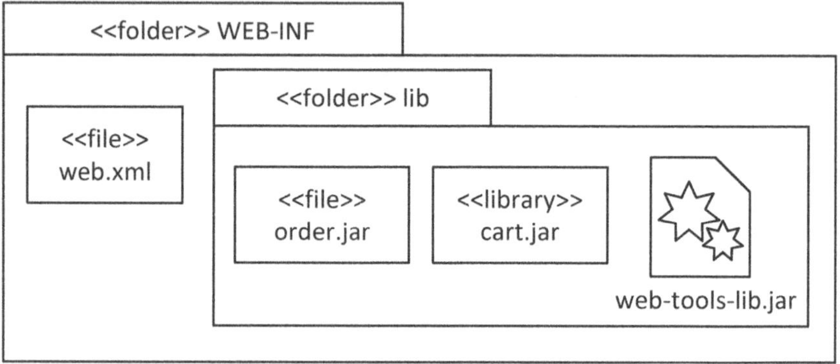

Figure 5.50: Example of Deployment Diagram

The diagram shown in figure 5.50 represents the directory structure of the WEB-INF folder in a Java web application, which is part of the standard layout for Java EE (Jakarta EE) projects. Inside the WEB-INF folder, there is a configuration file web.xml, and a subfolder named lib that contains library files. The lib folder includes order.jar (marked as a file), cart.jar (marked as a library), and web-tools-lib.jar (represented with a visual icon indicating it's a JAR file). These JAR files are dependencies used by the web application and are not accessible directly via the web, ensuring security and modularity in the application's deployment.

5.8.6. State Machine Diagram

It shows all possible states that an object of a class can have and which events cause the state to change. An event may be another object that sends a message. A change of state is called transition. State diagrams are drawn only for the classes that have a number of well defined states. Behavior of the class may be affected by different states.

Example: Elevator System as shown in figure 5.51.

Figure 5.51 shows a UML state machine diagram representing the behavior of an elevator system. It starts in the "On Ground Floor" state, and depending on user input or system conditions, it transitions to "Moving Up" when going up or "Moving Down" when descending. Upon arrival at a requested floor, the elevator enters an "Idle" state, where it waits for further input. If idle too long, it transitions to "Moving to Ground Floor", eventually returning to the "On Ground Floor" state upon arrival. The diagram captures key transitions like "go up," "go down," "arrival at floor," "arrival at ground floor," and "timeout," modeling how the elevator responds dynamically to usage.

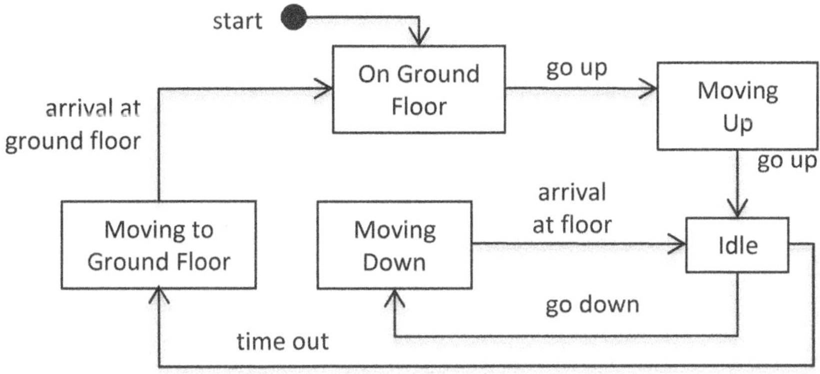

Figure 5.51: Example of State Machine Diagram

5.9. Worked out Examples of Complete Systems

5.9.1. Car Rental System

Problem Statement: There are mainly two types of users in the car rental system – driver and passenger (customer). Customer books a particular type of car for a specific number of travelers for a particular date. Customer has to pay in advance and after payment, a ticket will be provided to customer. Drivers get different salaries depending upon experience and customer feedback. Customers will be able to provide feedback only after completing a trip. The system has the following classes with corresponding attributes –

- Driver – userid, name, phone, email, license, experience

- Passenger – userid, name, address, phone, email, gender

- Car – regno, type, rate, capacity

- Ticket – ticketno, date, noofpassenger, fare, destination

- Feedback – rating, comments

Draw Use Case Diagram, Class Diagram and Sequence Diagram.

Solution:

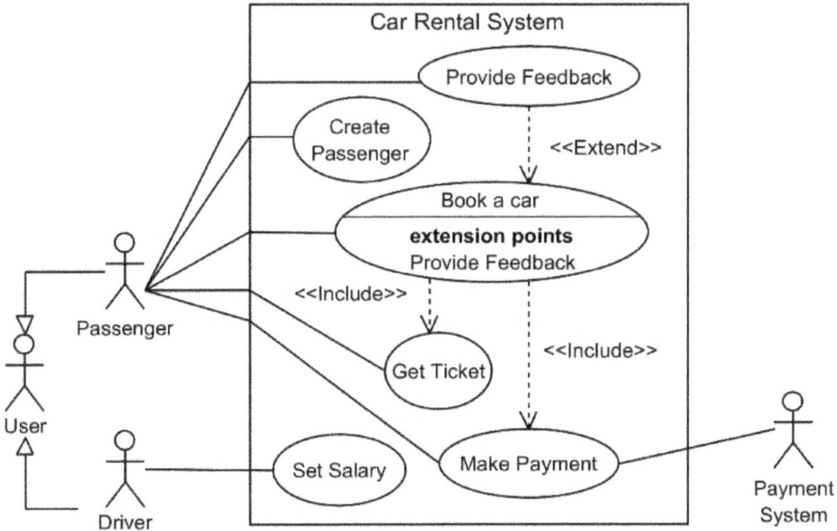

Figure 5.52: Use Case Diagram of Car Rental System

The **Use Case Diagram** in figure 5.52 represents a Car Rental System and outlines the interactions between different actors (users) and the system's functionalities. The main actors include User, Passenger, Driver, and an external Payment System. The User is a generalization of both Passenger and Driver, indicating that both inherit common user functionalities.

The Passenger can perform several actions:

- Create Passenger to register or create their profile.

- Book a car, which is the primary use case and includes the actions Get Ticket and Make Payment.

- Provide Feedback is an optional extension of Book a car, shown using the <<extend>> relationship and labeled as an extension point.

The Driver can perform the Set Salary use case, possibly to configure or view their compensation.

The Payment System is an external actor that interacts with the system during the Make Payment use case.

Overall, this diagram highlights how users interact with the system to rent cars, make payments, and provide feedback, with shared and optional activities clearly structured using <<include>> and <<extend>> relationships.

The **Class Diagram** for a Car Rental System depicts the system's structure through classes, their attributes, methods, and relationships.

Key Classes and Relationships:

1. User (abstract/general class):

   a. Attributes: userid, email, name, phone.

   b. It's a parent class to both Driver and Passenger (indicated by "IS A" relationships).

2. Driver (inherits from User):

   a. Attributes: license, experience (default 0).

   b. Methods: addDriver(...), getDriver(...).

   c. A Driver can drive one or more Cars (1..* multiplicity).

3. Passenger (inherits from User):

   a. Attributes: address, gender.

b. Methods: createPassenger(...), getPassenger(...).

c. A Passenger can book one or more Tickets.

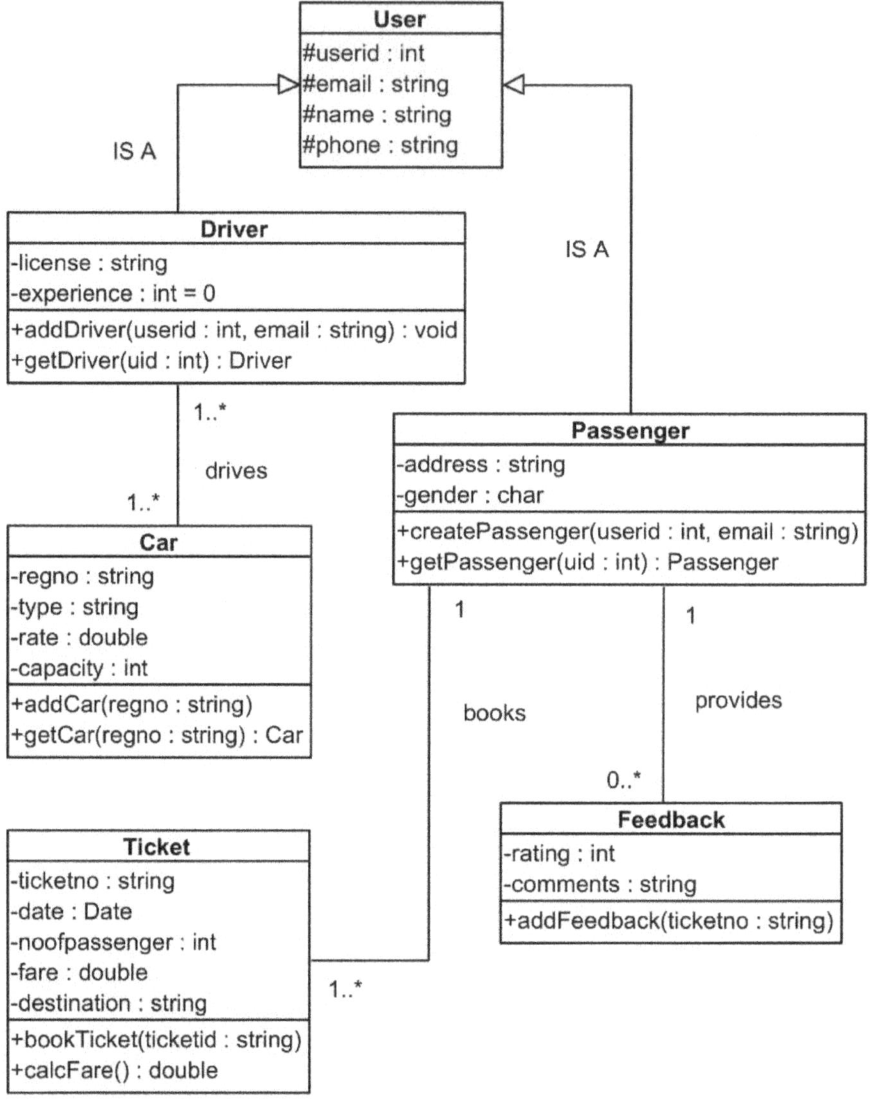

Figure 5.53: Class Diagram of Car Rental System

4. Car:

a. Attributes: regno, type, rate, capacity.

    b.   Methods: addCar(...), getCar(...).

    c.   A Car is associated with one or more Driver(s) (1..* multiplicity), indicating shared vehicle use.

5.   Ticket:

    d.   Attributes: ticketno, date, noofpassenger, fare, destination.

    e.   Methods: bookTicket(...), calcFare().

    f.   A Ticket is booked by a Passenger and is tied to one or more instances (1..*) of ticketing operations.

6.   Feedback:

    g.   Attributes: rating, comments.

    h.   Method: addFeedback(...).

    i.   Each Passenger can provide zero or more feedbacks for each Ticket (0..* multiplicity).

This diagram models how Users (specifically Passengers and Drivers) interact with entities like Cars, Tickets, and Feedback within the system. It shows inheritance, aggregation, and the cardinality of relationships, helping in understanding both data and functional structure.

The **Sequence Diagram** for a Car Rental System, shown in figure 5.54, visually represents the flow of interactions between objects over time for three main processes: Passenger Creation, Ticket Booking, and Feedback Submission.

<u>Passenger Creation (sd passenger creation)</u>

A Passenger initiates the process by calling createPassenger(userid, email). Upon success, the system performs a sequence of attribute-setting operations:

- setName(name)

- setAddress(address)

- setPhone(phone)

- setGender(gender)

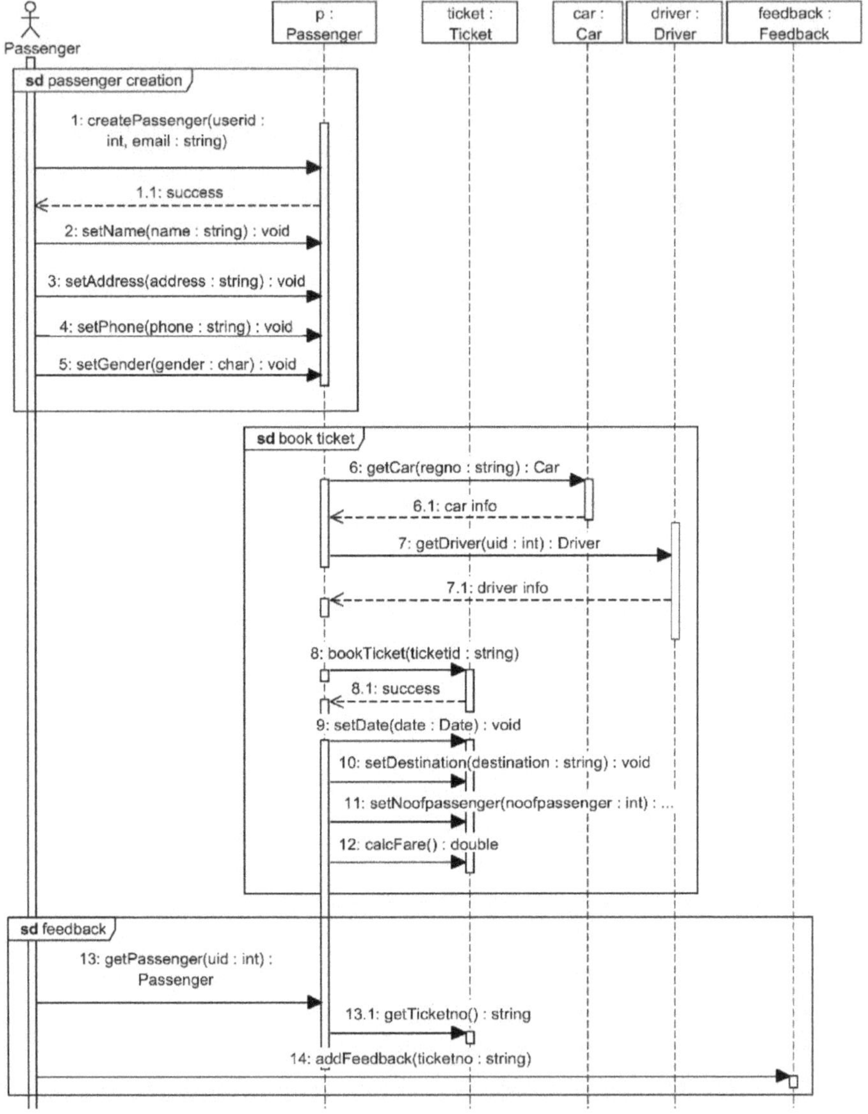

Figure 5.54: Sequence Diagram of Car Rental System

Ticket Booking (sd book ticket)

The passenger fetches a car using getCar(regno) from the Car object, and receives car info. Then, getDriver(uid) is called to retrieve the driver's info. The passenger books the ticket using bookTicket(ticketid), which returns a success acknowledgment. Additional ticket details are then set:

- setDate(date)

- setDestination(destination)

- setNoofpassenger(noofpassenger)

- Finally, calcFare() is called to compute the total fare.

<u>Feedback Submission (sd feedback)</u>

The system retrieves the passenger using getPassenger(uid). It then gets the associated ticket number using getTicketno(). Finally, feedback is submitted with addFeedback(ticketno) to the Feedback object.

This diagram shows a detailed time-ordered flow of messages between various system objects (Passenger, Ticket, Car, Driver, Feedback) as a passenger is created, a car is booked, and feedback is submitted. It clearly outlines method calls, their parameters, and the success responses for major user interactions within the system.

5.9.2. Online Examination System

Problem Statement: First of all students have to enter credentials for login (userid and password) in order to login into the exam system. In case of incorrect credentials, the students will be asked to enter them again. On successful login, the exam system will do the following –

- Select course code

- Start exam

- Finish exam

Examiners will be responsible for setting pass marks and negative marking rules. Also they will make the evaluation after exam is over. Exam system will generate an exam report after the exam is finished. Final result can be displayed by exam system only after completion of both generation of exam report and evaluation. Now students can take printout of the result.

Draw Use Case Diagram, Class Diagram and Sequence Diagram.

Solution:

For **Use Case Diagram**, followings are the considerations -

List of Actors: Student, Examiner, System

List of Use Cases: Login, Select Course, Perform Exam, Generate Exam Report, Evaluate Exam, Display Result, Print Result, Set Exam Rules

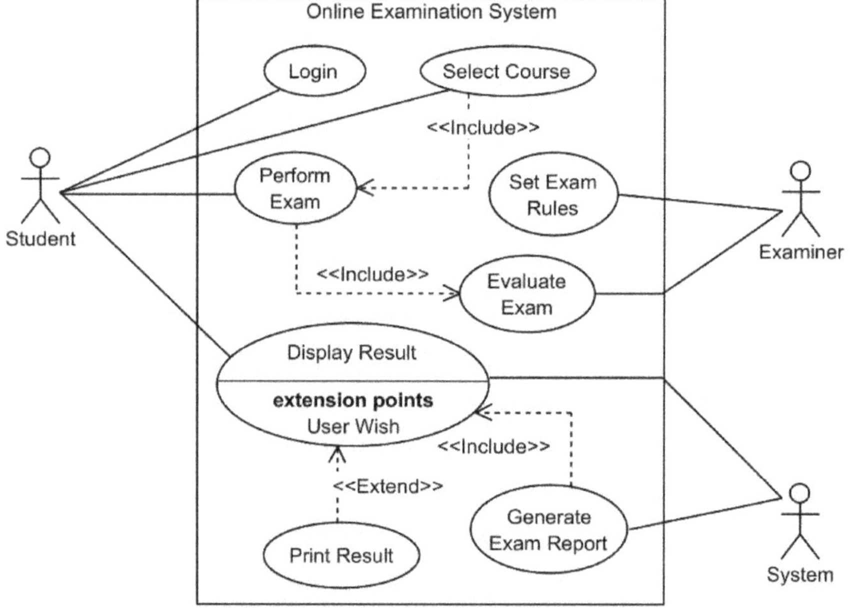

Figure 5.55: Use Case Diagram of Online Examination System

Relationships:

- Students will be associated with - Login, Select Course, Perform Exam (Start to Finish), Print Result, Display Result.

- Examiners will be associated with - Set Exam Rules, Evaluate Exam.

- System will Generate Exam Report, Display Result (after Generate Exam Report AND Evaluate Exam).

Notes:

- Login includes credential validation (retry on failure)

- Display Result is dependent on both: Generate Exam Report + Evaluate Exam

Figure 5.55 depicts the use case diagram.

For **Class Diagram**, followings are the considerations -

Classes and Their Roles

Student

    i.   Attributes:

        a.   userid: A unique ID to identify the student.

        b.   password: Used for login authentication.

    ii.   Methods:

        a.   login(): Allows the student to log into the system.

Examiner

    i.   Attributes:

        a.   examinerId: A unique ID for the examiner.

        b.   name: Name of the examiner.

Test - This is the central class that manages the overall exam process.

    i.   Attributes:

        a.   testCode: The code of the test selected for the exam.

        b.   passMarks: Minimum marks required to pass, set by the examiner.

        c.   fullMarks: Full marks set by Examiner.

ii. Methods:

  a. createTest(): Test created by Examiner

  b. setNegativeMarks(): Penalty for wrong answer.

  c. selectTest(): Allows the student to pick the test.

  d. startExam(): Begins the exam.

  e. finishExam(): Ends the exam.

  f. generateResult(): Creates a report of the exam after completion.

  g. displayResult(): Displays the final result, but only after both evaluation and report generation are done.

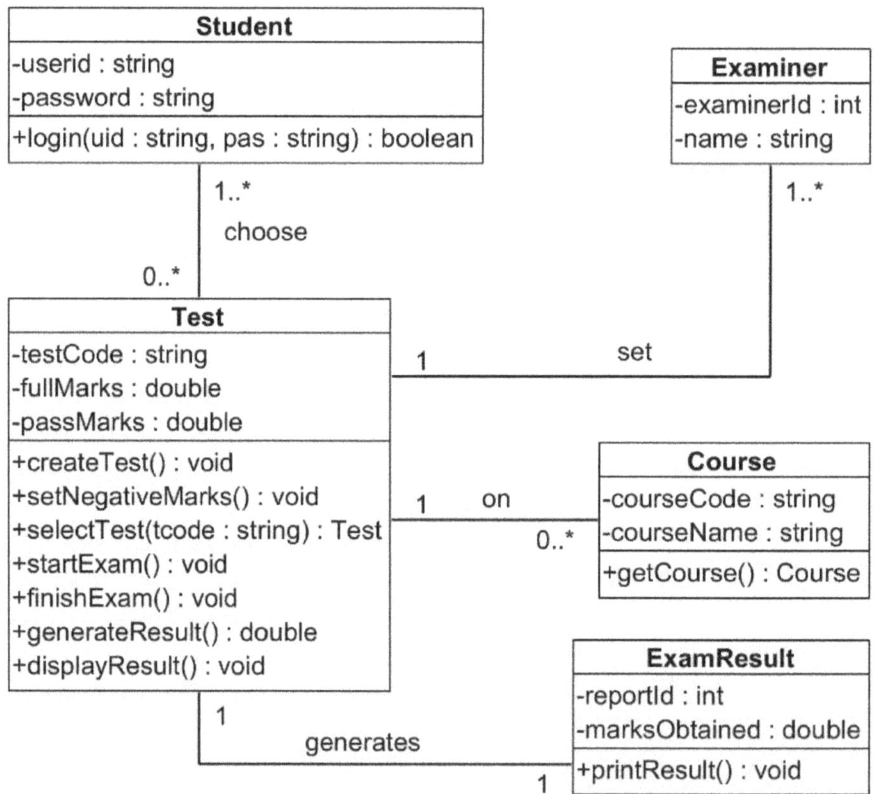

Figure 5.56: Class Diagram of Online Examination System

Course

    i.   Attributes:

        a.   courseCode: Unique identifier for each course.

        b.   courseName: name of the course.

    ii.   Methods:

        a.   createCourse(): allows to add new course.

ExamResult

    i.   Attributes:

        a.   reportId: Unique identifier for each report.

        b.   marksObtained: Total marks secured by the student.

    ii.   Methods:

        a.   printResult(): Lets the student print their exam result after it's available.

Relationships and Flow:

- Examiner sets the Test on Course.

- Student chooses a particular Test to take the exam.

- Test generates the ExamResult.

- Only after both evaluation and report generation, the Test object can display the result to the student.

- The Student can then print the result.

The overall class diagram is shown in figure 5.56.

For **Sequence diagram**, followings are the considerations -

The diagram shows how the different parts (Student, Examiner, System, Course, Test, ExamResult) interact step-by-step during three major activities:

- Setting up the Exam

- Taking the Exam

- Getting the Exam Result

First Part: set exam (Setting up the exam by the Examiner)

Step 1: The Examiner calls getCourse() to select the course for which the test is being set.

Step 2: The Examiner creates a new test using createTest().

Step 3: The Examiner sets the full marks for the test using setFullMarks(fullMarks: double).

Step 4: The Examiner sets the pass marks using setPassMarks(passMarks: double).

Step 5: The Examiner sets the negative marking rule using setNegativeMarks().

Second Part: take test (Student takes the test)

Step 6: The Student logs into the system by calling login(uid: string, pas: string): boolean. If login is successful:

Step 6.1: The student selects the test based on a test code with selectTest(tcode: string): Test.

Step 6.2: The exam starts with startExam().

Step 6.3: After answering all questions, the exam finishes with finishExam().

Third Part: get result (Student gets the result)

Step 7: After the exam is finished, the system retrieves the student ID using getUserid().

Step 8: The system generates the exam result using generateResult().

Step 9: The system retrieves the marks obtained using getMarksObtained().

Step 10: Finally, the Student prints the result using printResult().

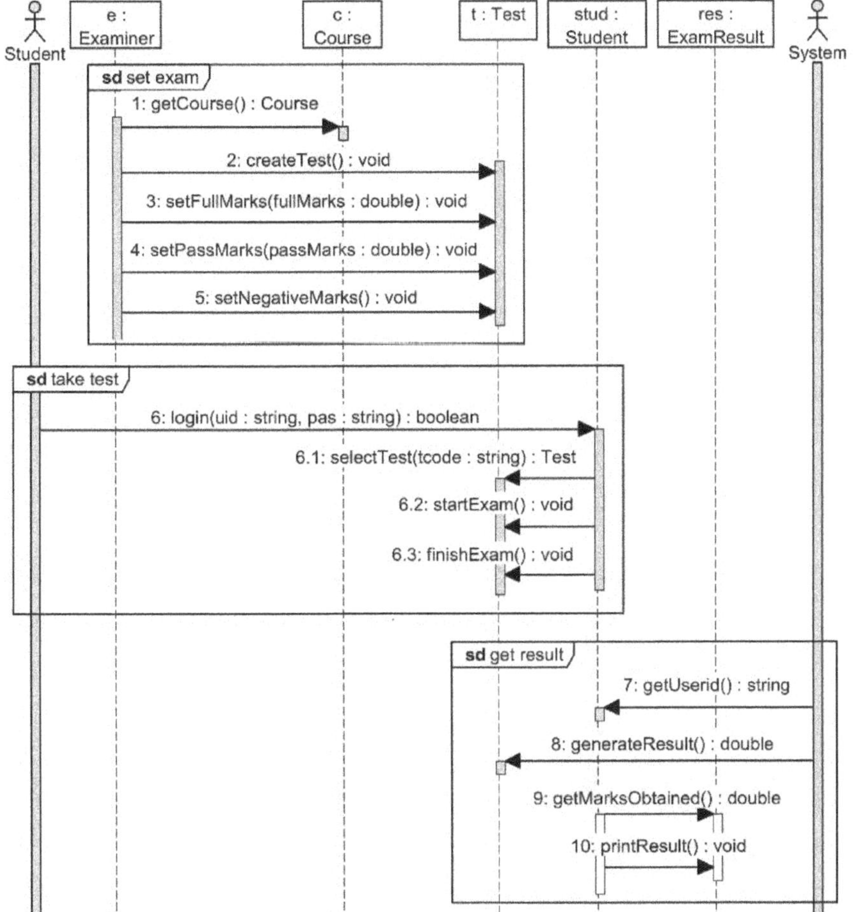

Figure 5.57: Sequence Diagram of Online Examination System

Important Points:

- The Examiner is only involved in setting the exam rules and preparing the test.

- The Student interacts heavily during the login, test-taking, and result retrieval phases.

- The System manages the exam start, exam finish, result generation, and displaying/printing parts.

- The Course, Test, and ExamResult classes are support classes to help manage the data and process flow.

5.9.3. Use case Diagram for ATM System

The system here is a Bank ATM that serves mainly two types of users:

Customer (regular ATM users)

ATM Technician (maintenance person)

It also interacts with the Bank itself.

Actors:

> Customer: They interact with the ATM for financial transactions like checking balance, depositing, withdrawing, transferring funds, etc.

> ATM Technician: They are responsible for maintenance, repairs, diagnostics, etc.

> Bank: Supports ATM operations like approving transactions and maintenance activities.

Main Use Cases (Processes):

> ATM Transaction (Core Use Case): Represents all main activities a customer can do at an ATM. It has extension points for providing help (in case users need ATM assistance).

> Customer Authentication: Before accessing transactions, customers must authenticate (login with card + PIN). It is included (mandatory part) before ATM transactions can happen.

> Check Balances, Deposit Funds, Withdraw Cash, Transfer Funds: These are the actual services available inside an ATM Transaction.

ATM Help: If a customer needs assistance during a transaction, they can trigger ATM Help (optional). This is an <<Extend>> relationship (optional extra behavior).

Maintenance Use Cases (Technician's Side):

Maintenance: Main process handled by the ATM Technician. It includes Replenishing (refill cash and supplies), Upgrades (software/hardware updates).

Repair: If the ATM has issues, the Technician can start Repair. It includes Diagnostics (run tests to find faults).

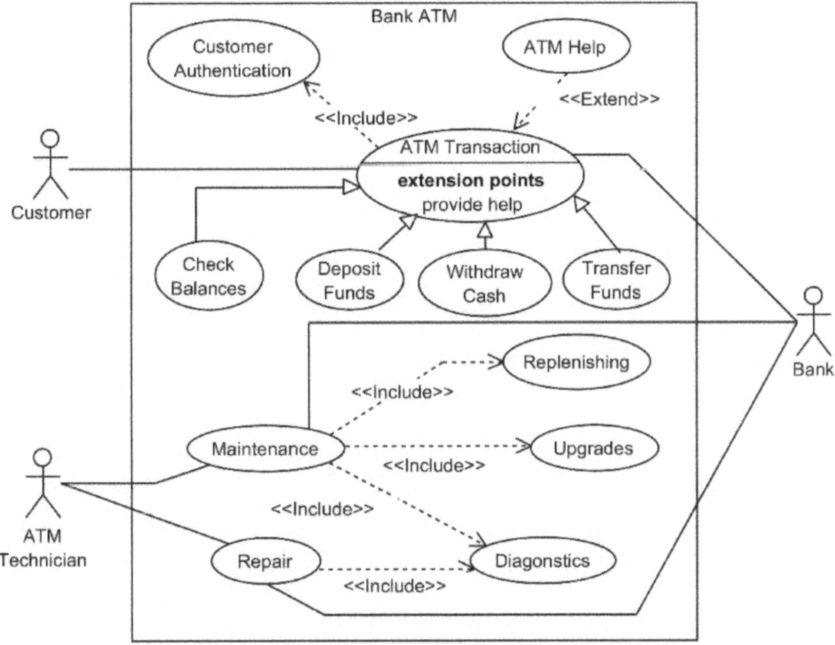

Figure 5.58: Use case Diagram for ATM System

Relationships:

<<Include>>: Means the included use case must happen as part of the main one. Example: Customer Authentication is always required before an ATM Transaction.

<<Extend>>: Means the additional use case may optionally happen based on some condition. Example: ATM Help is extended only if the customer needs help during the transaction.

<u>In Simple Terms:</u>

Customers: login → choose an operation → optionally get help → complete the transaction.

ATM Technicians: perform maintenance, repairs, diagnostics, upgrades.

Bank: backs operations behind the scenes.

5.9.4. Hotel Reservation System

Problem Statement: When a customer needs a room on specific dates, she first checks with the hotel reservation system whether any room is available in the hotel on those dates. If a room is available, then she fills up an application form that contains her personal data such as name, telephone number, address and her credit card information. The reservation system sends a request in a specified format to the credit card to check whether enough credit is available to pay the hotel bills. At the same time, a request in a specified format is sent out by the reservation system to the police to check if the customer is listed as a bad character. After getting favorable replies to both the queries, the system proceeds to book the room in the hotel database and creates a confirmation message which is sent back to the customer.

Draw Activity Diagram for Hotel Reservation System.

Solution:

The Activity Diagram shows the workflow for a hotel room reservation system. It shows how Customer, Credit Card Company, Reservation System, and Police interact.

Actors (Swimlanes):

- Customer: person trying to reserve the room.

- Credit Card: checks customer's financial status.

- Reservation System: manages availability and booking.

- Police: verifies customer's background (character check).

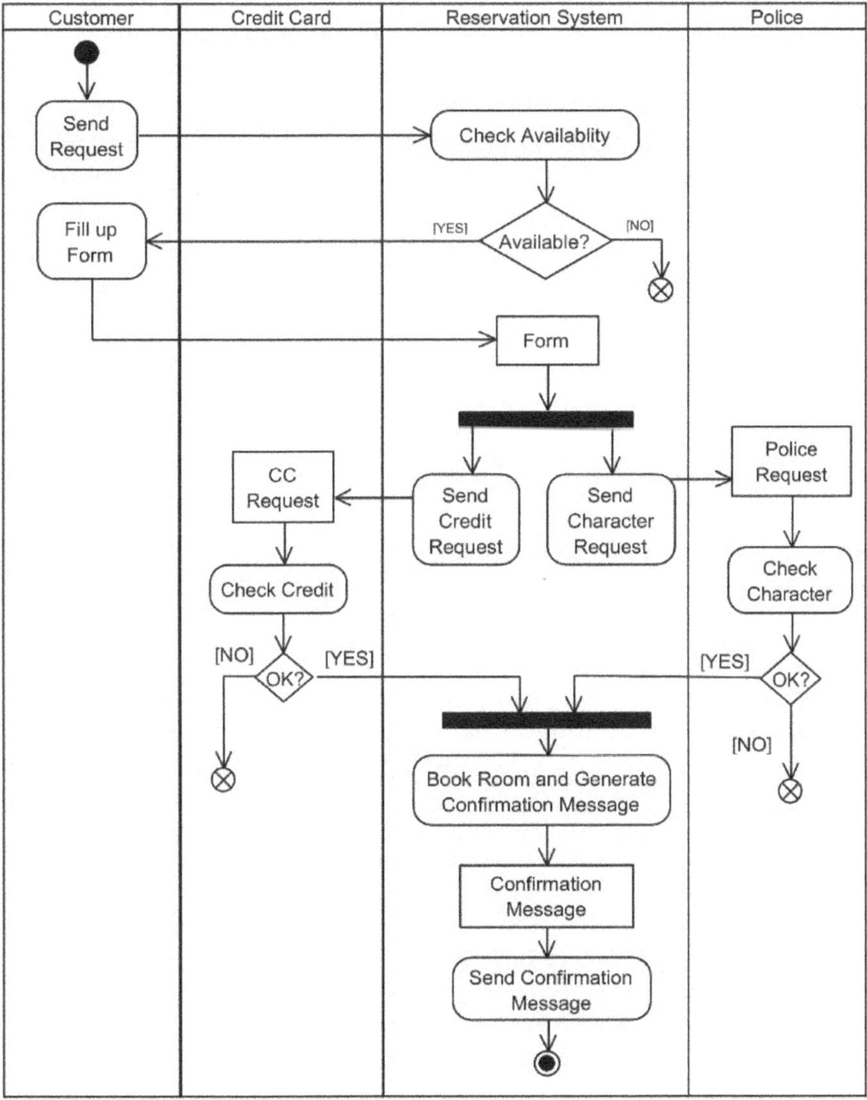

Figure 5.59: Activity Diagram for Hotel Reservation System

Activity Flow:

1. Customer Sends Request

    a. Customer initiates a booking request.

2. Reservation System Checks Availability

    a. System checks if a room is available.

3. Decision: Room Available?

    a. If NO: process terminates (end of line marked with an "X").

    b. If YES: proceed to next step.

4. Customer Fills up Form

    a. Customer fills a form with personal details.

5. Parallel Activities (Two processes happen simultaneously):

    a. Send Credit Request to the Credit Card company.

    b. Send Character Request to the Police department.

6. Credit Card Checks Credit:

    a. Verifies if customer's credit is acceptable.

    b. If NO: process terminates.

    c. If YES: continue.

7. Police Checks Character:

    a. Checks if customer has any criminal issues.

    b. If NO: process terminates.

    c. If YES: continue.

8. Reservation System Books Room:

    a. After both Credit and Character checks succeed, the room is booked.

9. Confirmation Message:

   a. Reservation system generates and sends a confirmation message to the customer.

10. Process Ends (final circle with border).

In Simple Words:

Customer → Checks availability → Fills form → Credit & Character verification → Book room → Send confirmation → Done!

5.10. Conclusion

Open Source Tools for UML Design

- StarUML (older versions) - Originally free and open-source (StarUML 1.x). Later versions are paid, but StarUML 1 is still usable for basic UML. Features: Class, Sequence, Activity diagrams, etc. Platform: Windows, MacOS, Linux (through Wine).

- Modelio - Full modeling tool, supports UML, BPMN, and SysML. Customizable with modules and plugins. Platform: Windows, Linux, MacOS.

- Umbrello UML Modeller - Part of the KDE project. Great for lightweight UML diagrams. Platform: Linux (native), Windows (port available).

- ArgoUML - One of the oldest open-source UML tools. Simple, intuitive (but looks old-fashioned). Platform: Java-based (works on Windows, Linux, Mac).

- Draw.io / Diagrams.net - Not purely "UML-focused" but very easy to draw UML diagrams. Completely free, open source. Platform: Web, Desktop app (Windows, MacOS, Linux).

- PlantUML - Text-based UML generation. You write simple code, and it generates diagrams. Great for embedding in codebases or documentation. Platform: Java-based, online editors available.

- Papyrus UML - Eclipse-based modeling environment. Very powerful for complex models (UML2). Heavy if you need just simple diagrams. Platform: Windows, Linux, MacOS.

Quick Recommendation:

- Want graphical drag-drop? → Try Modelio or Draw.io.

- Want code-based diagrams? → Use PlantUML.

- Need lightweight & simple? → Umbrello.

Object-Oriented Software Design (OOSD) is a foundational methodology that emphasizes modeling software systems as a collection of interacting objects, each defined by attributes and behaviors. This paradigm closely mirrors real-world systems, promoting better modularity, scalability, and reuse of code. Through key principles like encapsulation, inheritance, and polymorphism, OOSD supports the creation of software that is easier to maintain and extend. By organizing software into logical units (classes and objects), it enhances collaboration, clarity, and adaptability during development.

Unified Modeling Language (UML) serves as a powerful visual language for documenting, designing, and understanding object-oriented systems. It provides a standardized set of diagrams—such as class diagrams, use case diagrams, sequence diagrams, and activity diagrams—that help developers visualize system structure and behavior. UML bridges the gap between abstract design and implementation, facilitating communication among stakeholders and ensuring a well-defined system architecture. Together, OOSD and UML empower developers to build robust and well-structured software systems through clear and consistent design practices.

Chapter 6

Software Testing

6.1. Overview of Software Testing

Software testing is the process of evaluating and verifying that a software product or application does what it is supposed to do. The main objective is to find software bugs and ensure that the software is reliable and meets the requirements.

Error, Fault, Defect, Bug, and Failure – Difference

Error

A human mistake made by a developer, such as a typo or incorrect logic in the code. It occurs during the design or coding phase.

Example: A programmer accidentally writes a = b - c instead of a = b + c.

Fault

The result of an error in the code. It is an incorrect step, process, or data definition in a program.

Example: The wrong calculation (b − c) becomes part of the software's source code.

Defect

A flaw in the software that causes it to behave unexpectedly. It is often used interchangeably with fault.

Example: The incorrect logic is compiled into the software, and under certain inputs, it gives wrong results.

Bug

An informal term commonly used by developers and testers to refer to a defect or fault in the software.

Example: A tester reports a "bug" where a button doesn't perform the expected action due to a coding mistake.

Failure

Occurs when the software does not perform its intended function during execution, often due to a defect.

Example: The software crashes when a user tries to log in because of a previously undetected fault.

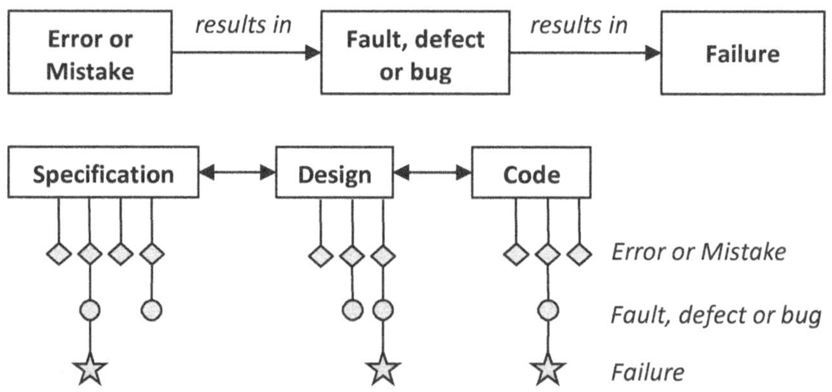

Figure 6.1: Error, Fault, Defect, Bug, and Failure

In Short:

- Error → Human action (during coding)

- Fault/Defect/Bug → Problem in the code

- Failure → Incorrect behavior during execution

Note:

- IEEE standard 1044, 1993 defined errors and faults as synonyms

- IEEE Revision of standard 1044 in 2010 introduced finer distinctions

Testing is the activity to detect errors from all the previous phases of a software project.

Importance of Software Testing:

- Detects defects early

- Ensures software quality

- Improves customer satisfaction

- Saves costs in the long run

Types of Software Testing

Manual Testing: Testing carried out manually by a tester without using any automated tools.

Automated Testing: Testing performed using automated tools to execute test cases.

Functional Testing:

- Unit Testing: Tests individual components.

- Integration Testing: Tests interaction between integrated units.

- System Testing: Tests the complete integrated system.

- Acceptance Testing: Validates the end-to-end business flow.

Non-functional Testing:

- Performance Testing: Assesses speed and responsiveness.

- Security Testing: Identifies vulnerabilities.

- Usability Testing: Measures ease of use.

- Compatibility Testing: Checks operation across different environments.

6.2. Software Testing Life Cycle (STLC)

The Software Testing Life Cycle (STLC) is a systematic process that ensures quality and effectiveness in software testing. It consists of several sequential phases, each with specific goals and deliverables.

1. Requirement Analysis:

- Understand and analyze testing requirements based on software specifications.

- Identify types of tests to be performed.

- Involve stakeholders to clarify doubts.

2. Test Planning:

- Create a testing strategy and define the scope of testing.

- Allocate resources and estimate time and cost.

- Determine testing tools, risk mitigation, and deliverables.

3. Test Case Design:

- Design detailed test cases and test scripts.

- Prepare test data.

- Review and baseline test cases.

4. Test Environment Setup:

- Prepare hardware, software, and network configuration.

- Set up tools and frameworks.

- Validate the environment with a smoke test.

5. Test Execution:

- Execute test cases.

- Log defects in a bug tracking system.

- Retest and perform regression testing as needed.

6. Test Closure:

- Evaluate exit criteria.

- Prepare a test summary report.

- Archive test artifacts and document lessons learned.

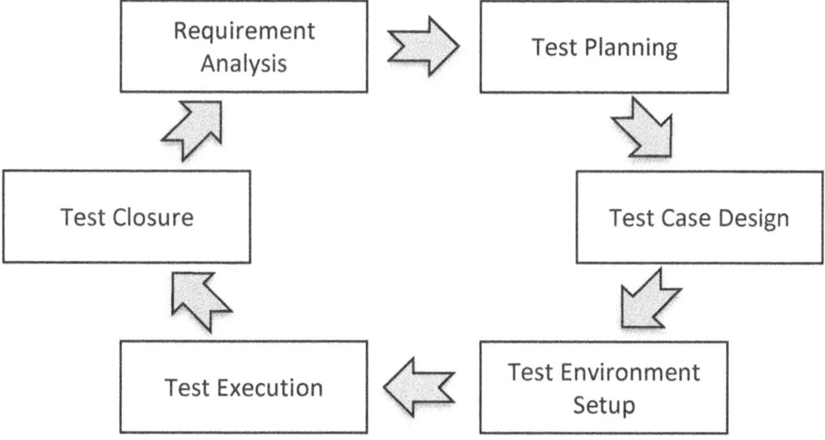

Figure 6.2: Software Testing Life Cycle

Here is a simple diagram representing the STLC phases:

Requirement Analysis → Test Planning → Test Case Design → Test Environment Setup → Test Execution → Test Closure

Each phase plays a crucial role in ensuring the software is thoroughly tested before release.

6.3. Testing Techniques

Black Box Testing: Focuses on inputs and outputs without knowing the internal code. Black Box testing is also known as **Functional testing**.

Black box testing, also known as behavioral testing, focuses on evaluating the functional requirements of a system without delving into its internal implementation details. In this approach, the system is treated as a "black box," meaning the tester is only concerned with the inputs and expected outputs, not how the system processes those inputs internally.

This type of testing is ideal for validating that the system behaves as intended under various conditions. In contrast, white box testing requires a thorough understanding of the system's internal structure and logic.

Black box testing is further classified into two primary techniques: Boundary Value Analysis (BVA), which tests the edges of input ranges, and Equivalence Class Partitioning (ECP) or Equivalence Class Analysis (ECA), which divides input data into valid and invalid partitions to reduce the number of test cases while maintaining coverage.

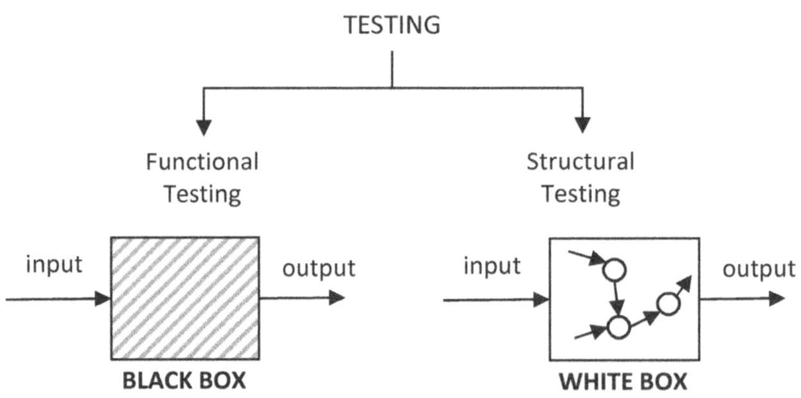

Figure 6.3: Software Testing Techniques

White Box Testing: Involves testing internal logic and code structure. White Box testing is also known as **Structural testing**. White box testing, sometimes referred to as glass box testing, is used to verify the functional requirements of a system by examining its internal structure and logic.

Unlike black box testing, it requires knowledge of the code and is often performed by developers. There are several key techniques in white box testing:

1. **Statement Coverage:** This ensures that every statement in the program is executed at least once. The goal is to verify that all lines of code are tested, as unexecuted code cannot be checked for potential errors.

2. **Branch Coverage:** Also known as edge testing, this technique involves designing test cases to evaluate all possible branches in the decision points of the code, ensuring each condition is tested with both true and false outcomes.

3. **Condition Coverage:** This method ensures that each individual condition within a decision is tested for both true and false outcomes. For example, in a condition like if (C1 AND C2 OR C3), each condition (C1, C2, and C3) would be tested separately with both true and false values. This provides more thorough testing than branch coverage.

4. **Path Coverage:** In this approach, test cases are designed to execute all linearly independent paths in the program at least once. The number of such paths is determined using a Control Flow Graph (CFG), making this technique particularly useful for identifying missing or redundant logic. CFG is thoroughly discussed in section 6.4.

Gray Box Testing: Combines black and white box approaches.

Exploratory Testing: Tester explores the application without predefined cases.

Regression Testing: Re-tests after changes to ensure existing functionalities work.

6.4. Cyclomatic Complexity using CFG

6.4.1. Control Flow Graph (CFG)

Definition:

A Control Flow Graph is a graphical representation of all paths that might be traversed through a program during its execution. Each node in the graph represents a block of code (a sequence of statements with no branches), and each directed edge represents the flow of control from one block to another.

Purpose in White Box Testing:

CFG helps visualize the structure of the code and identify all possible execution paths. It's a fundamental tool for analyzing path coverage in white box testing.

6.4.2. Cyclomatic Complexity

Definition:

Cyclomatic Complexity is a quantitative measure of the number of linearly independent paths through a program's source code.

Importance:

- o Helps determine the minimum number of test cases for full path coverage.

- o Indicates code complexity and potential maintainability.

Formula:

<u>Method 1</u>: The Cyclomatic complexity, V(G) for a flow graph G can be defined as

$$V(G) = E - N + 2$$

where, E is total number of edges in the flow graph

N is the total number of nodes in the flow graph.

<u>Method 2</u>: The Cyclomatic complexity V (G) for a flow graph G can be defined as

$$V(G) = P + 1$$

where, P is the number of predicate nodes contained in the flow G

<u>Method 3</u>: The Cyclomatic complexity, V(G) for a flow graph G can be defined as the total number of regions (R). Regions are the closed area by nodes and edges and the outside area of the graph.

$$V(G) = R$$

Note: All formulae must produce the same result for a particular problem.

<u>Example 1</u>:

Find out number of independent paths for the following function:

```c
int main(){
    int fact = 1, i, n;
    printf("Enter a number:\n");
    scanf("%d",$n);
    if(n>0){
        for(i=1;i<=n;i++)
            fact *= i;
    }
    printf("Factorial = %d\n",fact);
    return 0;
}
```

Solution:

Steps to solve the problem -

1) Number each statement in the program

```
1.  int main(){

2.      int fact = 1, i, n;

3.      printf("Enter a number:\n");

4.      scanf("%d",$n);

5.      if(n>0){

6.              for(i=1;i<=n;i++)

7.                      fact *= i;

8.      }

9.      printf("Factorial = %d\n",fact);

10.     return 0;

11. }
```

2) These numbers serve as nodes. Use them to draw the Control Flow Graph. An edge from one node to another exists if control transfers from one node to another.

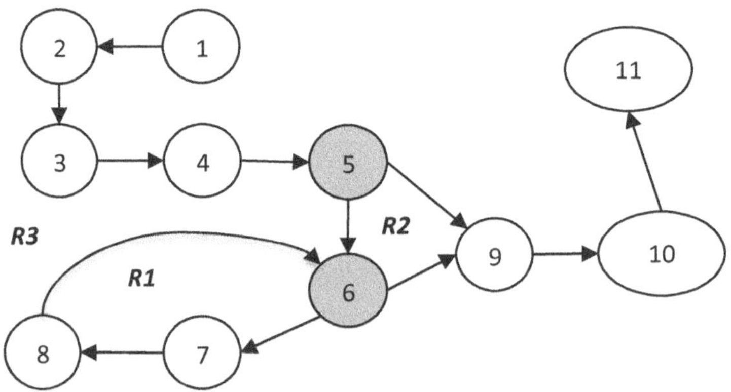

Figure 6.4: Control Flow Graph for Example 1

3) Apply the formula to calculate Cyclomatic Complexity.

$V(G) = E - N + 2 = 12 - 11 + 2 = 3$

$V(G) = P + 1 = 2 + 1 = 3$

$V(G) = R = 3$ (Regions are denoted by R1, R2 and R3 in figure 6.4)

4) Determine a basis set of linearly independent paths.

As $V(G) = 3$, there will be 3 independent paths as follows -

$1 \rightarrow 2 \rightarrow 3 \rightarrow 4 \rightarrow 5 \rightarrow 9 \rightarrow 10 \rightarrow 11$

$1 \rightarrow 2 \rightarrow 3 \rightarrow 4 \rightarrow 5 \rightarrow 6 \rightarrow 7 \rightarrow 8 \rightarrow 6 \rightarrow 9 \rightarrow 10 \rightarrow 11$

$1 \rightarrow 2 \rightarrow 3 \rightarrow 4 \rightarrow 5 \rightarrow 6 \rightarrow 7 \rightarrow 8 \rightarrow 6 \rightarrow \ldots 6 \rightarrow 9 \rightarrow 10 \rightarrow 11$

<u>Example 2:</u>

Find out number of independent paths for the following function:

```
void function1(){
    int n;
    printf("Enter a number:\n");
    scanf("%d",$n);
    while(n>0){
        if(n%5==0)
            printf("Output 1\n");
        else if(n%2==0)
            printf("Output 2\n");
        else
            printf("Output 3\n");
    }
```

```
        return;

    }
```

Solution:

Steps to solve the problem -

1) Number each statement in the program

```
1. void function1(){
2.     int n;
3.     printf("Enter a number:\n");
4.     scanf("%d",$n);
5.     while(n>0){
6.             if(n%5==0)
7.                     printf("Output 1\n");
8.             else if(n%2==0)
9.                     printf("Output 2\n");
10.            else
11.                    printf("Output 3\n");
12.    }
13.    return;
14. }
```

2) These numbers serve as nodes. Use them to draw the Control Flow Graph. An edge from one node to another exists if control transfers from one node to another.

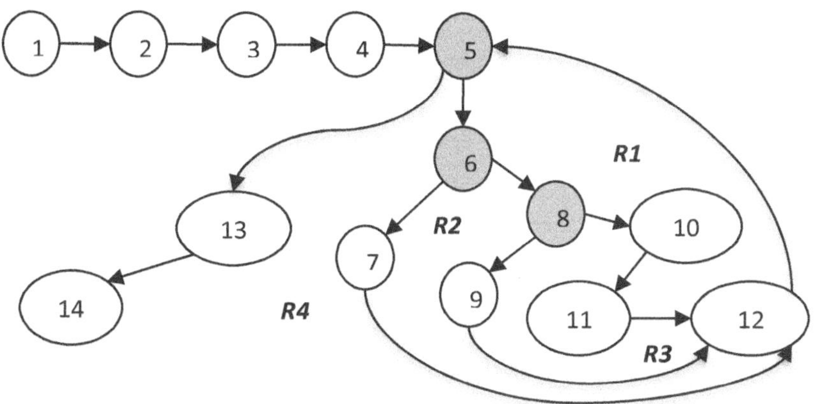

Figure 6.5: Control Flow Graph for Example 2

3) Apply the formula to calculate Cyclomatic Complexity.

$V(G) = E - N + 2 = 14 - 12 + 2 = 4$

$V(G) = P + 1 = 3 + 1 = 4$

$V(G) = R = 4$ (Regions are denoted by R1, R2, R3 and R4 in figure 6.5)

4) Determine a basis set of linearly independent paths.

As $V(G) = 4$, there will be 4 independent paths as follows -

$1 \rightarrow 2 \rightarrow 3 \rightarrow 4 \rightarrow 5 \rightarrow 13 \rightarrow 14$

$1 \rightarrow 2 \rightarrow 3 \rightarrow 4 \rightarrow 5 \rightarrow 6 \rightarrow 7 \rightarrow 12 \rightarrow 5 \rightarrow \ldots 13 \rightarrow 14$

$1 \rightarrow 2 \rightarrow 3 \rightarrow 4 \rightarrow 5 \rightarrow 6 \rightarrow 8 \rightarrow 9 \rightarrow 12 \rightarrow 5 \rightarrow \ldots 13 \rightarrow 14$

$1 \rightarrow 2 \rightarrow 3 \rightarrow 4 \rightarrow 5 \rightarrow 6 \rightarrow 8 \rightarrow 10 \rightarrow 11 \rightarrow 12 \rightarrow 5 \rightarrow \ldots 13 \rightarrow 14$

6.5. Case Studies

Case Study 1: E-Commerce Website Testing

Overview: Online shopping platform

Objectives:

- Validate user login and registration

- Test shopping cart functionality

- Test payment gateway integration

- Tools Used: Selenium, JIRA

Challenges:

- Browser compatibility

- Intermittent payment failures

Resolutions:

- Added cross-browser test scripts

- Simulated load to replicate payment issues

Case Study 2: Mobile App Testing

Overview: Food delivery application

Devices/OS Tested: Android and iOS

Testing Focus:

- Installation and updates

- GPS functionality

- Push notifications

Automation Tools: Appium, BrowserStack

Challenges:

- Device fragmentation

- Network variability

Solutions:

- Used cloud device farms

- Added offline support tests

Case Study 3: API Testing for FinTech Application

API Function: Handles financial transactions

Tools Used: Postman, Swagger

Testing Focus:

- Authentication and authorization

- Rate limiting

- Data integrity and security

Lessons Learned:

- Security testing is crucial

- Mock services helped isolate issues

6.6. Conclusion

Best Practices in Software Testing

- Write clear and concise test cases

- Automate repetitive tests

- Maintain test documentation

- Integrate testing into CI/CD pipelines

- Perform root cause analysis of bugs

Tools for Software Testing

- Selenium: Web automation

- JUnit/TestNG: Java-based unit testing

- Postman: API testing

- JMeter: Performance testing

- JIRA/Bugzilla: Bug tracking and project management

Software testing ensures the quality, functionality, and reliability of applications. By applying structured testing methods and tools, developers and testers can deliver better software. Staying updated with industry trends and tools is vital for continuous improvement.

Chapter 7

Software Project Management

7.1. Overview

Software Project Management (SPM) is the application of knowledge, tools, skills, and techniques to project activities to meet software development goals efficiently and effectively.

Software Project Management (SPM) is a technique to enable a group of software developers to work efficiently towards successful completion of the project.

In the context of software engineering, SPM focuses on managing all aspects of a software project from initiation to closure. This includes defining project scope, estimating cost and time, scheduling tasks, managing risks, ensuring quality, and leading teams to deliver software that meets customer requirements.

Objectives of Software Project Management

- Deliver software on time and within budget

- Meet or exceed quality expectations

- Effectively manage people, tools, and processes

- Minimize risks and handle changes efficiently

Why SPM Matters

Without structured project management, software teams often:

- Miss deadlines

- Overrun budgets

- Build products that fail to meet user needs

- Struggle with scope creep and uncontrolled changes

SPM provides a systematic framework to tackle these challenges, ensuring that projects are predictable, repeatable, and measurable.

7.2. Software Project Planning

Once a project is found to be feasible, the project planning has to be done. Project planning consists of the following essential activities -

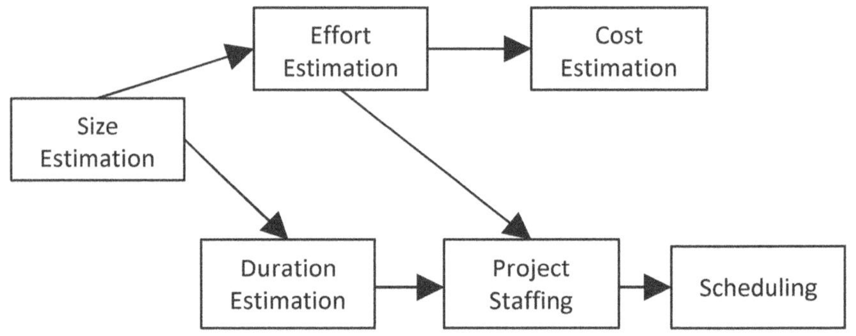

Figure 7.1: Software Project Planning

Estimation – the following activities have to be estimated –

1. Cost – how much it is going to cost to develop the product?

2. Duration – how long it is going to take to develop the product?

3. Effort – how much effort would be required to develop the product?

The effectiveness of all other planning activities are based on the accuracy of these estimations.

Staffing – staff organization and plan has to be made.

Scheduling – after the estimations are made, the schedules for manpower and other resources have to be done.

Risk Management – risk identification, analysis and abatement planning have to be done.

Miscellaneous Plans – several other plans such as quality assurance plan, configuration management plan have to be done.

7.3. Software Project Metrics

> *-   A software measure is a mapping from a set of objects in the software engineering world into a set of mathematical constructs such as numbers and vectors of numbers.*
>
> *-   McClure, 1994*

A software measurement is a technique or method that applies software measures to a class of software engineering objects to achieve predefined goals. A software measure is a simple quantitative measure derivable from any attribute of the software life cycle.

It is possible to quantify effort required in the development of a software system. Measures of effort help allocation of resources to test, modify and maintain a system. The benefit of software measurement is an identification of what might be done to improve the software process as well as the software entities derived from the process.

What Software Metric does

- Measure and predict software processes

- Measure and predict necessary resources for a project

- Measure and predict work products for a software development effort

- Quantify properties of existing and planned software products

Basic Consideration of Software Metrics

Five characteristics of software measurement can be identified as –

- Object of Measurement – ranges from products to processes and projects

- Purpose of Measurement – such as characterization, assessment, evaluation and prediction

- Source of Measurement – such as software designers, testers and managers

- Measured Property – such as cost, reliability, size, portability, maintainability of the software

- Context of Measurement – where the software artifacts are measured in different environments

Size Oriented Metrics

Size oriented metrics are derived from normalizing quantity and/or productivity size of the software. Let us consider that a software organization maintains simple records in a table of size oriented metrics as given in table 7.1. The table lists each software development project that has been completed with all corresponding measures. To develop metrics that can be assimilated with similar metrics from other projects, LOC has been chosen as the normalization value.

Project	LOC	Effort	Cost	Errors	People
Alpha	12,100	24	168K	134	3
Beta	27,200	62	440K	1224	5
Gamma	20,200	43	314K	10503	6

Table 7.1: Records of three different projects

From the rudimentary data contain in the table, a set of simple size-oriented metrics can be developed for each project such as –

- Errors per KLOC (thousand lines of code)

- Defects per KLOC

- Cost per KLOC

- Pages of documentation per KLOC etc.

Or, if person-months (Effort) is chosen for normalization, then size oriented metrics would be –

- Errors per person-months

- KLOC per person-months

- Cost per person-months etc.

Size oriented metrics are not universally accepted because of some controversy, such as –

- KLOC / LOC is subjective in nature

- It correlates poorly with efficiency and quality of code

- KLOC / LOC cannot be of equal weight for procedural programming and object oriented programming

- KLOC / LOC may be different for the same problem with different programmers, as shown in figure 7.2.

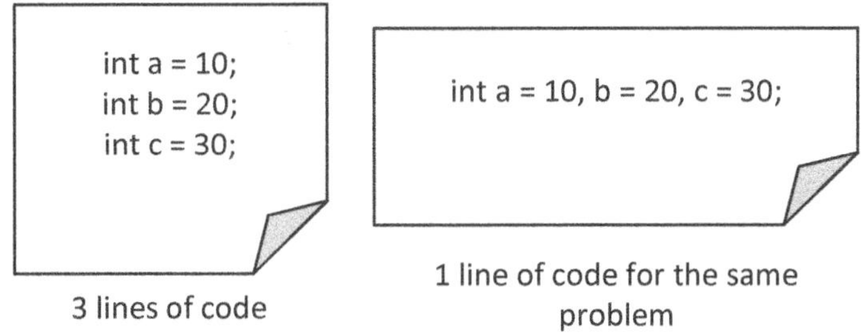

Figure 7.2: Different LOC for the same problem

To overcome this problem, we can use Function Point (FP) Oriented Metrics, which is discussed in detail in section 7.4. Let's have a look at the differences between Size Oriented Metrics (LOC) vs Function Point (FP) Oriented Metrics in table 7.2.

Size Oriented Metrics (LOC) vs Function Point (FP) Oriented Metrics

Lines of Code (LOC)	Function Point (FP)
Depends on programming language	Independent of programming language
Measures "how much code"	Measures "how much functionality"
Not good for early estimation	Can estimate early (even before coding)
Hard to compare between systems	Easier to compare between different systems

Table 7.2: Differences between LOC and FP

7.4. Function Point Analysis

Function Points (FP) measure the size of a software project based on the functionality it provides to the user, not based on the number of lines of code (LOC). It focuses on what the system does rather than how it is built.

In short: Function Points = A way to measure software based on features the user cares about.

A brief history of Function Point Analysis

The following shows a brief history of function points, beginning with the introduction of the concept by Alan Albrecht in 1979.

1979	FPs introduced by Alan Albrecht
1984	First FP guidelines
1986	First IFPUG Board of Directors
1994	CPM Release 4.0

2003   ISO standard

Details of Functions in Function Point Analysis

Function Point Analysis (FPA) is a method to break systems into smaller components for better understanding and analysis. In counting FP, there are 5 standard functions –

1. Internal Logical Files (ILF) – Tables maintained by the system

2. External Interface Files (EIF) – Data files used but maintained by another system

3. External Inputs (EI) – User entering data into a form

4. External Outputs (EO) – System generating a report

5. External Inquiries (EQ) – Search functions (no update to database)

Figure 7.3 shows the classification of different functions in Function Point Analysis.

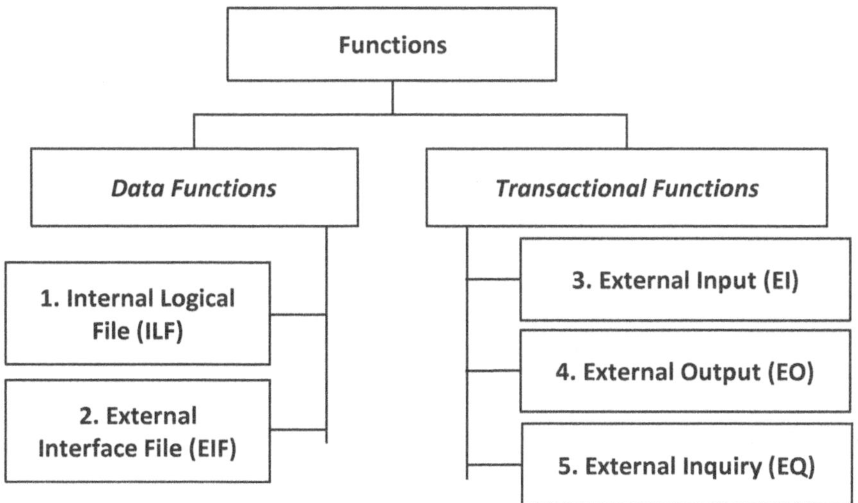

Figure 7.3: Classification functions in FPA

Figure 7.4 shows how Function Point Analysis classifies different types of interactions between an application and its users or external systems. Here, Application is the software system for which FPA will be calculated. It contains an Internal Logical File (ILF) — a database or file managed by the application.

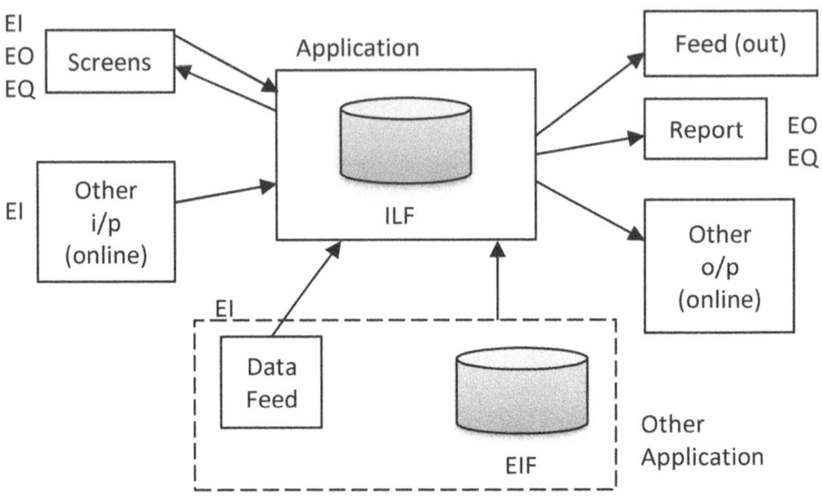

Figure 7.4: Interactions among functions in FPA

Users can input data (EI), receive outputs (EO), or query data (EQ) via screens. Data entered from online forms, APIs, etc. into the application. The application sends data feeds out to other systems via Feed (out). The application generates reports (EO) and handles report queries (EQ). Other online outputs from the application to users or systems. Data is coming into the application from another system (External Input). It is reading from EIF (External Interface File).

Some Definitions required to understand each of the functions -

- **User-Identifiable:** it refers to the defined requirements for processes and/or group of data and understood by both users and the developers.

- **Control Information:** this is the data that influences an elementary process of the application.

- **Elementary Process:** it is a smallest unit of activity that is meaningful to the user.

- **Data Element Type (DET):** it is a unique, user-recognizable, non-repeated field.

- **File Type Referenced (FTR):** a file that is referenced by a transaction.

- **Record Element Type (RET):** it is a user-recognizable sub-group of data elements within ILF or EIF.

Explanation of each function used in FPA

1. Internal Logical File (ILF)

An ILF is a user-identifiable group of logically related data or control information maintained within the boundary of the application. It is maintained through EI. An ILF should have one external input.

Example: Tables in RDBMS. Flat Files, Control Information, LDAP data stores etc.

Complexity Matrix and Weight Matrix for ILF is shown in figure 7.5.

No. of RET	No. of DET				Complexity	Weight
	1 - 19	20 - 50	> 50			
1	Simple	Simple	Average		Simple	7
2 – 5	Simple	Average	Complex		Average	10
> 5	Average	Complex	Complex		Complex	15

Figure 7.5: ILF Complexity Matrix and Weight Matrix

2. External Interface File (EIF)

An EIF is a user-identifiable group of logically related data or control information referenced by the application, but maintained within the boundary of the other application. The EIF is ILF of another application. An application may count a file / function as either ILF or EIF but not both.

Example: Tables in RDBMS, Flat Files, Control Information. LDAP data stores etc.

Complexity Matrix and Weight Matrix for EIF is shown in figure 7.6.

No. of	No. of DET				Complexity	Weight
RET	1 - 19	20 - 50	> 50		Complexity	Weight
1	Simple	Simple	Average		Simple	5
2 – 5	Simple	Average	Complex		Average	7
> 5	Average	Complex	Complex		Complex	10

Figure 7.6: EIF Complexity Matrix and Weight Matrix

3. External Input (EI)

An external input is an elementary process that processes the data or control information coming from outside of the application boundary.

Example: Data entry by users, Data / file feed by external application etc.

Complexity Matrix and Weight Matrix for EI is shown in figure 7.7.

No. of	No. of DET				Complexity	Weight
FTR	1 - 4	5 - 15	> 15		Complexity	Weight
< 2	Simple	Simple	Average		Simple	3
2	Simple	Average	Complex		Average	4
> 2	Average	Complex	Complex		Complex	6

Figure 7.7: EI Complexity Matrix and Weight Matrix

4. External Output (EO)

An external output is an elementary process that sends the data or control information outside of the application boundary.

Example: Report created by application etc.

Complexity Matrix and Weight Matrix for EO is shown in figure 7.8.

5. External Inquiry (EQ)

An external inquiry is an elementary process that deals with both input and output components and results in data retrieval from one more ILF and EIF.

Complexity Matrix and Weight Matrix for EQ is shown in figure 7.9.

No. of	No. of DET				Complexity	Weight
FTR	1 - 5	6 - 19	> 19		Complexity	Weight
< 2	Simple	Simple	Average		Simple	4
2 – 3	Simple	Average	Complex		Average	5
> 3	Average	Complex	Complex		Complex	7

Figure 7.8: EO Complexity Matrix and Weight Matrix

No. of	No. of DET				Complexity	Weight
FTR	1 - 5	6 - 19	> 19		Complexity	Weight
< 2	Simple	Simple	Average		Simple	3
2 – 3	Simple	Average	Complex		Average	4
> 3	Average	Complex	Complex		Complex	6

Figure 7.9: EQ Complexity Matrix and Weight Matrix

7.5. Calculating Effort Using FPA

Function Point Analysis helps you estimate the effort (time and cost) required to develop a software system early, even before coding starts.

Step-by-Step Process:

1. Calculate the Unadjusted Function Points (UFP)

First step is to count the number of Internal Logical Files (ILF), External Interface Files (EIF), External Inputs (EI), External Outputs (EO) and External Inquiries (EQ). Each has a weight based on complexity: Simple, Average, Complex → each type has different weight values as shown in the previous section.

Then add all the count of functions multiplied with their weight to get the UFP. UFP is the simple sum of all weights of all functions depending upon type, scope and boundary of the count.

2. Calculate the Value Adjustment Factor (VAF)

The VAF is based on 14 General System Characteristics (GSC) to rate the general functionality of the system being counted. The GSCs represent characteristics of the application. Each is weighted on a scale from 0 to 5 as follows –

0 – no influence   3 – average influence

1 – incidental influence   4 – significant influence

2 – moderate influence   5 – strong influence

The 14 GSCs are -

1) Data communication   8) Online update

2) Distributed data processing   9) Complex processing

3) Performance   10) Reusability

4 – Heavily used configuration   11) Installation ease

5) Transaction rate   12) Operational ease

6) Online data entry   13) Multiple sites

7) End user efficiency   14) Facilitate change

Evaluate 14 General System Characteristics (like reliability, performance, usability, etc.) with their factor rated from 0 to 5. Total Degree of Influence (TDI) is the sum of scores for the 14 factors.

Now the Value Adjustment Factor (VAF) can be calculated as -

$$\textbf{VAF} = \textbf{0.65} + (\textbf{0.01} \times \textbf{TDI})$$

3. Calculate the Adjusted Function Points (AFP)

Now adjust the UFP based on VAF as -

Adjusted Function Point = Unadjusted Function Point * Value Adjustment Factor. In short –

$$AFP = UFP \times VAF$$

Note: Adjusted Function Points (AFP) = the final software size measure.

4. Estimate Effort

Finally, an effort rate – the number of hours, days or months needed per function point can be used. Typical industry standard effort rates are -

- Simple apps: 3–5 hours per FP

- Medium complexity apps: 7–10 hours per FP

- Very complex apps: 10–15 hours per FP

The formula:

Effort (Person-Hours) = AFP × Hours per FP   [...... Formula 1]

Sometimes, Contribution Percentage is given instead of Hours per FP. In this scenario, Effort can be calculated as -

Development Platform FP = AFP × Contribution Percentage

Effort (Person-Months) = Development Platform FP / Productivity FP per Person-Month   [...... Formula 2]

Effort (Person-Hours) = Development Platform FP × hours per month / Productivity FP per Person-Month   [...... Formula 3]

Note: The effort rate (hours per FP) depends on your team's past data or industry averages. Productivity can vary by technology, team experience, and project complexity.

Function Points can also be used to estimate cost:

Cost = Effort × Cost per Person-Hour

Example Walkthrough

Example 1: Let's say UFP = 100, Total Degree of Influence = 30

Therefore, VAF = 0.65 + (0.01 × 30) = 0.95

AFP = 100 × 0.95 = 95

If effort rate = 7 hours per FP, then

Effort = 95 × 7 = 665 person-hours

So 665 person-hours would be the estimated effort.

Example 2: Student Management System (Small Project)

We are building a basic system that allows:

- Students to register.

- Admins to manage students and courses.

- Reports to be generated for enrolled students.

Step 1: Identify and Count the Function Types

Type	Description	Count	Complexity	Weight
External Inputs (EI)	Student Registration, Course Enrollment	5	Average	4
External Outputs (EO)	Generate Student Report, List of Courses	4	Average	5
External Inquiries (EQ)	Search Student by Name or ID	3	Simple	3
Internal Logical Files (ILF)	Student Database, Course Database	2	Average	7
External Interface Files (EIF)	University System feed for Courses	1	Simple	5

Using standard FP weights for "Average" and "Simple" complexity:

Step 2: Calculate the Unadjusted Function Points (UFP)

$$UFP = (5 \times 4) + (4 \times 5) + (3 \times 3) + (2 \times 7) + (1 \times 5)$$

$$= (20) + (20) + (9) + (14) + (5)$$

$$= 68$$

Therefore, Unadjusted Function Points (UFP) = 68

Step 3: Calculate the Value Adjustment Factor (VAF)

Suppose we evaluate the 14 general system characteristics (like performance, usability, security, etc.) and their total score is 32.

Using the VAF formula:

$$VAF = 0.65 + (0.01 \times 32) = 0.65 + 0.32 = 0.97$$

Step 4: Calculate the Adjusted Function Points (AFP)

$$AFP = UFP \times VAF = 68 \times 0.97 = 65.96 = 66 \text{ (approximately)}$$

Therefore, Adjusted Function Points = 66

Step 5: Estimate the Effort

Suppose based on past projects, your team productivity is around 7 hours per Function Point.

Thus, Effort = 66 × 7 = 462 person-hours

Therefore, Estimated Effort = 462 person-hours

Step 6: (Optional) Estimate Cost

If your team charges $30 per hour, then:

Cost = 462 × $30 = $13,860

Therefore, Estimated Project Cost = $13,860

Final Results Summary:

Item	Result
Unadjusted Function Points (UFP)	68
Value Adjustment Factor (VAF)	0.97
Adjusted Function Points (AFP)	66

Estimated Effort	462 person-hours
Estimated Cost (optional)	$13,860

Example 3: Problem Statement

The number of all types of functions in a project is given as follows:

	ILF	EIF	EI	EO	EQ
Simple	12	6	5	5	10
Average	14	14	15	11	6
Complex	20	20	0	12	11

Among all the General System Characteristics (GSC), three are having moderate influence (2), three are having average influence (3), two are having strong influence (5) and others are having no influence (0) on the system.

Other parameters are:

Contribution percentage = 70%

Productivity FP per Staff Month = 135

No of working days per month = 25

No of working hours per day = 6

Now perform the following:

    a.   Calculate the Adjusted Function Point.

    b.   Calculate the Effort in terms of person-months and person-hours.

Solution:

Input data are as follows -

	ILF	EIF	EI	EO	EQ
Simple / Low	12	6	5	5	10

| Average | 14 | 14 | 15 | 11 | 6 |
| Complex / High | 20 | 20 | 0 | 12 | 11 |

Weight values for each function are as follows -

	ILF	EIF	EI	EO	EQ
Simple / Low	7	5	3	4	3
Average	10	7	4	5	4
Complex / High	15	10	6	7	6

Unadjusted Function Point (UFP) for each Function can be calculated as -

UFP for ILF $= 12 \times 7 + 14 \times 10 + 20 \times 15 = 524$

UFP for EIF $= 6 \times 5 + 14 \times 7 + 20 \times 10 - 328$

UFP for EI $= 5 \times 3 + 15 \times 4 + 0 \times 6 = 75$

UFP for EO $= 5 \times 4 + 11 \times 5 + 12 \times 7 = 159$

UFP for EQ $= 10 \times 3 + 6 \times 4 + 11 \times 6 = 120$

Therefore, Total UFP is calculated as

UFP $= 524 + 328 + 75 + 159 + 120 = 1206$

Now, according to the problem, 3 GSCs are having weight 2, 3 are having weight 3, 2 are having weight 5.

So, Total Degree of Influence can be calculated as -

TDI $= 3 \times 2 + 3 \times 3 + 2 \times 5 = 25$

Now Value Adjustment Factor is calculated as -

VAF $= (25 \times 0.01) + 0.65 = 0.9$

Therefore, Adjusted Function Point (AFP) is calculated as -

AFP $=$ UFP $\times$ VAF $= 1208 \times 0.9 = 1087.2$ .... [Answer of part (a)]

Given

Contribution percentage = 70

Productivity FP per Staff Month = 135

No of working days per month = 25

No of working hours per day = 6

Now,

Development Platform FP = AFP × Contribution %

= 1085.4 × 70 /100

= 759.78

EFFORT = 759.78 / 135

= 5.628 person-months

= 759.78 × 25 × 6 / 135

= 844.2 person-hours ………… [Answer of part (b)]

Example 4: Bank Loan Management System

Problem Statement:

The five functions and their corresponding record element type (RET) and data element type (DET) are given as follows:

1. INTERNAL LOGICAL FILE (ILF)

SL	Description	No of Record Element Type (RET)	No of Data Element Type (DET)
1	Errror_Master	1	10
2	Op_balance_list	3	15
3	Acc_Transac	3	35
4	User_bank	2	23
5	Bank_rate	7	43

6	Bank_module	6	28
7	Recovery_module	5	18
8	Comp_module	2	12

2. EXTERNAL INTERFACE FILE (EIF)

SL	Description	No of Record Element Type (RET)	No of Data Element Type (DET)
1	Customer_Master	10	12
2	Property_Master	12	30
3	Savings_record	4	8
4	Salary_record	2	24
5	Police_record	2	55

3. EXTERNAL INPUT (EI)

SL	Description	No of File Type Referenced (FTR)	No of Data Element Type (DET)
1	Users_ Master	2	6
2	Usage_ Master	3	4
3	Loan_ Norm_Master	3	20
4	Loan_ Master	2	14
5	Account_ Master	2	2
6	Account_ Details	2	8

4.   EXTERNAL OUTPUT (EO)

SL	Description	No of File Type Referenced (FTR)	No of Data Element Type (DET)
1	User_List	1	3
2	List_permittedLoans	1	8
3	List_LoanSanctioned	1	7
4	List_Loansrepaid	1	7
5	List_interestincome	3	7
6	List_Loansoutstanding	4	8
7	List_Defaulters	1	8
8	List_NonPerfAssets	2	8
9	List_LoansRemNPAlist	2	8

5.　EXTERNAL INQUIRY (EQ)

SL	Description	No of File Type Referenced (FTR)	No of Data Element Type (DET)
1	List_Locations	2	3
2	List_Departments	1	22
3	List_Land/Plate	1	4
4	List_Bill Frequency	5	7

General System Characteristics (GSC) weights are given as follows:

Sl	Name	Wt	Sl	Name	Wt
1	Data Communications	5	8	On-Line Data Update	2
2	Distributed Functions	5	9	Complex Processing	0
3	Performance	4	10	Reusability	1
4	Heavily Used Configuration	2	11	Installation Ease	1
5	Transaction Rate	4	12	Operational Ease	1
6	On-Line Data Entry	5	13	Multiple Sites	2
7	End User Efficiency	5	14	Facilitate change	3

Other parameters are:

- Contribution percentage = 60%

- Productivity FP per Staff Month = 120

- No of working days per month = 20

- No of working hours per day = 7

- Team Charges = Rs. 250 per person-hour

Now perform the following:

a. Calculate the Adjusted Function Point.

b. Calculate the Effort in terms of person-months and person-hours.

c. Calculate the total Cost of the Project.

Solution:

Step 1: Identify and Count the Function Types

First of all, the complexity of each and every function is determined. This is done taking references from the complexity matrices given in figure 7.5 for ILF, figure 7.6 for EIF, figure 7.7 for EI, figure 7.8 for EO and figure 7.9 for EQ.

1. Internal Logical File (ILF)

SL	Description	No of RET	No of DET	Complexity
1	Errror_Master	1	10	Simple
2	Op_balance_list	3	15	Simple
3	Acc_Transac	3	35	Average
4	User_bank	2	23	Average
5	Bank_rate	7	43	Complex
6	Bank_module	6	28	Complex
7	Recovery_module	5	18	Simple
8	Comp_module	2	12	Simple

Therefore,

Count of functions for ILF is Simple = 4, Average = 2, Complex = 2

Total Function Point for ILF = (4 × 7) + (2 × 10) + (2 × 15) = 78

2. External Interface File (EIF)

SL	Description	No of RET	No of DET	Complexity
1	Customer_Master	10	12	Average
2	Property_Master	12	30	Complex
3	Savings_record	4	8	Simple
4	Salary_record	2	24	Average

5	Police_record	2	55	Complex

Therefore,

Count of functions for EIF is Simple = 1, Average = 2, Complex = 2

Total Function Point for EIF = (1 × 5) + (2 × 7) + (2 × 10) = 39

3. External Input (EI)

SL	Description	No of FTR	No of DET	Complexity
1	Users_ Master	2	6	Average
2	Usage_ Master	3	4	Average
3	Loan_ Norm_Master	3	20	Complex
4	Loan_ Master	2	14	Average
5	Account_ Master	2	2	Simple
6	Account_ Details	2	8	Average

Therefore,

Count of functions for EI is Simple = 1, Average = 4, Complex = 1

Total Function Point for EI = (1 × 3) + (4 × 4) + (1 × 6) = 25

4. External Output (EO)

SL	Description	No of FTR	No of DET	Complexity
1	User_List	1	3	Simple
2	List_permitted Loans	1	8	Simple
3	List_Loan Sanctioned	1	7	Simple
4	List_Loans repaid	1	7	Simple
5	List_interest income	3	7	Average
6	List_Loans outstanding	4	8	Complex

7	List_Defaulters	1	8	Simple
8	List_NonPerfAssets	2	8	Average
9	List_LoansRemNPAlist	2	8	Average

Therefore,

Count of functions for EO is Simple = 5, Average = 3, Complex = 1

Total Function Point for EO = (5 × 4) + (3 × 5) + (1 × 7) = 42

5. External Inquiry (EQ)

SL	Description	No of FTR	No of DET	Complexity
1	List_Locations	2	3	Simple
2	List_Departments	1	22	Average
3	List_Land/Plate	1	4	Simple
4	List_Bill Frequency	5	7	Complex

Therefore,

Count of functions for EQ is Simple = 2, Average = 1, Complex = 1

Total Function Point for EQ = (2 × 3) + (1 × 4) + (1 × 6) = 16

Step 2: Calculate the Unadjusted Function Points (UFP)

UFP = (78) + (39) + (25) + (42) + (16) = 200

Therefore, Unadjusted Function Points = 200

Step 3: Calculate the Value Adjustment Factor (VAF)

From the given data in the problem, TDI is calculated as -

TDI = 5 + 5 + 4 + 2 + 4 + 5 + 5 + 2 + 0 + 1 + 1 + 1 + 2 + 3 = 40

Using the VAF formula:

VAF = 0.65 + (0.01 × 40) = 0.65 + 0.4 = 1.05

Step 4: Calculate the Adjusted Function Points (AFP)

$AFP = UFP \times VAF = 200 \times 1.05 = 210$

Therefore, Adjusted Function Points = 210   … [Answer of part (a)]

Step 5: Estimate the Effort

Given

Contribution percentage = 60

Productivity FP per Staff Month = 120

No of working days per month = 20

No of working hours per day = 7

Now,

Development Platform FP $= AFP \times$ Contribution %

$= 210 \times 60 / 100$

$= 126$

EFFORT $= 126 / 120$

$= 1.05$ person-months

$= 126 \times 20 \times 7 / 120$

$= 147$ person-hours   ………… [Answer of part (b)]

Step 6: Estimate Cost

If the Team Charges = Rs. 250 per person-hour, then:

Cost = 147 × Rs. 250 = Rs. 36,750

Therefore, Estimated Project Cost = Rs. 36,750 … [Answer of part (c)]

7.6. Project Scheduling

Overview

Project Scheduling in software engineering is a structured approach to plan, execute, and track project tasks within defined timeframes and resource limits.

Tools like PERT and CPM support scheduling under uncertainty, while Gantt charts help visualize the final timeline, progress, and dependencies.

Project scheduling is the process of determining:

- What tasks need to be done
- When they should be started and finished
- Who should perform them
- How they are interrelated

In software engineering, scheduling is critical to on-time delivery, effective resource usage, and cost control.

Objectives of Project Scheduling

- Break down the project into manageable tasks
- Assign start and end dates to each task
- Establish task dependencies
- Assign resources (people, tools, budget)
- Identify milestones and deadlines
- Monitor and control progress
- Generate a Gantt chart as the outcome

Table 7.3 demonstrates the core components of a project schedule.

Component	Description
Activities/Tasks	Individual work units like "Design UI", "Write test cases"
Duration	Estimated time to complete each task
Dependencies	Which tasks rely on others to begin or finish
Milestones	Key events such as "Requirements Approved"
Resources	Who or what is needed (developers, testers, tools)
Start and End Dates	Scheduling timeframes for tasks
Slack/Float	Extra time a task can delay without affecting project finish
Critical Path	Longest path of dependent tasks — determines project length

Table 7.3: Core Components of a Project Schedule

Steps in Project Scheduling

Step 1: Define Project Activities (Work Breakdown Structure - WBS)

Break the project into manageable parts:

- Major Phases → Modules → Tasks

Example (for a web application):

- Phase: Requirements
    - o   Task: Conduct Interviews
    - o   Task: Document Requirements
- Phase: Design
    - o   Task: Design UI

o   Task: Review Architecture

Step 2: Estimate Task Duration

Techniques used:

- Expert Judgment

- Historical Data

- Three-Point Estimation:

  Expected Time = (O + 4M + P) / 6, where: O = optimistic, M = most likely, P = pessimistic estimates

Step 3: Determine Task Dependencies

Use tools like Dependency Tables or Precedence Diagrams to find:

- Finish-to-Start (FS)   Task B starts after Task A ends

- Start-to-Start (SS) – Task B starts when Task A starts

- Finish-to-Finish (FF) – Task B finishes when Task A finishes

Step 4: Create Network Diagram

This is a graphical representation of the order of tasks, used for critical path analysis.

Step 5: Calculate the Critical Path

Critical Path is the longest sequence of dependent tasks with zero slack.

Any delay in critical path tasks will delay the project.

Step 6: Assign Resources

Allocate: Developers, Testers, Designers, Equipment and Tools

Step 7: Develop the Schedule (Gantt Chart or Calendar View)

Use scheduling software to input: Tasks, Durations, Dependencies, and Resources

Generate a Gantt Chart – a visual timeline that shows: Task bars, Milestones, Dependencies, Progress

Step 8: Monitor and Control

During execution:

- Track progress

- Update actual vs. planned dates

- Recalculate schedule if needed

- Reschedule on changes (e.g., delays, scope changes)

The overall process of Project Scheduling is depicted in figure 7.10.

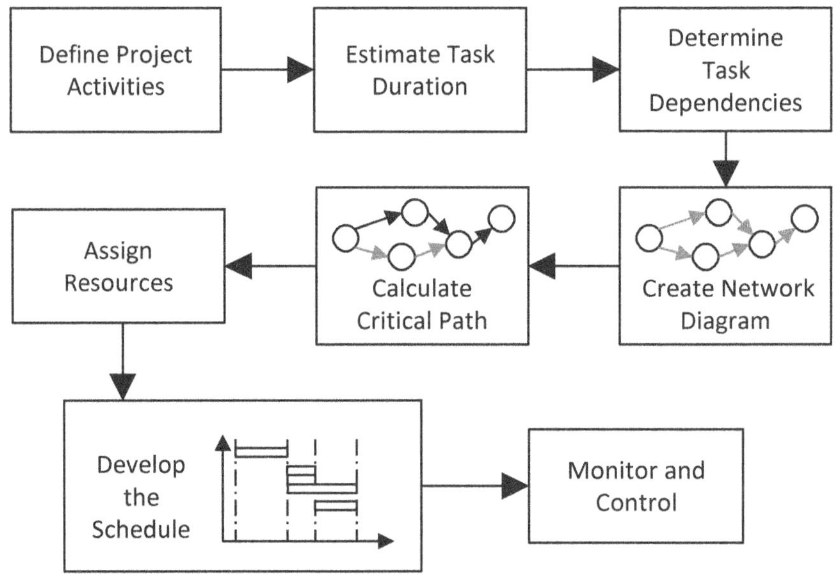

Figure 7.10: Steps in Project Scheduling

Project Scheduling Techniques

Software project scheduling techniques help plan, allocate resources, and track task progress to ensure the project is delivered on time and within scope. The right technique depends on the project size, complexity, team workflow, and uncertainty. Table 7.4 shows the summary of Project Scheduling Techniques.

Technique	Description
Gantt Chart	Visual timeline; most commonly used
PERT (Program Evaluation Review Technique)	Uses probabilistic time estimates
CPM (Critical Path Method)	Determines the longest path of dependent activities
Resource Leveling	Adjusts schedule to resolve resource conflicts
Agile Burn-Down Chart	In Agile, tracks completed vs remaining work over time

Table 7.4: Project Scheduling Techniques

1. Gantt Chart

A Gantt chart is a horizontal bar chart that visually represents the project schedule.

Features:

- Tasks are listed vertically
- Time is shown on the horizontal axis
- Bars represent task duration
- Dependencies shown with arrows
- Milestones marked as symbols (like diamonds)

Use Cases:

- Ideal for linear, well-defined projects
- Widely used in Waterfall methodology

Example:

Design UI |■■■■■■■

Backend Dev | ■■■■■■■■■

Testing | ■■■■■

Advantages:

- Easy to understand

- Visual progress tracking

- Shows overlapping tasks and timelines

Limitations:

- Becomes complex for large projects

- Doesn't handle uncertainty well

2. PERT (Program Evaluation and Review Technique)

A probabilistic technique that estimates task durations using three values:

- Optimistic (O)

- Most Likely (M)

- Pessimistic (P)

Formula: TE = (O + 4M + P) / 6

This formula gives more weight to the most likely estimate. It helps manage incomplete or uncertain information.

<u>Variance and Standard Deviation</u> - PERT also allows you to quantify risk:

Variance (σ^2) of a task is given by -

$$\sigma^2 = [(P - O) / 6]^2$$

where, Standard Deviation (σ) = (P − O) / 6

and, the Expected Variation = Sum of all Standard Deviations (σ) for the activities on critical path only.

This helps in calculating the probability of completing the entire project on time using the normal distribution.

Use Cases:

- Useful in research or innovative software projects

- Suitable when exact durations are uncertain

Advantages:

- Incorporates uncertainty

- Provides risk analysis through variance and standard deviation

- Can be used to compute on-time delivery probability

Limitations:

- Estimations can be subjective

- Requires skilled input for accuracy

3. CPM (Critical Path Method)

A technique to determine the longest sequence of dependent tasks (the critical path) that defines the shortest possible project duration.

Use Cases:

- Best for projects with predictable task durations

- Suitable for high-dependency tasks (e.g., waterfall projects)

Advantages:

- Identifies tasks that directly affect deadline

- Highlights slack (time flexibility)

- Helps focus on high-risk areas

Limitations:

- Doesn't account for duration uncertainty
- Assumes fixed estimates

4. Resource Leveling

Adjusts the schedule so that resources are not over-allocated — spreading work more evenly.

Use Cases:

- When resources (e.g., developers) are shared across tasks
- Useful in small teams with limited personnel

Advantages:

- Avoids bottlenecks due to resource overuse
- Makes workload realistic

Limitations:

- May extend the project duration
- Requires rescheduling of dependent tasks

5. Milestone Chart

A schedule showing only key events or milestones (e.g., "Design Complete", "Testing Begins").

Use Cases:

- Best for executive reporting
- Suitable for monitoring high-level goals

Advantages:

- Simple to read
- Focuses on deliverables and deadlines

Limitations:

- Doesn't show task-level details

- Can't track ongoing work

6. *Task Network Diagram (Activity Network Diagram)*

A graphical representation of tasks (nodes) and their dependencies (arrows).

- Used in both PERT and CPM

- Shows task sequence and parallelism

Use Cases:

- Helpful in identifying bottlenecks and task concurrency

- Used before generating a Gantt chart

Advantages:

- Shows full task flow and logic

- Supports critical path identification

Limitations:

- Can get complex for large projects

7. *Kanban Board (Agile Technique)*

A visual tool for tracking task status (To Do, In Progress, Done).

Use Cases:

- Suitable for Agile, Scrum, DevOps teams

- Continuous delivery pipelines

Advantages:

- Promotes real-time collaboration

- Helps limit work-in-progress

- Encourages fast feedback loops

Limitations:

- Doesn't focus on exact time duration

- Not ideal for deadline-driven projects

8. *Agile Burndown Chart*

A graph that shows work remaining vs. time for a sprint or release.

Use Cases:

- Used in Agile and Scrum to track sprint progress

Advantages:

- Quick overview of completion rate

- Helps with predictive forecasting

Limitations:

- Limited to Agile environments

- Doesn't show dependencies

Note: The choice of project scheduling technique depends on your development approach, project complexity, and resource availability. Many real-world software projects use a combination:

- PERT/CPM for early planning

- Gantt charts for tracking

- Kanban/Burndown for Agile sprints

Comparison Table:

Technique	Handles Uncertainty	Shows Dependencies	Good for Agile	Time Estimation	Visual Tracking
Gantt Chart	NO	**YES**	NO	**YES**	**YES**
PERT	**YES**	**YES**	NO	**YES** (probabilistic)	NO
CPM	NO	**YES**	NO	**YES** (deterministic)	NO
Resource Leveling	NO	**YES**	**YES**	**YES**	NO
Milestone Chart	NO	NO	**YES**	**YES**	**YES**
Task Network Diagram	NO	**YES**	NO	**YES**	**YES**
Kanban	NO	NO	**YES**	NO	**YES**
Burndown Chart	NO	NO	**YES**	NO	**YES**

Table 7.5: Comparison of Project Scheduling Techniques

Detailed Critical Path Method (CPM)

Network Representation - Each activity of the project is represented as an arrow or directional arc pointing to the direction of progress in the project. The nodes in the network represent the precedence relationships among the activities / tasks. Rules for constructing the network –

- Each activity is represented by one and only one arrow in the network.

- Each activity must be identified by two distinct end nodes.

- A dummy activity can be used to represent two concurrent activities.

- Figure 7.11 shows how dummy activity can be used.

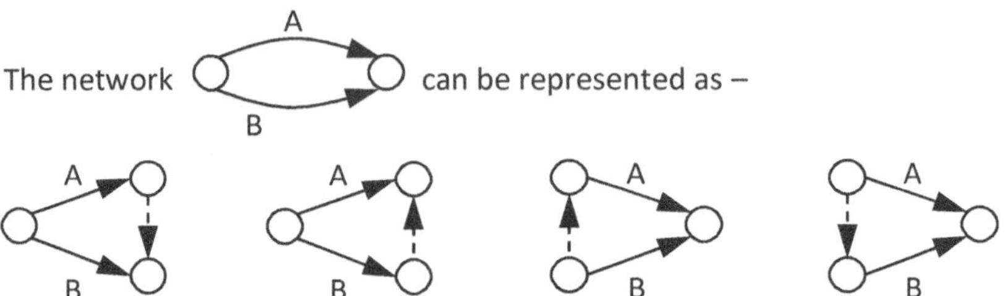

Figure 7.11: Use of Dummy Activity

An example of using dummy is shown in figure 7.12 –

Precedence: (i) A, B < C (ii) B < E

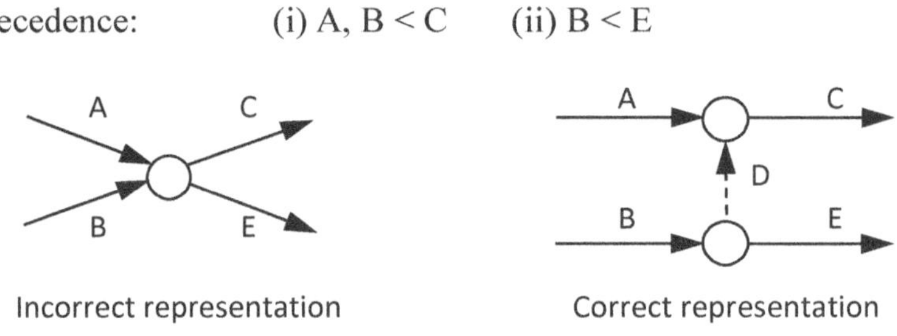

Figure 7.12: Example of Dummy Activity

The ultimate goal in the CPM is the construction of the time schedule for the project. It produces the following information –

- Total duration required to complete the project

- Categorization of the project activities / task as critical and non-critical

An activity is said to be critical when there is no leeway (freedom or flexibility) in determining its start and finish time. A non-critical activity allows some scheduling slack so that the start time of the activity may be advanced or delayed without affecting the completion date of the entire project. An event can be defined as a point in time at which some activities are terminated and other activities are started.

$\Box j$ = earliest occurrence time of event j

Δj = latest occurrence time of event j

Dij = Duration of activity i, j

The critical path involves two phases – Forward Pass and Backward Pass. These are shown in figure 7.13.

An activity Dij is said to be critical if it satisfies the following conditions

$\Delta j = \Box j$

$\Delta i = \Box i$

$\Delta j - \Delta i = \Box j - \Box i = Dij$

Slack time can be calculated as –

$\Delta j - \Delta i$ or $\Box j - \Box i$ [both must be equal]

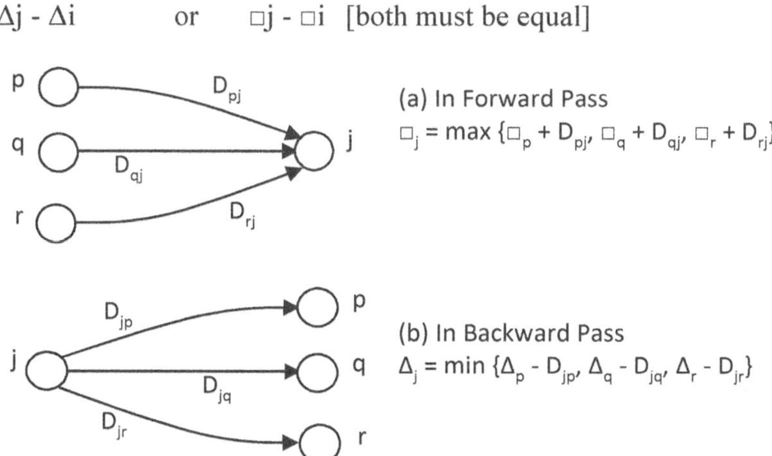

Figure 7.13: Slack Time calculation in Forward and Backward Pass

7.7. Project Scheduling Examples

7.7.1. Example1: activity and duration (days) are given below -

A	B	C	D	E	F	G	H
1	4	2	1	5	5	6	2

Precedence Rules: A<D; B<E; C<F; D,E<G; F,G<H;

Solution:

The activity network diagram is drawn as follows (figure 7.14) –

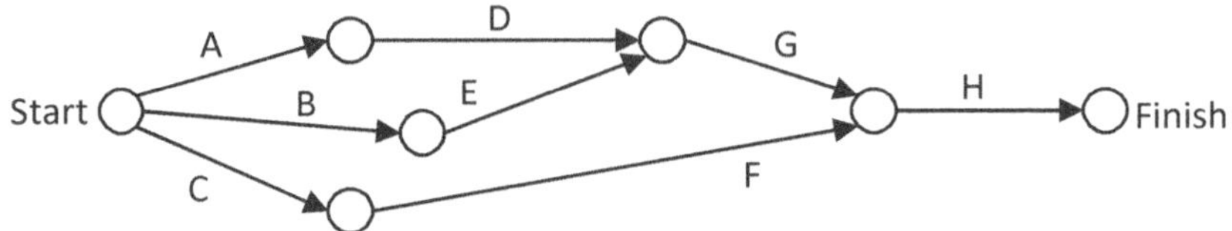

Figure 7.14: Activity Network Diagram for Example 1

Next, the Network calculations are done for both forward and backward pass. The detailed calculation is shown in table 7.6.

Task Name	Dura-tion	Prece-dence	Forward Pass		Backward Pass		Slack Time (ST)
			Early Start (ES)	Early Finish (EF)	Late Start (LS)	Late Finish (LF)	
A	1	---	0	1	7	8	7
B	4	---	0	4	0	4	0
C	2	---	0	2	8	10	8
D	1	A	1	2	8	9	7
E	5	B	4	9	4	9	0
F	5	C	2	7	10	15	8
G	6	D, E	9	15	9	15	0
H	2	F, G	15	17	15	17	0

Table 7.6: Network calculations for Example 1

Calculation mechanism as shown in table 7.6:

In forward pass, Early Start (ES) and Early Finish (EF) are considered and the calculations are made from Start to Finish. ES for a task is calculated as per the dependency or precedence rule. EF for a task is calculated as EF = ES + Duration. The forward pass calculations are shown in figure 7.15.

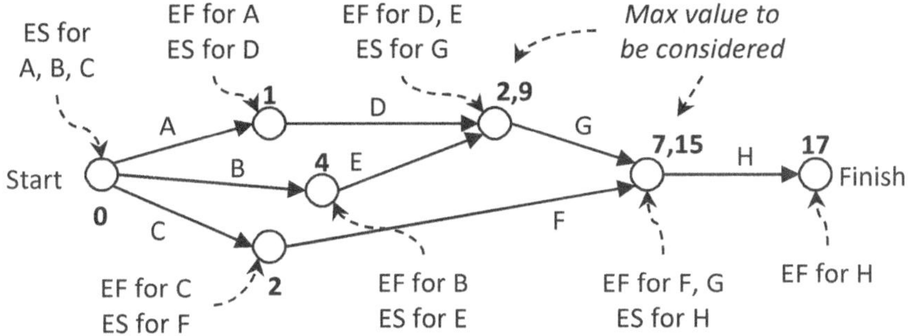

Figure 7.15: Forward Pass Calculations

In backward pass, Late Start (LS) and Late Finish (LF) are considered and the calculations are made from Finish to Start. LF for a task is calculated from the forward pass values and dependency or precedence rule. LS for a task is calculated as LS = LF - Duration. The backward pass calculations are shown in figure 7.16.

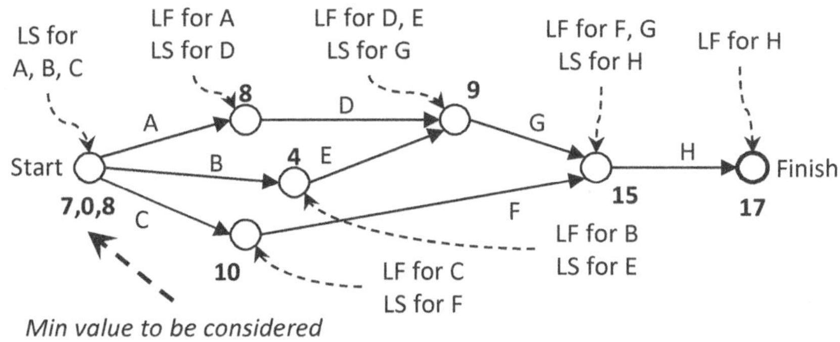

Figure 7.16: Backward Pass Calculations

Slack Time (ST) is calculated as:

ST = LS - ES or ST = LF - EF (both must produce the same result).

The project will be completed in 17 days. The activity network including critical activities (double line) are shown in figure 7.17.

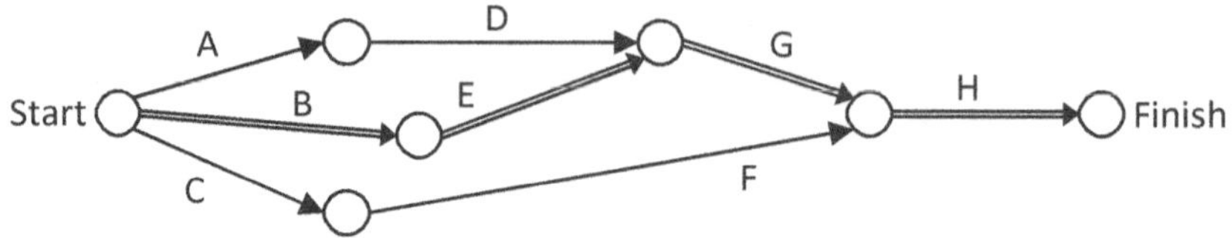

Figure 7.17: Critical Path for Example 1

Critical path: B → E → G → H. So, the activities B, E, G and H cannot be delayed. Notice that the slack time for critical activities is zero (0).

Following is the Gantt Chart for the Example 1 (figure 7.18) –

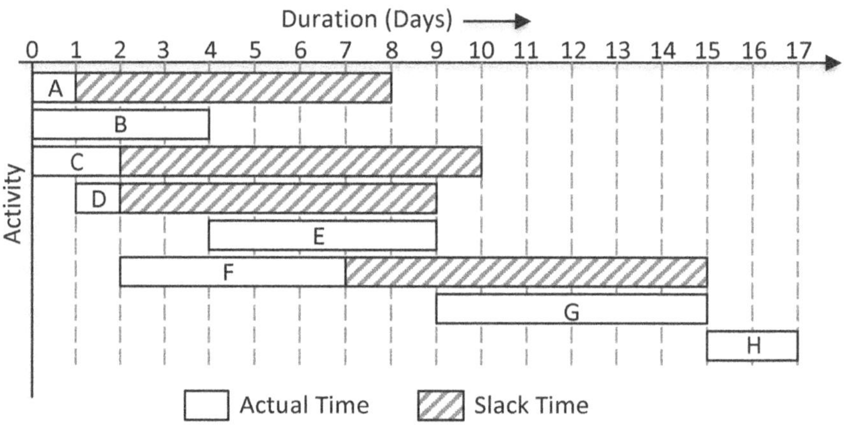

Figure 7.18: Gantt Chart for Example 1

7.7.2. Example 2: Followings are the activities of a project with their corresponding precedence and duration:

Activity	Precedence	Duration (Days)		
		Optimistic (O)	Most Likely (M)	Pessimistic (P)
A	—	1	1	7
B	—	1	4	7
C	—	2	2	8

D	A	1	1	1
E	B	2	5	14
F	C	2	5	8
G	D, E	3	6	15
H	F, G	1	2	3

Table 7.7: Input data for Example 2

Now do the following:

a.   Draw the activity diagram.

b.   Determine the critical path.

c.   Find expected project completion (μ) and expected variation (σ).

d.   Draw the Gantt Chart.

Solution:

First of all, the actual duration of each activity is calculated as -

$$\textbf{Duration} = (\textbf{ O } + \textbf{4M} + \textbf{ P }) / \textbf{6}$$

The result is shown in table 7.8.

Activity	Preced- ence	All Durations (Days)			
		O	M	P	Duration
A	—	1	1	7	(1+4×1+7)/6 = 2
B	—	1	4	7	(1+4×4+7)/6 = 4
C	—	2	2	8	(2+4×2+8)/6 = 3
D	A	1	1	1	(1+4×1+1)/6 = 1
E	B	2	5	14	(2+4×5+14)/6 = 6
F	C	2	5	8	(2+4×5+8)/6 = 5
G	D, E	3	6	15	(3+4×6+15)/6 = 7
H	F, G	1	2	3	(1+4×2+3)/6 = 2

Table 7.8: Duration calculations for Example 2

The activity network is exactly the same as example 1, so refer to figure 7.14. The Network calculations are shown in table 7.9. Notations are as usual and same as example 1.

Activity	Duration	Precedence	ES	EF	LS	LF	ST
A	2	---	0	2	7	9	7
B	4	---	0	4	0	4	0
C	3	---	0	3	9	12	9
D	1	A	2	3	9	10	7
E	6	B	4	10	4	10	0
F	5	C	3	8	12	17	9
G	7	D, E	10	17	10	17	0
H	2	F, G	17	19	17	19	0

Table 7.9: Network calculations for Example 2

Expected completion of the project (μ) = 19 days

Now, we know that, Variance = σ^2(Activity) = $[\,(\,P - O\,)\,/\,6\,]^2$

Expected variation (σ)　= $\pm\sqrt{(\,\sum_{i=0}^{n} \text{Variance(i)}\,)}$,

    where i denotes the critical activity only

$$= \pm\sqrt{[\sigma^2(B) + \sigma^2(E) + \sigma^2(G) + \sigma^2(H)]}$$

$$= \pm\sqrt{[1+4+4+1]}$$

$$= \pm\,3.019 \text{ days}$$

Therefore, the expected completion of the project (μ) = 19 days may vary by $\pm$ 3 days.

Finally, the Gantt Chart will be the same as example 1 (figure 7.18).

7.7.3. Example 3: Followings are the activities of a project with their corresponding precedence and duration:

Sl.	Activity	Preced ence	Duration (days)		
			Optimis tic (O)	Most Likely (M)	Pessimi stic (P)
1	DB Design	---	1	2	3
2	System Design	---	2	4	12
3	DB Creation	1	1	2	9
4	UI Coding	2	1	7	7
5	Backend Coding	2	4	7	10
6	DB Integration	3, 4	2	3	4
7	System Integration	3, 4	3	10	11
8	System Testing	2, 7	3	4	5
9	DB Testing	6	1	2	3
10	System Demo	5, 6, 8	1	3	5

Table 7.10: Input data for Example 3

Now do the following:

a. Draw the activity diagram.

b. Determine the critical path.

c. Find expected project completion (μ) and expected variation (σ).

d. Draw the Gantt Chart.

Solution:

First of all, the actual duration of each activity is calculated as -

$$\text{Duration} = (O + 4M + P)/6$$

The result is shown in table 7.11.

Sl	Activity	Preced.	O	M	P	Duration
1	DB Design	---	1	2	3	2
2	System Design	---	2	4	12	5
3	DB Creation	1	1	2	9	3
4	UI Coding	2	1	7	7	6
5	Backend Coding	2	4	7	10	7
6	DB Integration	3, 4	2	3	4	3
7	System Integration	3, 4	3	10	11	9

8	System Testing	2, 7	3	4	5	**4**
9	DB Testing	6	1	2	3	**2**
10	System Demo	5, 6, 8	1	3	5	**3**

Table 7.11: Duration calculations for Example 3

The activity network diagram is drawn as follows (figure 7.19) –

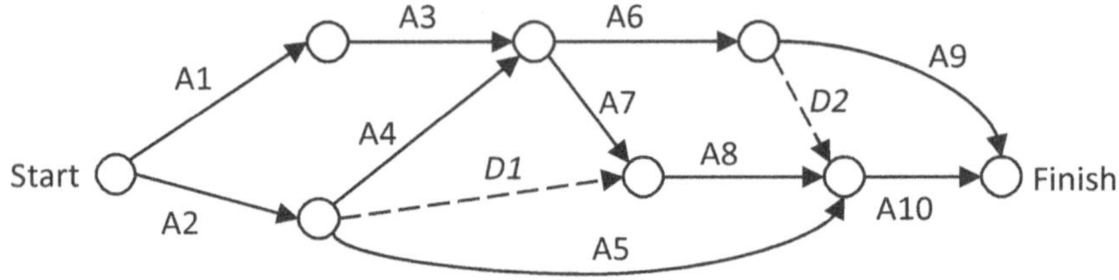

Figure 7.19: Activity Network Diagram for Example 3

Next, the Network calculations are done for both forward and backward pass. The detailed calculation is shown in table 7.12. Notations are as usual and same as previous examples.

Sl	Activity	Preced.	Dur	ES	EF	LS	LF	ST
A1	DB Design	---	2	0	2	6	8	**6**
A2	System Design	---	5	0	5	0	5	**0**
A3	DB Creation	1	3	2	5	8	11	**6**
A4	UI Coding	2	6	5	11	5	11	**0**
A5	Backend Coding	2	7	5	12	17	24	**12**
A6	DB Integration	3, 4	3	11	14	21	24	**10**
A7	Sys. Integration	3, 4	9	11	20	11	20	**0**
A8	System Testing	2, 7	4	20	24	20	24	**0**
A9	DB Testing	6	2	14	16	25	27	**11**
A10	System Demo	5, 6, 8	3	24	27	24	27	**0**
D1	Dummy 1	---	0	5	5	20	20	**15**
D2	Dummy 2	---	0	14	14	24	24	**10**

Table 7.12: Network calculations for Example 3

In forward pass, Early Start (ES) and Early Finish (EF) are considered and the calculations are made from Start to Finish. ES for a task is calculated as per the dependency or precedence rule. EF for a task is calculated as EF = ES + Duration. In backward pass, Late Start (LS) and Late Finish (LF) are considered and the calculations are made from Finish to Start. LF for a task is calculated from the forward pass values and dependency or precedence rule. LS for a task is calculated as LS = LF - Duration.

Slack Time (ST) is calculated as:

ST = LS - ES or ST = LF - EF (both must produce the same result).

The project will be completed in 27 working days. The activity network including critical activities (double line) are shown in figure 7.20.

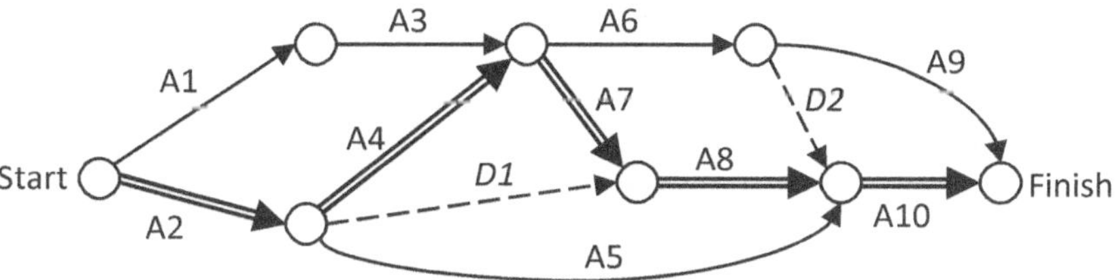

Figure 7.20: Critical Path for Example 3

Critical path: A2 → A4 → A7 → A8 → A10.

So, the activities A2, A4, A7, A8, A10 cannot be delayed. Notice that the slack time for critical activities is zero (0), and the slack time for dummy activities is always non-zero.

Expected Variation (σ)

$$= \pm\sqrt{[\sigma^2(A2) + \sigma^2(A4) + \sigma^2(A7) + \sigma^2(A8) + \sigma^2(A10)]}$$

$$= \pm\, 2.472 \text{ days}$$

Therefore, the expected completion of the project (μ) = 27 days may vary by ± 2.5 days.

Following is the Gantt Chart for the Example 3 (figure 7.21). This Gantt Chart is generated from GanttProject software.

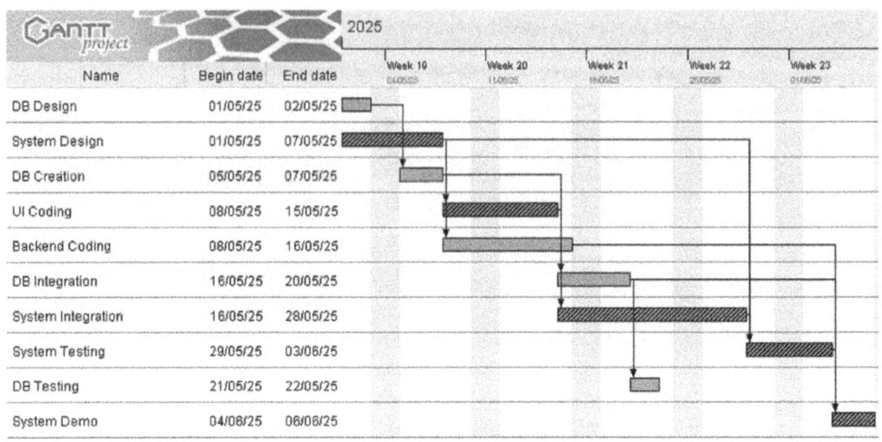

Figure 7.21: Gantt Chart for Example 3

7.7.4. Example 4: An Example solved with the help of GanttProject (an open-source software)

Followings are the resource chart to be used in the project (table 7.13):

SL	Initial	Resource Name	Std. Rate
1	PM	Project Manager	Rs. 500/-
2	TL	Team Lead	Rs. 350/-
3	PH	Programmer Head	Rs. 300/-
4	P1	Programmer 1	Rs. 200/-
5	P2	Programmer 2	Rs. 150/-
6	P3	Programmer 3	Rs. 150/-
7	P4	Programmer 4	Rs. 130/-
8	T1	Tester1	Rs. 230/-
9	T2	Tester2	Rs. 250/-
10	T3	Tester3	Rs. 200/-
11	T4	Tester4	Rs. 200/-

Table 7.13: Resource data for Example 4

Followings are the activities of a project with their corresponding precedence and duration (table 7.14):

SL	Activity	Predece-ssor	Responsibility	Duration
1	Platform Analysis	---	PM, TL	5 days
2	Package Analysis	---	PH, P2	3 days
3	Modularization	1, 2	PH, TL	2 days
4	Code Module 1	3	P1, P4	8 days
5	Code Module 2	3	P2, P3	10 days
6	Code Module 3	4, 5	PH, P1, P3, P4	7 days
7	Test Module 1	4	T1, T3	2 days
8	Test Module 2	5	T2, T4	3 days
9	Test Module 3	6	T1, T2, T4	3 days
10	Integration	7, 8, 9	PM, TL, PH	5 days

Table 7.14: Task data for Example 4

Some information about the project:

Project Name: Project Omega   Company: CEMK

Project Start Date: 02 June, 2025

The company has 6 working days (Mon - Sat)

Solution:

Open the GanttProject and create New Project. Now set project properties as shown in figure 7.22 and 7.23. You may add other properties also as per the problem statement. For example, resource roles etc.

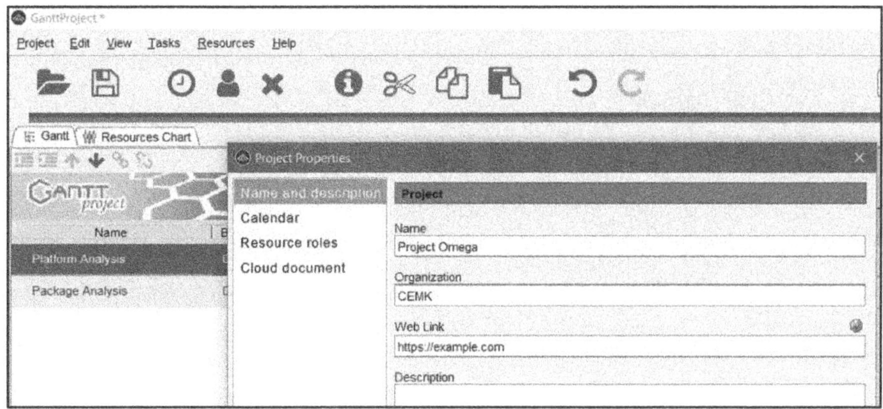

Figure 7.22: Project Description for Example 4

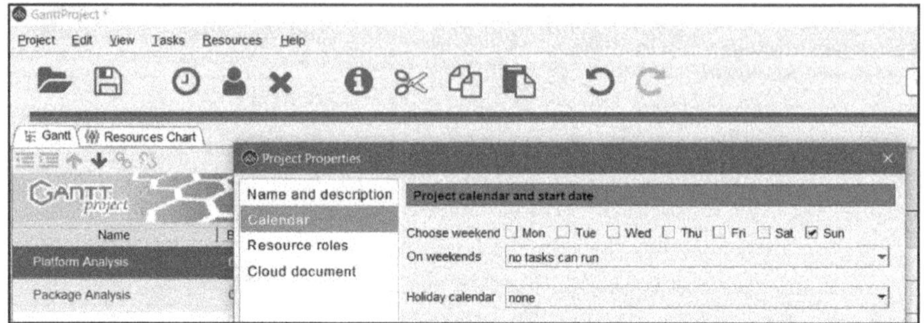

Figure 7.23: Setting Calendar for Example 4

Now go to the Resource tab and set all the resources as per table 7.13. This is shown in figure 7.24.

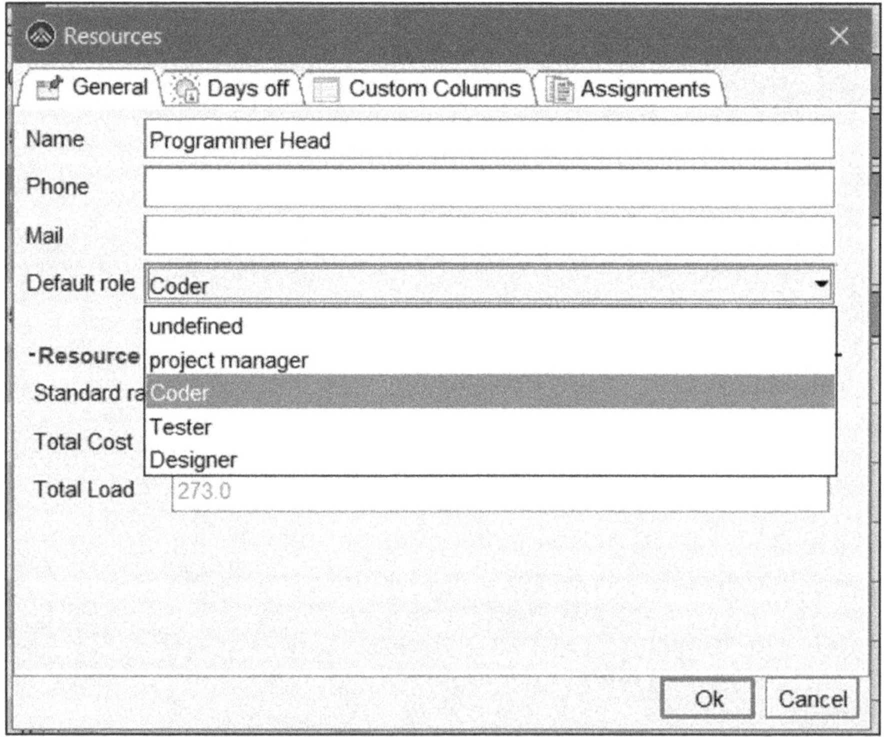

Figure 7.24: Setting Resources for Example 4

Next step is to go to the Task tab and all data for each task as per data given in table 7.14. This is shown in figure 7.25, 7.26 and 7.27.

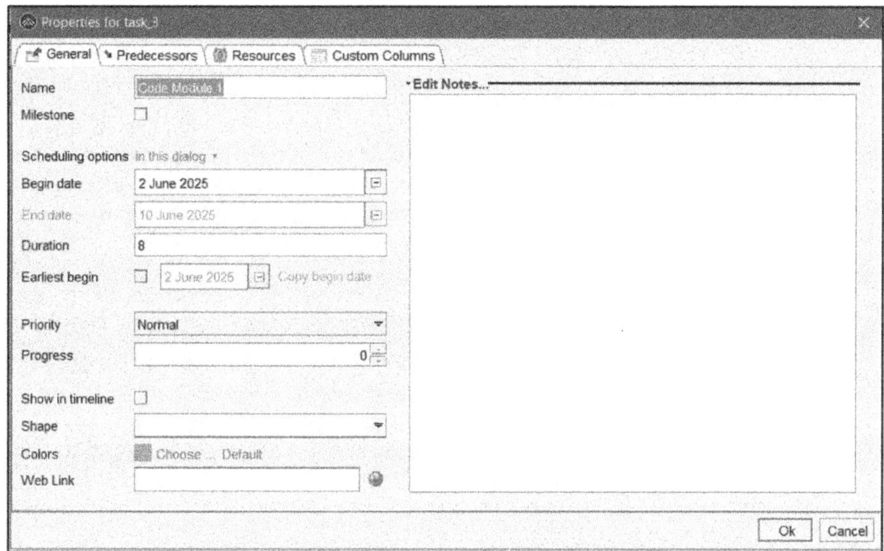

Figure 7.25: Setting General Task detail for Example 4

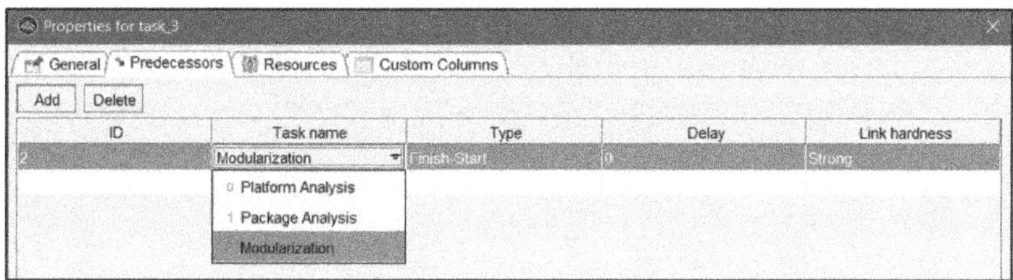

Figure 7.26: Setting Task - Predecessors detail for Example 4

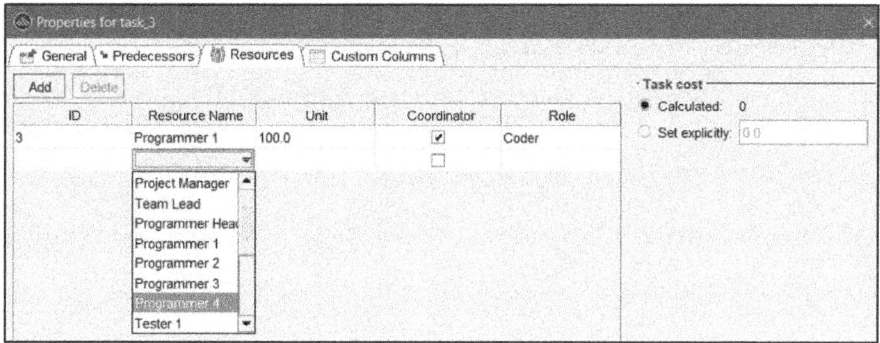

Figure 7.27: Setting Task detail - Resources for Example 4

Once all the inputs are given, the Gantt Chart and Resource Chart are generated automatically. Figure 7.28 and 7.29 shows them.

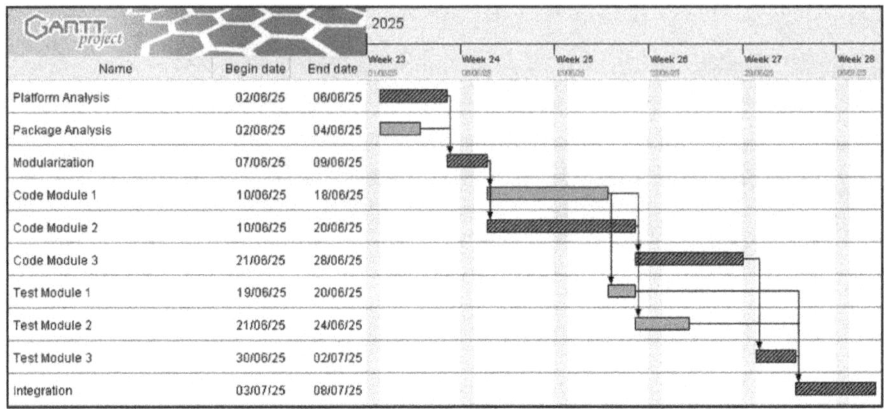

Figure 7.28:Gantt Chart for Example 4

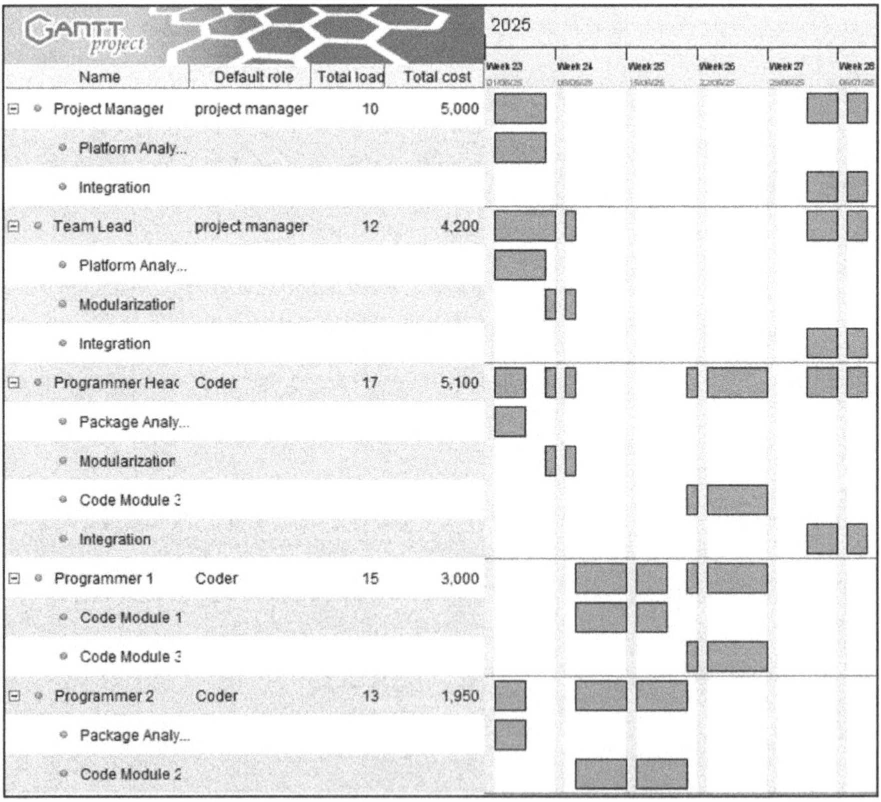

Figure 7.29: Resource Chart (partial) detail for Example 4

7.8. Conclusion

Tools Used to Create Gantt Charts:

- Microsoft Project

- Excel (with bar charts)

- Trello (with plugins)

- ClickUp / Jira / Monday.com

- OpenProject or GanttProject (Free / OpenSource tools)

Software Project Management is a specialized branch of project management focused on the planning, execution, monitoring, and completion of software development projects. It involves defining project scope, estimating effort and cost, setting realistic timelines, and ensuring the right allocation of resources. A key goal of SPM is to deliver software that meets user requirements within the constraints of time, budget, and quality. This is achieved through careful planning, effective team coordination, and systematic risk management.

The process of software project management includes various phases such as requirement analysis, scheduling (using tools like Gantt charts or PERT), progress tracking, and quality assurance. Techniques like Function Point Analysis or the Critical Path Method help in effort estimation and project scheduling. Agile methodologies and tools like Scrum, Kanban, and Jira are also widely used to improve flexibility and responsiveness. Ultimately, good software project management leads to successful project delivery, improved customer satisfaction, and more efficient use of development resources.

Summary of the Book

The Software Engineering Handbook – From Theory to Practice provides a structured and practical overview of the key principles, models, and techniques essential for developing high-quality software systems. Spanning the software development lifecycle, this handbook bridges theoretical concepts with hands-on practices suitable for both students and early-career professionals in computer science and engineering.

1. Introduction to Software Engineering

The handbook begins by laying a strong foundation in software engineering, discussing its evolution, importance, and core concepts such as software processes, development methodologies (Waterfall, Agile, Spiral), and the distinction between software engineering and programming. It introduces readers to the software development life cycle (SDLC) and the role of software engineering in building reliable, scalable, and maintainable systems.

2. Software Requirements Specification (SRS) Document

This chapter emphasizes the critical phase of requirement gathering and documentation. It introduces the structure of a good SRS document, techniques for eliciting requirements, and the importance of clarity and completeness. Real-world examples and templates are provided to help students practice writing effective SRS documents.

3. Software Data Modeling

Here, the focus shifts to the representation of system data using models. The chapter introduces Entity-Relationship (ER) modeling, and the transition from logical to physical data models. It explores how these models facilitate communication between stakeholders and guide database and system design.

4. Function Oriented Software Design using UML

This section explores the traditional function-oriented approach to software design, emphasizing modularization, design techniques such as data flow-based decomposition using data flow diagrams (DFDs), data dictionary, decision trees and decision tables. Students learn how to transform requirements into a functional system architecture.

5. Object Oriented Software Design (UML)

This chapter transitions into modern design methodologies using the Unified Modeling Language (UML). It covers use case diagrams, class diagrams, sequence diagrams, activity diagrams, communication diagrams, and other UML diagrams providing a comprehensive understanding of how object-oriented design supports encapsulation, inheritance, and polymorphism including lots of visual examples. Practical case studies are included to reinforce diagramming and modeling skills.

6. Software Testing

An essential part of the development cycle, software testing is covered in depth, from unit and integration testing to system and acceptance testing. The chapter explores black-box and white-box testing techniques, test case design, and defect tracking. Hands-on examples help students design, execute, and evaluate test plans.

7. Software Project Management

The final chapter addresses the managerial aspects of software projects. It covers project planning, scheduling (using Gantt and PERT charts) etc. Emphasis is placed on real-world tools and techniques, including agile project management and team collaboration practices.

Conclusion

Together, these chapters form a complete journey from foundational theory to practical application in software engineering. The handbook aims not only to equip readers with technical proficiency but also to develop a mindset of quality, precision, and continuous improvement—core traits of a successful software engineer.

www.ingramcontent.com/pod-product-compliance
Lightning Source LLC
Chambersburg PA
CBHW041304120726
48005CB00014B/1864